OF MICE AND MEN
CANNERY ROW

John Steinbeck was born in 1902 at Salinas' California, the son of an Irish mother and a half-German father. He was educated at Stanford University, and afterwards led a roving life, becoming in turn ranch hand, carpenter's mate, painter's apprentice, chemist, labourer, and newspaper man – until, when caretaker of an estate which was snow-bound for eight months in the year, he began seriously to write. *Tortilla Flat*, his fourth book, but the first to attract attention, was published in 1935. After that he wrote a number of books – novels, stories, and plays – many of which have been successfully filmed. These include *The Grapes of Wrath, Forgotten Village, Sea of Cortez, The Moon is Down, The Wayward Bus, The Pearl, A Russian Journal, East of Eden, Once There Was a War*, and *Winter of Our Discontent*; his last books were *Travels with Charley* and *America and the Americans*. He was in England during the war on the staff of the *Daily Express*. In 1962 he was awarded the Nobel Prize for Literature. He died in 1969.

Also available in Penguins:

THE GRAPES OF WRATH
TORTILLA FLAT

Not for sale in the U.S.A. or Canada

OF MICE AND MEN
and
CANNERY ROW

JOHN STEINBECK

PENGUIN BOOKS

IN ASSOCIATION WITH

WILLIAM HEINEMANN LTD

Penguin Books Ltd, Harmondsworth, Middlesex, England
Penguin Books Australia Ltd, Ringwood, Victoria, Australia

—

Of Mice and Men first published by William Heinemann Ltd, 1937
Cannery Row first published by William Heinemann Ltd, 1945
First published in Penguin Books 1949
Reprinted 1951, 1953, 1955, 1957, 1958 ,1960, 1961, 1963, 1964,
1965, 1968 (twice), 1969, 1970 (twice)

—

Copyright © John Steinbeck, 1937, 1945

—

Made and printed in Great Britain
by Cox & Wyman Ltd,
London, Reading and Fakenham
Set in Monotype Baskerville

Of Mice and Men

OF MICE AND MEN

A FEW miles south of Soledad, the Salinas River drops in close to the hill-side bank and runs deep and green. The water is warm too, for it has slipped twinkling over the yellow sands in the sunlight before reaching the narrow pool. On one side of the river the golden foothill slopes curve up to the strong and rocky Gabilan mountains, but on the valley side the water is lined with trees – willows fresh and green with every spring, carrying in their lower leaf junctures the debris of the winter's flooding; and sycamores with mottled, white, recumbent limbs and branches that arch over the pool. On the sandy bank under the trees the leaves lie deep and so crisp that a lizard makes a great skittering if he runs among them. Rabbits come out of the brush to sit on the sand in the evening, and the damp flats are covered with the night tracks of 'coons, and with the spread pads of dogs from the ranches, and with the split-wedge tracks of deer that come to drink in the dark.

There is a path through the willows and among the sycamores, a path beaten hard by boys coming down from the ranches to swim in the deep pool, and beaten hard by tramps who come wearily down from the highway in the evening to jungle-up near water. In front of the low horizontal limb of a giant sycamore there is an ash-pile made by many fires; the limb is worn smooth by men who have sat on it.

*

EVENING of a hot day started the little wind to moving among the leaves. The shade climbed up the hills toward the top. On the sand-banks the rabbits sat as quietly as little grey, sculptured stones. And then from the direction of the state highway came the sound of footsteps on crisp sycamore leaves. The rabbits hurried noiselessly for cover. A stilted heron laboured up into the air and pounded down river. For a moment the place was lifeless, and then two men

7

emerged from the path and came into the opening by the green pool. They had walked in single file down the path, and even in the open one stayed behind the other. Both were dressed in denim trousers and in denim coats with brass buttons. Both wore black, shapeless hats and both carried tight blanket rolls slung over their shoulders. The first man was small and quick, dark of face, with restless eyes and sharp, strong features. Every part of him was defined: small, strong hands, slender arms, a thin and bony nose. Behind him walked his opposite, a huge man, shapeless of face, with large, pale eyes, with wide, sloping shoulders; and he walked heavily, dragging his feet a little, the way a bear drags his paws. His arms did not swing at his sides, but hung loosely and only moved because the heavy hands were pendula.

The first man stopped short in the clearing, and the follower nearly ran over him. He took off his hat and wiped the sweat-band with his forefinger and snapped the moisture off. His huge companion dropped his blankets and flung himself down and drank from the surface of the green pool; drank with long gulps, snorting into the water like a horse. The small man stepped nervously beside him.

'Lennie!' he said sharply. 'Lennie, for God's sakes don't drink so much.' Lennie continued to snort into the pool. The small man leaned over and shook him by the shoulder. 'Lennie. You gonna be sick like you was last night.'

Lennie dipped his whole head under, hat and all, and then he sat up on the bank and his hat dripped down on his blue coat and ran down his back. 'Tha's good,' he said. 'You drink some, George. You take a good big drink.' He smiled happily.

George unslung his bundle and dropped it gently on the bank. 'I ain't sure it's good water,' he said. 'Looks kinda scummy.'

Lennie dabbled his big paw in the water and wiggled his fingers so the water arose in little splashes; rings widened across the pool to the other side and came back again. Lennie watched them go. 'Look, George. Look what I done.'

George knelt beside the pool and drank from his hand with quick scoops. 'Tastes all right,' he admitted. 'Don't really seem to be running, though. You never oughta drink water when it ain't running, Lennie,' he said hopelessly. 'You'd drink out of a gutter if you was thirsty.' He threw a scoop of water into his face and rubbed it about with his hand, under his chin and around the back of his neck. Then he replaced his hat, pushed himself back from the river, drew up his knees and embraced them. Lennie, who had been watching, imitated George exactly. He pushed himself back, drew up his knees, embraced them, looked over to George to see whether he had it just right. He pulled his hat down a little more over his eyes, the way George's hat was.

George stared morosely at the water. The rims of his eyes were red with sun glare. He said angrily: 'We could just as well of rode clear to the ranch if that bastard bus-driver knew what he was talkin' about. "Jes' a little stretch down the highway," he says. "Jes' a little stretch." God damn near four miles, that's what it was! Didn't wanta stop at the ranch gate, that's what. Too God damn lazy to pull up. Wonder he isn't too damn good to stop in Soledad at all. Kicks us out and says: "Jes' a little stretch down the road." I bet it was *more* than four miles. Damn hot day.'

Lennie looked timidly over to him. 'George?'

'Yeah, what ya want?'

'Where we goin', George?'

The little man jerked down the brim of his hat and scowled over at Lennie. 'So you forgot that awready, did you? I gotta tell you again, do I? Jesus Christ, you're a crazy bastard!'

'I forgot,' Lennie said softly. 'I tried not to forget. Honest to God I did, George.'

'O.K. – O.K. I'll tell ya again. I ain't got nothing to do. Might jus' as well spen' all my time tellin' you things and then you forget 'em, and I tell you again.'

'Tried and tried,' said Lennie, 'but it didn't do no good. I remember about the rabbits, George.'

'The hell with the rabbits. That's all you ever can remember is them rabbits. O.K.! Now you listen and this time you got to remember so we don't get in no trouble. You remember settin' in that gutter on Howard Street and watchin' that blackboard?'

Lennie's face broke into a delighted smile. 'Why sure, George. I remember that . . . but . . . what'd we do then? I remember some girls come by and you says . . . you says . . .'

'The hell with what I says. You remember about us goin' into Murray and Ready's, and they give us work cards and bus tickets?'

'Oh, sure, George. I remember that now.' His hands went quickly into his side coat pockets. He said gently: 'George . . . I ain't got mine. I musta lost it.' He looked down at the ground in despair.

'You never had none, you crazy bastard. I got both of 'em here. Think I'd let you carry your own work card?'

Lennie grinned with relief. 'I . . . I thought I put it in my side pocket.' His hand went into the pocket again.

George looked sharply at him. 'What'd you take outa that pocket?'

'Ain't a thing in my pocket,' Lennie said cleverly.

'I know there ain't. You got it in your hand. What you got in your hand – hidin' it?'

'I ain't got nothin', George. Honest.'

'Come on, give it here.'

Lennie held his closed hand away from George's direction. 'It's on'y a mouse, George.'

'A mouse? A live mouse?'

'Uh-uh. Jus' a dead mouse, George. I didn't kill it. Honest! I found it. I found it dead.'

'Give it here,' said George.

'Aw, leave me have it, George.'

'*Give it here!*'

Lennie's closed hand slowly obeyed. George took the mouse and threw it across the pool to the other side, among the brush. 'What you want of a dead mouse, anyways?'

'I could pet it with my thumb while we walked along,' said Lennie.

'Well, you ain't petting no mice while you walk with me. You remember where we're goin' now?'

Lennie looked startled and then in embarrassment hid his face against his knees. 'I forgot again.'

'Jesus Christ,' George said resignedly. 'Well – look, we're

gonna work on a ranch like the one we come from up north.'

'Up north?'

'In Weed.'

'Oh, sure. I remember. In Weed.'

'That ranch we're goin' to is right down there about a quarter-mile. We're gonna go in an' see the boss. Now, look – I'll give him the work tickets, but you ain't gonna say a word. You jus' stand there and don't say nothing. If he finds out what a crazy bastard you are, we won't get no job, but if he sees ya work before he hears ya talk, we're set. Ya got that?'

'Sure, George. Sure I got it.'

'O.K. Now when we go in to see the boss, what you gonna do?'

'I . . . I,' Lennie thought. His face grew tight with thought. 'I . . . ain't gonna say nothin'. Jus' gonna stan' there.'

'Good boy. That's swell. You say that over two, three times so you won't forget it.'

Lennie droned to himself softly: 'I ain't gonna say nothin' . . . I ain't gonna say nothin' . . . I ain't gonna say nothin'.'

'O.K.,' said George. 'An' you ain't gonna do no bad things like you done in Weed, neither.'

Lennie looked puzzled. 'Like I done in Weed?'

'Oh, so ya forgot that too, did ya? Well, I ain't gonna remind ya, fear ya do it again.'

A light of understanding broke on Lennie's face. 'They run us outa Weed,' he exploded triumphantly.

'Run us out, hell,' said George disgustedly. 'We run. They was lookin' for us, but they didn't catch us.'

Lennie giggled happily. 'I didn't forget that, you bet.'

George lay back on the sand and crossed his hands under his head, and Lennie imitated him, raising his head to see whether he were doing it right. 'God, you're a lot of trouble,' said George. 'I could get along so easy and so nice if I didn't have you on my tail. I could live so easy and maybe have a girl.'

For a moment Lennie lay quiet, and then he said hopefully: 'We gonna work on a ranch, George.'

'Awright. You got that. But we're gonna sleep here because I got a reason.'

The day was going fast now. Only the tops of the Gabilan mountains flamed with the light of the sun that had gone from the valley. A water-snake slipped along the pool, its head held up like a little periscope. The reeds jerked slightly in the current. Far off toward the highway a man shouted something, and another man shouted back. The sycamore limbs rustled under a little wind that died immediately.

'George – why ain't we goin' on to the ranch and get some supper? They got supper at the ranch.'

George rolled on his side. 'No reason at all for you. I like it here. To-morra we're gonna go to work. I seen thrashin' machines on the way down. That means we'll be bucking grain-bags, bustin' a gut. Tonight I'm gonna lay right here and look up. I like it.'

Lennie got up on his knees and looked down at George. 'Ain't we gonna have no supper?'

'Sure we are, if you gather up some dead willow sticks. I got three cans of beans in my bundle. You get a fire ready. I'll give you a match when you get the sticks together. Then we'll heat the beans and have supper.'

Lennie said: 'I like beans with ketchup.'

'Well, we ain't got no ketchup. You go get wood. An' don't you fool around. It'll be dark before long.'

Lennie lumbered to his feet and disappeared in the brush. George lay where he was and whistled softly to himself. There were sounds of splashings down the river in the direction Lennie had taken. George stopped whistling and listened. 'Poor bastard,' he said softly, and then went on whistling again.

In a moment Lennie came crashing back through the brush. He carried one small willow stick in his hand. George sat up. 'Aw right,' he said brusquely. 'Gi'me that mouse!'

But Lennie made an elaborate pantomime of innocence. 'What mouse, George? I ain't got no mouse.'

George held out his hand. 'Come on. Give it to me. You ain't puttin' nothing over.'

Lennie hesitated, backed away, looked wildly at the brush

line as though he contemplated running for his freedom. George said coldly: 'You gonna give me that mouse or do I have to sock you?'

'Give you what, George?'

'You know God damn well what. I want that mouse.'

Lennie reluctantly reached into his pocket. His voice broke a little. 'I don't know why I can't keep it. It ain't nobody's mouse. I didn't steal it. I found it lyin' right beside the road.'

George's hand remained outstretched imperiously. Slowly, like a terrier who doesn't want to bring a ball to its master, Lennie approached, drew back, approached again. George snapped his fingers sharply, and at the sound Lennie laid the mouse in his hand.

'I wasn't doin' nothing bad with it, George. Jus' stroking it.'

George stood up and threw the mouse as far as he could into the darkening brush, and then he stepped to the pool and washed his hands. 'You crazy fool. Don't you think I could see your feet was wet where you went across the river to get it?' He heard Lennie's whimpering cry and wheeled about. 'Blubberin' like a baby? Jesus Christ! A big guy like you.' Lennie's lip quivered and tears started in his eyes. 'Aw, Lennie!' George put his hand on Lennie's shoulder. 'I ain't takin' it away jus' for meanness. That mouse ain't fresh, Lennie; and besides, you've broke it pettin' it. You get another mouse that's fresh and I'll let you keep it a little while.'

Lennie sat down on the ground and hung his head dejectedly. 'I don't know where there is no other mouse. I remember a lady used to give 'em to me – ever' one she got. But that lady ain't here.'

George scoffed. 'Lady, huh? Don't even remember who that lady was. That was your own Aunt Clara. An' she stopped givin' 'em to ya. You always killed 'em.'

Lennie looked sadly up at him. 'They was so little,' he said apologetically. 'I'd pet 'em, and pretty soon they bit my fingers and I pinched their heads a little and then they was dead – because they was so little.'

'I wish't we'd get the rabbits pretty soon, George. They ain't so little.'

'The hell with the rabbits. An' you ain't to be trusted with no live mice. Your Aunt Clara give you a rubber mouse and you wouldn't have nothing to do with it.'

'It wasn't no good to pet,' said Lennie.

The flame of the sunset lifted from the mountain-tops and dusk came into the valley, and a half-darkness came in among the willows and the sycamores. A big carp rose to the surface of the pool, gulped air, and then sank mysteriously into the dark water again, leaving widening rings on the water. Overhead the leaves whisked again and little puffs of willow cotton blew down and landed on the pool's surface.

'You gonna get that wood?' George demanded. 'There's plenty right up against the back of that sycamore. Floodwater wood. Now you get it.'

Lennie went behind the tree and brought out a litter of dried leaves and twigs. He threw them in a heap on the old ash-pile and went back for more and more. It was almost night now. A dove's wings whistled over the water. George walked to the fire pile and lighted the dry leaves. The flame cracked up among the twigs and fell to work. George undid his bindle and brought out three cans of beans. He stood them about the fire, close in against the blaze, but not quite touching the flame.

'There's enough beans for four men,' George said.

Lennie watched him from over the fire. He said patiently: 'I like 'em with ketchup.'

'Well, we ain't got any,' George exploded. 'Whatever we ain't got, that's what you want. God a'mighty, if I was alone I could live so easy. I could go get a job an' work, an' no trouble. No mess at all, and when the end of the month come I could take my fifty bucks and go into town and get whatever I want. Why, I could stay in a cat-house all night. I could eat any place I want, hotel or any place, and order any damn thing I could think of. An' I could do all that every damn month. Get a gallon of whisky, or set in a pool-room and play cards or shoot pool. Lennie knelt and looked over the fire at the angry George. And Lennie's face was drawn with terror. 'An' whatta I got?' George went on furiously. 'I got you! You can't keep a job and you lose me ever' job I get. Jus' keep me shovin' all over the country all the time. An' that ain't the worst. You get in trouble. You do bad things and I got to get you out.' His voice rose nearly to a shout. 'You crazy son-of-a-bitch. You keep me in hot water all the time.' He took on the elaborate manner of little girls when they are mimicking one another. 'Jus' wanted to feel that girl's dress – jus' wanted to pet it like it was a mouse . . . Well, how the hell did she know you jus' wanted to feel her dress? She jerks back and you hold on like it was a mouse. She yells and we got to hide in a irrigation ditch all day with guys lookin' for us, and we got to sneak out in the dark and get outta the country. All the time somethin' like that – all the time. I wisht I could put you in a cage with about a million mice and let you have fun.' His anger left him suddenly. He looked across the fire at Lennie's anguished face, and then he looked ashamedly at the flames.

It was quite dark now, but the fire lighted the trunks of the trees and the curving branches overhead. Lennie crawled slowly and cautiously around the fire until he was close to George. He sat back on his heels. George turned the bean-cans so that another side faced the fire. He pretended to be unaware of Lennie so close beside him.

'George,' very softly. No answer. 'George!'

'Whatta you want?'

'I was only foolin', George. I don't want no ketchup. I wouldn't eat no ketchup if it was right here beside me.'

'If it was here, you could have some.'

'But I wouldn't eat none, George. I'd leave it all for you. You could cover your beans with it and I wouldn't touch none of it.'

George still stared morosely at the fire. 'When I think of the swell time I could have without you, I go nuts. I never get no peace.'

Lennie still knelt. He looked off into the darkness across the river. 'George, you want I should go away and leave you alone?'

'Where the hell could you go?'

'Well I could. I could go off in the hills there. Some place I'd find a cave.'

'Yeah? How'd you eat. You ain't got sense enough to find nothing to eat.'

'I'd find things, George. I don't need no nice food with ketchup. I'd lay out in the sun and nobody'd hurt me. An' if I foun' a mouse, I could keep it. Nobody'd take it away from me.'

George looked quickly and searchingly at him. 'I been mean, ain't I?'

'If you don' want me I can go off in the hills an' find a cave. I can go away any time.'

'No – look! I was jus' foolin', Lennie. Course I want you to stay with me. Trouble with mice is you always kill 'em.' He paused. 'Tell you what I'll do, Lennie. First chance I get I'll give you a pup. Maybe you wouldn't kill *it*. That'd be better than mice. And you could pet it harder.'

Lennie avoided the bait. He had sensed his advantage. 'If you don't want me, you only jus' got to say so, and I'll go off in those hills there – right up in those hills and live by myself. An' I won't get no mice stole from me.'

George said: 'I want you to stay with me, Lennie. Jesus Christ, somebody'd shoot you for a coyote if you was by yourself. No, you stay with me. Your Aunt Clara wouldn't like you running off by yourself, even if she is dead.'

Lennie spoke craftily: 'Tell me – like you done before.'

'Tell you what?'

'About the rabbits.'

George snapped: 'You ain't gonna put nothing over on me.'

Lennie pleaded: 'Come on, George. Tell me. Please, George. Like you done before.'

'You get a kick outta that, don't you. A'right, I'll tell you, and then we'll eat our supper . . .'

George's voice became deeper. He repeated his words rhythmically as though he had said them many times before. 'Guys like us, that work on ranches, are the loneliest guys in the world. They got no family. They don't belong no place. They come to a ranch an' work up a stake and then they go inta town and blow their stake, and the first thing you know they're poundin' their tail on some other ranch. They ain't got nothing to look ahead to.'

Lennie was delighted. 'That's it – that's it. Now tell how it is with us.'

George went on. 'With us it ain't like that. We got a future. We got somebody to talk to that gives a damn about us. We don't have to sit in no bar-room blowin' in our jack jus' because we got no place else to go. If them other guys gets in jail they can rot for all anybody gives a damn. But not us.'

Lennie broke in. *'But not us! An' why? Because . . . because I got you to look after me, and you got me to look after you, and that's why.'* He laughed delightedly. 'Go on now, George.'

'You got it by heart. You can do it yourself.'

'No, you. I forget some a' the things. Tell about how it's gonna be.'

'O.K. Some day – we're gonna get the jack together and we're gonna have a little house and a couple of acres an' a cow and some pigs and . . .'

'An' live off the fatta the lan'', Lennie shouted. 'An' have *rabbits.* Go on, George! Tell about what we're gonna have in the garden and about the rabbits in the cages and about the rain in the winter and the stove, and how thick the cream is on the milk like you can hardly cut it. Tell about that, George.'

'Why'n't you do it yourself. You know all of it.'

'No . . . you tell it. It ain't the same if I tell it. Go on . . . George. How I get to tend the rabbits.'

'Well,' said George. 'We'll have a big vegetable patch and a rabbit-hutch and chickens. And when it rains in the winter, we'll just say the hell with goin' to work, and we'll build up a fire in the stove and set around it an' listen to the rain comin' down on the roof – Nuts!' He took out his pocket-knife. 'I ain't got time for no more.' He drove his knife through the top of one of the bean-cans, sawed out the top, and passed the can to Lennie. Then he opened a second can. From his side pocket he brought out two spoons and passed one of them to Lennie.

They sat by the fire and filled their mouths with beans and chewed mightily. A few beans slipped out of the side of Lennie's mouth. George gestured with his spoon. 'What you gonna say tomorrow when the boss asks you questions?'

Lennie stopped chewing and swallowed. His face was concentrated. 'I . . . I ain't gonna . . . say a word.'

'Good boy! That's fine, Lennie! Maybe you're gettin' better. When we get the coupla acres I can let you tend the rabbits all right. 'Specially if you remember as good as that.'

Lennie choked with pride. 'I can remember,' he said.

George motioned with his spoon again.

'Look, Lennie. I want you to look around here. You can remember this place, can't you? The ranch is about a quarter-mile up that way. Just follow the river.'

'Sure,' said Lennie. 'I can remember this. Di'n't I remember about not gonna say a word?'

''Course you did. Well, look. Lennie – if you jus' happen to get in trouble like you always done before, I want you to come right here an' hide in the brush.'

'Hide in the brush,' said Lennie slowly.

'Hide in the brush till I come for you. Can you remember that?'

'Sure I can, George. Hide in the brush till you come.'

'But you ain't gonna get in no trouble, because if you do, I won't let you tend the rabbits.' He threw his empty bean-can off into the brush.

'I won't get in no trouble, George. I ain't gonna say a word.'

'O.K. Bring your bundle over here by the fire. It's gonna be nice sleepin' here. Lookin' up, and the leaves. Don't build up no more fire. We'll let her die down.'

They made their beds on the sand, and as the blaze dropped from the fire the sphere of light grew smaller; the curling branches disappeared and only a faint glimmer showed where the tree-trunks were. From the darkness Lennie called: 'George – you asleep?'

'No. Whatta you want?'

'Let's have different colour rabbits, George.'

'Sure we will,' George said sleepily. 'Red and blue and green rabbits, Lennie. Millions of 'em.'

'Furry ones, George, like I seen in the fair in Sacramento.'

'Sure, furry ones.'

''Cause I can jus' as well go away, George, an' live in a cave.'

'You can jus' as well go to hell,' said George. 'Shut up now.'

The red light dimmed on the coals. Up the hill from the river a coyote yammered, and a dog answered from the other side of the stream. The sycamore leaves whispered in a little night breeze.

*

THE bunk-house was a long, rectangular building. Inside, the walls were white-washed and the floor unpainted. In three walls there were small, square windows, and, in the fourth, a solid door with a wooden latch. Against the walls were eight bunks, five of them made up with blankets and the other three showing their burlap ticking. Over each bunk there was nailed an apple-box with the opening forward so that it made two shelves for the personal belongings of the occupant of the bunk. And these shelves were loaded with little articles, soap and talcum-powder, razors and those Western magazines ranch-men love to read and scoff at and secretly believe. And there were medicines on the shelves, and little vials, combs; and from nails on the box sides, a few neckties. Near one wall there was a black cast-iron stove, its stove-pipe going straight up through the ceiling. In the middle of the room stood a big square table littered with playing-cards, and around it were grouped boxes for the players to sit on.

At about ten o'clock in the morning the sun threw a bright dust-laden bar through one of the side windows, and in and out of the beam flies shot like rushing stars.

The wooden latch raised. The door opened and a tall, stoop-shouldered old man came in. He was dressed in blue jeans and he carried a big push-broom in his left hand. Behind him came George, and behind George, Lennie.

'The boss was expectin' you last night,' the old man said. 'He was sore as hell when you wasn't here to go out this morning.' He pointed with his right arm, and out of the sleeve came a round stick-like wrist, but no hand. 'You can have them two beds there,' he said, indicating two bunks near the stove.

George stepped over and threw his blankets down on the burlap sack of straw that was a mattress. He looked into the box shelf and then picked a small yellow can from it. 'Say. What the hell's this?'

'I don't know,' said the old man.

'Says "positively kills lice, roaches, and other scourges". What the hell kind of bed you giving us, anyways? We don't want no pants rabbits.'

The old swamper shifted his broom and held it between his elbow and his side while he held out his hand for the can. He studied the label carefully. 'Tell you what . . .' he said finally, 'last guy that had this bed was a blacksmith – hell of a nice fella and as clean a guy as you want to meet. Used to wash his hands even *after* he ate.'

'Then how come he got grey-backs?' George was working up a slow anger. Lennie put his bindle on the neighbouring bunk and sat down. He watched George with open mouth. 'Tell you what,' said the old swamper. 'This here black-smith – name of Whitey – was the kind of guy that would put that stuff around even if there wasn't no bugs – just to make sure, see? Tell you what he used to do . . . At meals he'd peel his boil' potatoes, an' he'd take out ever' little spot, no matter what kind, before he'd eat it. And if there was a red splotch on an egg, he'd scrape it off. Finally quit about the food. That's the kinda guy he was – clean. Used ta dress up Sundays even when he wasn't going no place, put on a necktie even, and then set in the bunk-house.'

'I ain't so sure,' said George sceptically. 'What did you say he quit for?'

The old man put the yellow can in his pocket, and he rubbed his bristly white whiskers with his knuckles. 'Why . . . he . . . just quit, the way a guy will. Says it was the food. Just wanted to move. Didn't give no other reason but the food. Just says "gimme my time" one night, the way any guy would.'

George lifted his tick and looked underneath it. He leaned over and inspected the sacking closely. Immediately Lennie got up and did the same with his bed. Finally George seemed satisfied. He unrolled his bindle and put things on the shelf, his razor and bar of soap, his comb and bottle of pills, his liniment and leather wrist-band. Then he made his bed up neatly with blankets. The old man said: 'I guess the boss'll be out here in a minute. He was sure burned when you wasn't here this morning. Come right in when we was eatin' breakfast and says: "Where the hell's them new men?" An' he give the stable buck hell, too.'

George patted a wrinkle out of his bed, and then sat down. 'Give the stable buck hell?' he asked.

'Sure. Ya see the stable buck's a nigger.'

'Nigger, huh?'

'Yeah. Nice fella, too. Got a crooked back where a horse kicked him. The boss gives him hell when he's mad. But the stable buck don't give a damn about that. He reads a lot. Got books in his room.'

'What kind of a guy is the boss?' George asked.

'Well, he's a pretty nice fella. Gets pretty mad sometimes, but he's pretty nice. Tell ya what – know what he done Christmas? Brang a gallon of whisky right in here and says: "Drink hearty, boys. Christmas comes but once a year."'

'The hell he did! Whole gallon?'

'Yes, sir. Jesus, we had fun. They let the nigger come in that night. Little skinner name of Smitty took after the nigger. Done pretty good, too. The guys wouldn't let him use his feet, so the nigger got him. If he coulda used his feet, Smitty says he woulda killed the nigger. The guys said on account of the nigger's got a crooked back, Smitty can't use his feet.' He paused in relish of the memory. 'After that the guys went into Soledad and raised hell. I didn't go in there. I ain't got the poop no more.'

Lennie was just finishing making his bed. The wooden latch raised again and the door opened. A little stocky man stood in the open doorway. He wore blue jean trousers, a flannel shirt, a black, unbuttoned vest, and a black coat. His thumbs were stuck in his belt, on each side of a square steel buckle. On his head was a soiled brown Stetson hat, and he wore high-heeled boots and spurs to prove he was not a labouring man.

The old swamper looked quickly at him, and then shuffled to the door rubbing his whiskers with his knuckles as he went. 'Them guys just come,' he said, and shuffled past the boss and out the door.

The boss stepped into the room with the short, quick steps of a fat-legged man. 'I wrote Murray and Ready I wanted two men this morning. You got your work slips?' George reached into his pocket and produced the slips and handed them to the boss. 'It wasn't Murray and Ready's fault. Says right here on the slip that you was to be here for work this morning.'

George looked down at his feet. 'Bus-driver give us a bum steer,' he said. 'We hadda walk ten miles. Says we was here when we wasn't. We couldn't get no rides in the morning.'

The boss squinted his eyes. 'Well, I had to send out the grain teams short two buckers. Won't do any good to go out now till after dinner.' He pulled his time-book out of his pocket and opened it where a pencil was stuck between the leaves. George scowled meaningfully at Lennie, and Lennie nodded to show that he understood. The boss licked his pencil. 'What's your name?'

'George Milton.'

'And what's yours?'

George said: 'His name's Lennie Small.'

The names were entered in the book. 'Le's see, this is the twentieth, noon the twentieth.' He closed the book. 'Where you boys been working?'

'Up around Weed,' said George.

'You, too?' to Lennie.

'Yeah, him too,' said George.

The boss pointed a playful finger at Lennie. 'He ain't much of a talker, is he?'

'No, he ain't, but he's sure a hell of a good worker. Strong as a bull.'

Lennie smiled to himself. 'Strong as a bull,' he repeated.

George scowled at him, and Lennie dropped his head in shame at having forgotten.

The boss said suddenly: 'Listen, Small!' Lennie raised his head. 'What can you do?'

In a panic, Lennie looked at George for help. 'He can do anything you tell him,' said George. 'He's a good skinner. He can rassel grain-bags, drive a cultivator. He can do anything. Just give him a try.'

The boss turned to George. 'Then why don't you let him answer? Why you trying to put over?'

George broke in loudly: 'Oh! I ain't saying he's bright. He ain't. But I say he's a God damn good worker. He can put up a four-hundred-pound bale.'

The boss deliberately put the little book in his pocket. He hooked his thumbs in his belt and squinted one eye nearly closed. 'Say – what you sellin'?'

'Huh?'

'I said what stake you got in this guy? You takin' his pay away from him?'

'No, 'course I ain't. Why ya think I'm sellin' him out?'

'Well, I never seen one guy take so much trouble for another guy. I just like to know what your interest is.'

George said: 'He's my . . . cousin. I told his old lady I'd take care of him. He got kicked in the head by a horse when he was a kid. He's awright. Just ain't bright. But he can do anything you tell him.'

The boss turned half away. 'Well, God knows he don't need any brains to buck barley bags. But don't you try to put nothing over, Milton. I got my eye on you. Why'd you quit in Weed?'

'Job was done,' said George promptly.

'What kinda job?'

'We . . . we was diggin' a cesspool.'

'All right. But don't try to put nothing over, 'cause you can't get away with nothing. I seen wise guys before. Go on out with the grain teams after dinner. They're pickin' up barley at the threshing machine. Go out with Slim's team.'

'Slim?'

'Yeah. Big tall skinner. You'll see him at dinner.' He turned abruptly and went to the door, but before he went out he turned and looked for a long moment at the two men.

When the sound of his footsteps had died away, George turned on Lennie. 'So you wasn't gonna say a word. You was gonna leave your big flapper shut and leave me do the talkin'. Damn near lost us the job.'

Lennie stared helplessly at his hands. 'I forgot, George.'

'Yeah, you forgot. You always forget, an' I got to talk you out of it.' He sat down heavily on the bunk.

'Now he's got his eye on us. Now we got to be careful and not make no slips. You keep your big flapper shut after this.' He fell morosely silent.

'George.'

'What you want now?'

'I wasn't kicked in the head with no horse, was I, George?'

'Be a damn good thing if you was,' George said viciously. 'Save ever'body a hell of a lot of trouble.'

'You said I was your cousin, George.'

'Well, that was a lie. An' I'm damn glad it was. If I was a relative of yours I'd shoot myself.' He stopped suddenly, stepped to the open front door and peered out. 'Say, what the hell you doin' listenin'?'

The old man came slowly into the room. He had his broom in his hand. And at his heels there walked a drag-footed sheep-dog, grey of muzzle, and with pale, blind old eyes. The dog struggled lamely to the side of the room and lay down, grunting softly to himself and licking his grizzled, moth-eaten coat. The swamper watched him until he was settled. 'I wasn't listenin'. I was jus' standin' in the shade a minute scratchin' my dog. I jus' now finished swampin' out the wash-house.'

'You was pokin' your big ears into our business,' George said. 'I don't like nobody to get nosey.'

The old man looked uneasily from George to Lennie, and then back. 'I jus' come there,' he said. 'I didn't hear nothing you guys was sayin'. I ain't interested in nothing you was sayin'. A guy on a ranch don't never listen nor he don't ast no questions.'

'Damn right he don't,' said George, slightly mollified, 'not if he wants to stay workin' long.' But he was reassured by the swamper's defence. 'Come on in and set down a minute,' he said. 'That's a hell of an old dog.'

'Yeah. I had 'im ever since he was a pup. God, he was a good sheep-dog when he was younger.' He stood his broom against the wall and he rubbed his white bristled cheek with his knuckles. 'How'd you like the boss?' he asked.

'Pretty good. Seemed awright.'

'He's a nice fella,' the swamper agreed. 'You got to take him right.'

At that moment a young man came into the bunk-house; a thin young man with a brown face, with brown eyes and a head of tightly curled hair. He wore a work glove on his left hand, and, like the boss, he wore high-heeled boots. 'Seen my old man?' he asked.

The swamper said: 'He was here jus' a minute ago, Curley. Went over to the cook-house, I think.'

'I'll try to catch him,' said Curley. His eyes passed over the new men and he stopped. He glanced coldly at George and then at Lennie. His arms gradually bent at the elbows and his hands closed into fists. He stiffened and went into a slight crouch. His glance was at once calculating and pugnacious. Lennie squirmed under the look and shifted his feet nervously. Curley stepped gingerly close to him. 'You the new guys the old man was waitin' for?'

'We just come in,' said George.

'Let the big guy talk.'

Lennie twisted with embarrassment.

George said: 'S'pose he don't want to talk?'

Curley lashed his body around. 'By Christ, he's gotta talk when he's spoke to. What the hell are you gettin' into it for?'

'We travel together,' said George coldly.

'Oh, so it's that way.'

George was tense and motionless. 'Yeah, it's that way.'

Lennie was looking helplessly to George for instruction.

'An' you won't let the big guy talk, is that it?'

'He can talk if he wants to tell you anything.' He nodded slightly to Lennie.

'We jus' come in,' said Lennie softly.

Curley stared levelly at him. 'Well, nex' time you answer when you're spoke to.' He turned towards the door and walked out, and his elbows were still bent out a little.

George watched him out, and then he turned back to the swamper. 'Say, what the hell's he got on his shoulder? Lennie didn't do nothing to him.'

The old man looked cautiously at the door to make sure no one was listening. 'That's the boss's son,' he said quietly. 'Curley's pretty handy. He done quite a bit in the ring. He's a lightweight, and he's handy.'

'Well, let him be handy,' said George. 'He don't have to take after Lennie. Lennie didn't do nothing to him. What's he got against Lennie?'

The swamper considered: '– Well – tell you what. Curley's like a lot of little guys. He hates big guys. He's alla time picking scraps with big guys. Kind of like he's mad at 'em because he ain't a big guy. You seen little guys like that, ain't you? Always scrappy?'

'Sure,' said George. 'I seen plenty tough little guys. But this Curley better not make no mistakes about Lennie. Lennie ain't handy, but this Curley punk is gonna get hurt if he messes around with Lennie.'

'Well, Curley's pretty handy,' the swamper said sceptically. 'Never did seem right to me. S'pose Curley jumps a big guy an' licks him. Ever'body says what a game guy Curley is. And s'pose he does the same thing and gets licked. Then ever'body says the big guy oughtta pick somebody his own size, and maybe they gang up on the big guy. Never did seem right to me. Seems like Curley ain't givin' nobody a chance.'

George was watching the door. He said ominously: 'Well, he better watch out for Lennie. Lennie ain't no fighter, but Lennie's strong and quick and Lennie don't know no rules.' He walked to the square table and sat down on one of the boxes. He gathered some of the cards together and shuffled them.

The old man sat down on another box. 'Don't tell Curley I said none of this. He'd slough me. He just don't give a damn. Won't ever get canned 'cause his old man's the boss.'

George cut the cards and began turning them over, look-ing at each one and throwing it down on a pile. He said: 'This guy Curley sounds like a son-of-a-bitch to me. I don't like mean little guys.'

'Seems to me like he's worse lately,' said the swamper. 'He got married a couple of weeks ago. Wife lives over in the boss's house. Seems like Curley is cockier'n ever since he got married.'

George grunted: 'Maybe he's showin' off for his wife.'

The swamper warmed to his gossip. 'You seen that glove on his left hand.'

'Yeah. I seen it.'

'Well, that glove's fulla vaseline.'

'Vaseline? What the hell for?'

'Well, I tell ya what, Curley says he's keepin' that hand soft for his wife.'

George studied the cards absorbedly. 'That's a dirty thing to tell around,' he said.

The old man was reassured. He had drawn a derogatory statement from George. He felt safe now, and he spoke more confidently. 'Wait'll you see Curley's wife.'

George cut the cards again and put out a solitaire lay, slowly and deliberately. 'Purty?' he asked casually.

'Yeah. Purty . . . but . . .'

George studied his cards. 'But what?'

'Well – she got the eye.'

'Yeah? Married two weeks and got the eye? Maybe that's why Curley's pants is full of ants.'

'I seen her give Slim the eye. Slim's a jerkline skinner. Hell of a nice fella. Slim don't need to wear no high-heeled boots on a grain team. I seen her give Slim the eye. Curley never seen it. An' I seen her give Carlson the eye.'

George pretended a lack of interest. 'Looks like we was gonna have fun.'

The swamper stood up from his box. 'Know what I think?' George did not answer. 'Well, I think Curley's mar-ried . . . a tart.'

'He ain't the first,' said George. 'There's plenty done that.'

The old man moved toward the door, and his ancient dog lifted his head and peered about, and then got painfully to his feet to follow. 'I gotta be settin' out the washbasins for the guys. The teams'll be in before long. You guys gonna buck barley?'

'Yeah.'

'You won't tell Curley nothing I said?'

'Hell, no.'

'Well, you look her over, mister. You see if she ain't a tart.' He stepped out the door into the brilliant sunshine.

George laid down his cards thoughtfully, turned his piles of three. He built four clubs on his ace pile. The sun square was on the floor now, and the flies whipped through it like sparks. A sound of jingling harness and the croak of heavy-laden axles sounded from outside. From the distance came a clear call. 'Stable Buck – ooh, sta-able Buck!' And then: 'Where the hell is that God damn nigger?'

George stared at his solitaire lay, and then he flounced the cards together and turned around to Lennie. Lennie was lying down on the bunk watching him.

'Look, Lennie! This here ain't no set-up. I'm scared. You gonna have trouble with that Curley guy. I seen that kind before. He was kinda feelin' you out. He figures he's got you scared and he's gonna take a sock at you the first chance he gets.'

Lennie's eyes were frightened. 'I don't want no trouble,' he said plaintively. 'Don't let him sock me, George.'

George got up and went over to Lennie's bunk and sat down on it. 'I hate that kinda bastard,' he said. 'I seen plenty of 'em. Like the old guy says, Curley don't take no chances. He always wins.' He thought for a moment. 'If he tangles with you, Lennie, we're gonna get the can. Don't make no mistake about that. He's the boss's son. Look, Lennie. You try to keep away from him, will you? Don't never speak to him. If he comes in here you move clear to the other side of the room. Will you do that, Lennie?'

'I don't want no trouble,' Lennie mourned. 'I never done nothing to him.'

'Well, that won't do you no good if Curley wants to plug

himself up for a fighter. Just don't have nothing to do with him. Will you remember?'

'Sure, George. I ain't gonna say a word.'

The sound of the approaching grain teams was louder, thud of big hooves on hard ground, drag of brakes, and the jingle of trace chains. Men were calling back and forth from the teams. George, sitting on the bunk beside Lennie, frowned as he thought. Lennie asked timidly: 'You ain't mad, George?'

'I ain't mad at you. I'm mad at this here Curley bastard. I hoped we was gonna get a little stake together – maybe a hundred dollars.' His tone grew decisive. 'You keep away from Curley, Lennie.'

'Sure I will, George. I won't say a word.'

'Don't let him pull you in – but – if the son-of-a-bitch socks you – let 'im have it.'

'Let 'im have what, George?'

'Never mind, never mind. I'll tell you when. I hate that kind of a guy. Look, Lennie, if you get in any kind of trouble, you remember what I told you to do?'

Lennie raised up on his elbow. His face contorted with thought. Then his eyes moved sadly to George's face. 'If I get in any trouble, you ain't gonna let me tend the rabbits.'

'That's not what I meant. You remember where we slep' last night? Down by the river?'

'Yeah. I remember. Oh, sure I remember! I go there an' hide in the brush.'

'Hide till I come for you. Don't let nobody see you. Hide in the brush by the river. Say that over.'

'Hide in the brush by the river, down in the brush by the river.'

'If you get in trouble.'

'If I get in trouble.'

A brake screeched outside. A call came: 'Stable – Buck. Oh! Sta-able Buck.'

George said: 'Say it over to yourself, Lennie, so you won't forget it.'

Both men glanced up, for the rectangle of sunshine in the

doorway was cut off. A girl was standing there looking in. She had full, rouged lips and wide-spaced eyes, heavily made up. Her finger-nails were red. Her hair hung in little rolled clusters, like sausages. She wore a cotton house dress and red mules, on the insteps of which were little bouquets of red ostrich feathers. 'I'm lookin' for Curley,' she said. Her voice had a nasal, brittle quality.

George looked away from her and then back. 'He was in here a minute ago, but he went.'

'Oh!' She put her hands behind her back and leaned against the door-frame so that her body was thrown forward. 'You're the new fellas that just come, ain't ya?'

'Yeah.'

Lennie's eyes moved down over her body, and although she did not seem to be looking at Lennie, she bridled a little. She looked at her finger-nails. 'Sometimes Curley's in here,' she explained.

George said brusquely: 'Well, he ain't now.'

'If he ain't, I guess I better look some place else,' she said playfully.

Lennie watched her, fascinated. George said: 'If I see him, I'll pass the word you was looking for him.'

She smiled archly and twitched her body. 'Nobody can't blame a person for lookin',' she said. There were footsteps behind her, going by. She turned her head. 'Hi, Slim,' she said.

Slim's voice came through the door. 'Hi, Good-lookin'.'

'I'm tryin' to find Curley, Slim.'

'Well, you ain't tryin' very hard. I seen him goin' in your house.'

She was suddenly apprehensive. ''Bye, boys,' she called into the bunk-house, and she hurried away.

George looked around at Lennie. 'Jesus, what a tramp,' he said. 'So that's what Curley picks for a wife.'

'She's purty,' said Lennie defensively.

'Yeah, and she's sure hidin' it. Curley got his work ahead of him. Bet she'd clear out for twenty bucks.'

Lennie still stared at the doorway where she had been. 'Gosh, she was purty.' He smiled admiringly. George looked quickly down at him and then he took him by an ear and shook him.

'Listen to me, you crazy bastard,' he said fiercely. 'Don't you even take a look at that bitch. I don't care what she says and what she does. I seen 'em poison before, but I never seen no piece of jail bait worse than her. You leave her be.'

Lennie tried to disengage his ear. 'I never done nothing, George.'

'No, you never. But when she was standin' in the doorway showin' her legs, you wasn't lookin' the other way, neither.'

'I never meant no harm, George. Honest I never.'

'Well, you keep away from her, 'cause she's a rat-trap if I ever seen one. You let Curley take the rap. He let himself in for it. Glove fulla vaseline,' George said disgustedly. 'An I bet he's eatin' raw eggs and writin' to the patent medicine houses.'

Lennie cried out suddenly: 'I don' like this place, George. This ain't no good place. I wanna get outa here.'

'We gotta keep it till we get a stake. We can't help it, Lennie. We'll get out jus' as soon as we can. I don't like it no better than you do.' He went back to the table and set out a new solitaire hand. 'No, I don't like it,' he said. 'For two bits I'd shove out of here. If we can get jus' a few dollars in the poke we'll shove off and go up the American River and pan gold. We can make maybe a couple of dollars a day there, and we might hit a pocket.'

Lennie leaned eagerly toward him. 'Le's go, George. Le's get outa here. It's mean here.'

'We gotta stay,' George said shortly. 'Shut up now. The guys'll be comin' in.'

From the wash-room near by came the sound of running water and rattling basins. George studied the cards. 'Maybe we oughtta wash up,' he said. 'But we ain't done nothing to get dirty.'

A tall man stood in the doorway. He held a crushed Stetson hat under his arm while he combed his long, black, damp hair straight back. Like the others, he wore blue jeans and a short denim jacket. When he had finished combing his hair he moved into the room, and he moved with a majesty only achieved by royalty and master craftsmen. He was a jerkline skinner, the prince of the ranch, capable of driving ten, sixteen, even twenty mules with a single line to the leaders. He was capable of killing a fly on the wheeler's butt with a bull whip without touching the mule. There was a gravity in his manner and a quiet so profound that all talk stopped when he spoke. His authority was so great that his word was taken on any subject, be it politics or love. This was Slim, the jerkline skinner. His hatchet face was ageless. He might have been thirty-five or fifty. His ear heard more than was said to him, and his slow speech had overtones not of thought, but of understanding beyond thought. His hands, large and lean, were as delicate in their action as those of a temple dancer.

He smoothed out his crushed hat, creased it in the middle and put it on. He looked kindly at the two in the bunkhouse. 'It's brighter'n a bitch outside,' he said gently. 'Can't hardly see nothing in here. You the new guys?'

'Just come,' said George.

'Gonna buck barley?'

'That's what the boss says.'

Slim sat down on a box across the table from George. He studied the solitaire hand that was upside-down to him. 'Hope you get on my team,' he said. His voice was very gentle. 'I gotta pair of punks on my team that don't know a barley bag from a blue ball. You guys ever bucked any barley?'

'Hell, yes,' said George. 'I ain't nothing to scream about, but that big bastard there can put up more grain alone than most pairs can.'

Lennie, who had been following the conversation back and forth with his eyes, smiled complacently at the compliment. Slim looked approvingly at George for having given the compliment. He leaned over the table and snapped the corner of a loose card. 'You guys travel around together?' His tone was friendly. It invited confidence without demanding it.

'Sure,' said George. 'We kinda look after each other.' He indicated Lennie with his thumb. 'He ain't bright. Hell of a good worker, though. Hell of a nice fella, but he ain't bright. I've knew him for a long time.'

Slim looked through George and beyond him. 'Ain't many guys travel around together,' he mused. 'I don't know why. Maybe ever'body in the whole damn world is scared of each other.'

'It's a lot nicer to go around with a guy you know,' said George.

A powerful, big-stomached man came into the bunkhouse. His head still dripped water from the scrubbing and dousing. 'Hi, Slim,' he said, and then stopped and stared at George and Lennie.

'These guys jus' come,' said Slim by way of introduction.

'Glad to meet ya,' the big man said. 'My name's Carlson.'

'I'm George Milton. This here's Lennie Small.'

'Glad ta meet ya,' Carlson said again. 'He ain't very small.' He chuckled softly at his joke. 'Ain't small at all,' he repeated. 'Meant to ask you, Slim – how's your bitch? I seen she wasn't under your wagon this morning.'

'She slang her pups last night,' said Slim. 'Nine of 'em. I drowned four of 'em right off. She couldn't feed that many.'

'Got five left, huh?'

'Yeah, five. I kept the biggest.'

'What kinda dogs you think they're gonna be?'

'I dunno,' said Slim. 'Some kinda shepherds, I guess. That's the most kind I seen around here when she was in heat.'

Carlson went on: 'Got five pups, huh. Gonna keep all of 'em?'

'I dunno. Have to keep 'em a while so they can drink Lulu's milk.'

Carlson said thoughtfully: 'Well, looka here, Slim. I been thinkin'. That dog of Candy's is so God damn old he can't hardly walk. Stinks like hell, too. Ever' time he comes into the bunk-house I can smell him for two, three days. Why'n't you get Candy to shoot his old dog and give him one of the pups to raise up. I can smell that dog a mile away. Got no

T—B

teeth, damn near blind, can't eat. Candy feeds him milk.
He can't chew nothing else.'

George had been staring intently at Slim. Suddenly a
triangle began to ring outside, slowly at first, and then faster
and faster until the beat of it disappeared into one ringing
sound. It stopped as suddenly as it had started.

'There she goes,' said Carlson.

Outside, there was a burst of voices as a group of men
went by.

Slim stood up slowly and with dignity. 'You guys better
come on while they's still something to eat. Won't be nothing left in a couple of minutes.'

Carlson stepped back to let Slim precede him, and then
the two of them went out the door.

Lennie was watching George excitedly. George rumpled
his cards into a messy pile. 'Yeah!' George said, 'I heard
him, Lennie. I'll ask him.'

'A brown and white one,' Lennie cried excitedly.

'Come on. Le's get dinner. I don't know whether he got a
brown and white one.'

Lennie didn't move from his bunk. 'You ask him right
away, George, so he won't kill no more of 'em.'

'Sure. Come on now, get up on your feet.'

Lennie rolled off his bunk and stood up, and the two of
them started for the door. Just as they reached it, Curley
bounced in.

'You seen a girl around here?' he demanded angrily.

George said coldly: ''Bout half an hour ago maybe.'

'Well, what the hell was she doin'?'

George stood still, watching the angry little man. He said
insultingly: 'She said – she was lookin' for you.'

Curley seemed really to see George for the first time. His
eyes flashed over George, took in his height, measured his
reach, looked at his trim middle. 'Well, which way'd she
go?' he demanded at last.

'I dunno,' said George. 'I didn' watch her go.'

Curley scowled at him, and turning, hurried out of the
door.

George said: 'Ya know, Lennie, I'm scared I'm gonna

tangle with that bastard myself. I hate his guts. Jesus Christ! Come on. They won't be a damn thing left to eat.'

They went out the door. The sunshine lay in a thin line under the window. From a distance there could be heard a rattle of dishes.

After a moment the ancient dog walked lamely in through the open door. He gazed about with mild, half-blind eyes. He sniffed, and then lay down and put his head between his paws. Curley popped into the doorway again and stood looking into the room. The dog raised his head, but when Curley jerked out, the grizzled head sank to the floor again.

*

ALTHOUGH there was evening brightness showing through the windows of the bunk-house, inside it was dusk. Through the open door came the thuds and occasional clangs of a horse-shoe game, and now and then the sound of voices raised in approval or derision.

Slim and George came into the darkening bunk-house together. Slim reached up over the card-table and turned on the tin-shaded electric light. Instantly the table was brilliant with light, and the cone of the shade threw its brightness straight downward, leaving the corners of the bunkhouse still in dusk. Slim sat down on a box and George took his place opposite.

'It wasn't nothing,' said Slim. 'I would of had to drowned most of 'em, anyways. No need to thank me about that.'

George said: 'It wasn't much to you, maybe, but it was a hell of a lot to him. Jesus Christ, I don't know how we're gonna get him to sleep in here. He'll want to sleep right out in the barn with 'em. We'll have trouble keepin' him from getting right in the box with them pups.'

'It wasn't nothing,' Slim repeated. 'Say, you sure was right about him. Maybe he ain't bright, but I never seen such a worker. He damn near killed his partner buckin' barley. There ain't nobody can keep up with him. God Almighty, I never seen such a strong guy.'

George spoke proudly. 'Jus' tell Lennie what to do an'

he'll do it if it don't take no figuring. He can't think of nothing to do himself, but he sure can take orders.'

There was a clang of horse-shoe on iron stake outside and a little cheer of voices.

Slim moved back slightly so the light was not on his face. 'Funny how you an' him string along together.' It was Slim's calm invitation to confidence.

'What's funny about it?' George demanded defensively.

'Oh, I dunno. Hardly none of the guys ever travel together. I hardly never seen two guys travel together. You know how the hands are, they just come in and get their bunk and work a month, and then they quit and go out alone. Never seem to give a damn about nobody. It jus' seems kinda funny a cuckoo like him and a smart little guy like you travellin' together.'

'He ain't no cuckoo,' said George. 'He's dumb as hell, but he ain't crazy. An' I ain't so bright neither, or I wouldn't be buckin' barley for my fifty and found. If I was bright, if I was even a little bit smart, I'd have my own little place, an' I'd be bringin' in my own crops, 'stead of doin' all the work and not getting what comes up outa the ground.' George fell silent. He wanted to talk. Slim neither encouraged nor discouraged him. He just sat back quiet and receptive.

'It ain't so funny, him an' me goin' aroun' together,' George said at last. 'Him and me was both born in Auburn. I knowed his Aunt Clara. She took him when he was a baby and raised him up. When his Aunt Clara died, Lennie just come along with me out workin'. Got kinda used to each other after a little while.'

'Um,' said Slim.

George looked over at Slim and saw the calm, God-like eyes fastened on him. 'Funny,' said George. 'I used to have a hell of a lot of fun with 'im. Used to play jokes on 'im 'cause he was too dumb to take care of 'imself. But he was too dumb even to know he had a joke played on him. I had fun. Made me seem God damn smart alongside of him. Why, he'd do any damn thing I tol' him. If I tol' him to walk over a cliff, over he'd go. That wasn't so damn much fun after a while. He never got mad about it, neither. I've beat the hell outa him, and he couda bust every bone in my body jus' with his han's, but he never lifted a finger against me.' George's voice was taking on the tone of confession. 'Tell you what made me stop that. One day a bunch of guys was standin' around up on the Sacramento River. I was feelin' pretty smart. I turns to Lennie and says: "Jump in." An' he jumps. Couldn't swim a stroke. He damn near drowned before we could get him. An' he was so damn nice to me for pullin' him out. Clean forgot I told him to jump in. Well, I ain't done nothing like that no more.'

'He's a nice fella,' said Slim. 'Guy don't need no sense to be a nice fella. Seems to me sometimes it jus' works the other way around. Take a real smart guy and he ain't hardly ever a nice fella.'

George stacked the scattered cards and began to lay out his solitaire hand. The shoes thudded on the ground outside. At the windows the light of the evening still made the window squares bright.

'I ain't got no people,' George said. 'I seen the guys that go around on the ranches alone. That ain't no good. They don't have no fun. After a long time they get mean. They get wantin' to fight all the time.'

'Yeah, they get mean,' Slim agreed. 'They get so they don't want to talk to nobody.'

'Course Lennie's a God damn nuisance most of the time,' said George. 'But you get used to goin' around with a guy an' you can't get rid of him.'

'He ain't mean,' said Slim. 'I can see Lennie ain't a bit mean.'

'Course he ain't mean. But he gets in trouble alla time because he's so God damn dumb. Like what happened in Weed . . .' He stopped, stopped in the middle of turning over a card. He looked alarmed and peered over at Slim. 'You wouldn't tell nobody.'

'What'd he do in Weed?' Slim asked calmly.

'You wouldn' tell? – no, course you wouldn'.'

'What'd he do in Weed?' Slim asked again.

'Well, he seen this girl in a red dress. Dumb bastard like he is, he wants to touch ever'thing he likes. Just wants to feel it. So he reaches out to feel this red dress an' the girl lets out a squawk, and that gets Lennie all mixed up, and he holds on 'cause that's the only thing he can think to do. Well, this girl squawks and squawks. I was jus' a little bit off, and I heard all the yellin', so I comes running, an' by that time Lennie's so scared all he can think to do is jus' hold on. I socked him over the head with a fence picket to make him let go. He was so scairt he couldn't let go of that dress. And he's so God damn strong, you know.'

Slim's eyes were level and unwinking. He nodded very slowly. 'So what happens?'

George carefully built his line of solitaire cards. 'Well, that girl rabbits in an' tells the law she been raped. The guys in Weed start a party out to lynch Lennie. So we sit in a irrigation ditch under water all the rest of that day. Got on'y our heads sticking outa water, an' up under the grass that sticks out from the side of the ditch. An' that night we scrammed outa there.'

Slim sat in silence for a moment. 'Didn't hurt the girl none, huh?' he asked finally.

'Hell, no. He just scared her. I'd be scared too if he grabbed me. But he never hurt her. He jus' wanted to touch that red dress, like he wants to pet them pups all the time.'

'He ain't mean,' said Slim. 'I can tell a mean guy a mile off.'

'Course he ain't, and he'll do any damn thing I . . .'

Lennie came in through the door. He wore his blue denim coat over his shoulders like a cape, and he walked hunched way over.

'Hi, Lennie,' said George. 'How do you like the pup now?'

Lennie said breathlessly: 'He's brown an' white jus' like I wanted,' He went directly to his bunk and lay down and turned his face to the wall and drew up his knees.

George put down his cards very deliberately. 'Lennie,' he said sharply.

Lennie twisted his neck and looked over his shoulder. 'Huh? What you want, George?'

'I tol' you you couldn't bring that pup in here.'

'What pup, George? I ain't got no pup.'

George went quickly to him, grabbed him by the shoulder and rolled him over. He reached down and picked the tiny puppy from where Lennie had been concealing it against his stomach.

Lennie sat up quickly. 'Give 'um to me, George.'

George said: 'You get right up an' take this pup back to the nest. He's gotta sleep with his mother. You want to kill him? Just born last night an' you take him out of the nest. You take him back or I'll tell Slim not to let you have him.'

Lennie held out his hands pleadingly. 'Give 'um to me, George. I'll take 'um back. I didn't mean no harm, George. Honest I didn't. I jus' wanted to pet 'um a little.'

George handed the pup to him. 'Awright. You get him back there quick, and don't you take him out no more. You'll kill him, the first thing you know.' Lennie fairly scuttled out of the room.

Slim had not moved. His calm eyes followed Lennie out the door. 'Jesus,' he said. 'He's jes' like a kid, ain't he?'

'Sure he's jes' like a kid. There ain't no more harm in him than a kid neither, except he's so strong. I bet he won't come in here to sleep tonight. He'd sleep right alongside that box in the barn. Well – let 'im. He ain't doin' no harm out there.' It was almost dark outside now. Old Candy, the swamper, came in and went to his bunk, and behind him struggled his old dog. 'Hello, Slim. Hello, George. Didn't neither of you play horse-shoes?'

'I don't like to play ever' night,' said Slim.

Candy went on: 'Either you guys got a slug of whisky? I gotta gut ache.'

'I ain't,' said Slim. 'I'd drink it myself if I had, an' I ain't got a gut ache neither.'

'Gotta bad gut ache,' said Candy. 'Them God damn turnips give it to me. I knowed they was going to before I ever eat 'em.'

The thick-bodied Carlson came in out of the darkening yard. He walked to the other end of the bunk-house and turned on the second shaded light. 'Darker'n'hell in here,' he said. 'Jesus, how that nigger can pitch shoes.'

'He's plenty good,' said Slim.

'Damn right he is,' said Carlson. 'He don't give nobody else a chance to win . . .' He stopped and sniffed the air, and still sniffing, looked down at the old dog. 'God Awmighty that dog stinks. Get him outa here, Candy! I don't know nothing that stinks so bad as an old dog. You gotta get him out.'

Candy rolled to the edge of his bunk. He reached over and patted the ancient dog, and he apologized: 'I been around him so much I never notice how he stinks.'

'Well, I can't stand him in here,' said Carlson. 'That stink hangs around even after he's gone.' He walked over with his heavy-legged stride and looked down at the dog. 'Got no teeth,' he said. 'He's all stiff with rheumatism. He ain't no good to you, Candy. An' he ain't no good to himself. Why'n't you shoot him, Candy?'

The old man squirmed uncomfortably. 'Well – hell! I had him so long. Had him since he was a pup. I herded sheep with him.' He said proudly: 'You wouldn't think it to look at him now, but he was the best damn sheep dog I ever seen.'

George said: 'I seen a guy in Weed that had an Airedale could herd sheep. Learned it from the other dogs.'

Carlson was not to be put off. 'Look, Candy. This ol' dog jus' suffers hisself all the time. If you was to take him out and shoot him right in the back of the head' – he leaned over and pointed – 'right there, why he'd never know what hit him.'

Candy looked about unhappily. 'No,' he said softly. 'No, I couldn't do that. I had 'im too long.'

'He don't have no fun,' Carlson insisted. 'And he stinks to beat hell. Tell you what. I'll shoot him for you. Then it won't be you that does it.'

Candy threw his legs off his bunk. He scratched the white stubble whiskers on his cheek nervously. 'I'm so used too him,' he said softly. 'I had him from a pup.'

'Well, you ain't bein' kind to him keepin' him alive,' said Carlson. 'Look, Slim's bitch got a litter right now. I bet Slim would give you one of them pups to raise up, wouldn't you, Slim?'

The skinner had been studying the old dog with his calm eyes. 'Yeah,' he said. 'You can have a pup if you want to.' He seemed to shake himself free for speech. 'Carl's right, Candy. That dog ain't no good to himself. I wisht somebody'd shoot me if I get old an' a cripple.'

Candy looked helplessly at him, for Slim's opinions were law. 'Maybe it'd hurt him,' he suggested. 'I don't mind takin' care of him.'

Carlson said: 'The way I'd shoot him, he wouldn't feel nothing. I'd put the gun right there.' He pointed with his toe. 'Right back of the head. He wouldn't even quiver.'

Candy looked for help from face to face. It was quite dark outside now. A young labouring man came in. His sloping shoulders were bent forward and he walked heavily on his heels, as though he carried the invisible grain bag. He went to his bunk and put his hat on his shelf. Then he picked a pulp magazine from his shelf and brought it to the light over the table. 'Did I show you this, Slim?' he asked.

'Show me what?'

The young man turned to the back of the magazine, put it down on the table and pointed with his finger. 'Right there, read that.' Slim bent over it. 'Go on,' said the young man. 'Read it out loud.'

'"Dear Editor:"' Slim read slowly. '"I read your mag for six years and I think it is the best on the market. I like stories by Peter Rand. I think he is a whing-ding. Give us more like the "Dark Rider". I don't write many letters. Just thought I would tell you I think your mag is the best dime's worth I ever spent."'

Slim looked up questioningly. 'What you want me to read that for?'

Whit said: 'Go on. Read the name at the bottom.'

Slim read: '"Yours for success, William Tenner."' He glanced up at Whit again. 'What you want me to read that for?'

Whit closed the magazine impressively. 'Don't you remember Bill Tenner? Worked here about three months ago.'

Slim thought . . . 'Little guy?' he asked. 'Drove a cultivator?'

'That's him,' Whit cried. 'That's the guy!'

'You think he's the guy wrote this letter?'

'I know it. Bill and me was in here one day. Bill had one of them books that just come. He was lookin' in it and he says: "I wrote a letter. Wonder if they put it in the book!" but it wasn't there. Bill says: "Maybe they're savin' it for later." An' that's just what they done. There it is.'

'Guess you're right,' said Slim. 'Got it right in the book.' George held out his hand for the magazine. 'Let's look at it?'

Whit found the place again, but he did not surrender his hold on it. He pointed out the letter with his forefinger. And then he went to his box shelf and laid the magazine carefully in. 'I wonder if Bill seen it,' he said. 'Bill and me worked in that patch of field peas. Run cultivators, both of us. Bill was a hell of a nice fella.'

During the conversation Carlson had refused to be drawn in. He continued to look down at the old dog. Candy watched him uneasily. At last Carlson said: 'If you want me to, I'll put the old devil out of his misery right now and get it over with. Ain't nothing left for him. Can't eat, can't see, can't even walk without hurtin'.'

Candy said hopefully: 'You ain't got no gun.'

'The hell I ain't. Got a Luger. It won't hurt him none at all.'

Candy said: 'Maybe tomorra. Le's wait till tomorra.'

'I don't see no reason for it,' said Carlson. He went to his bunk, pulled his bag from underneath it, and took out a Luger pistol. 'Le's get it over with,' he said. 'We can't sleep with him stinkin' around in here.' He put the pistol in his hip pocket.

Candy looked a long time at Slim to try to find some reversal. And Slim gave him none. At last Candy said softly and hopelessly: 'Awright – take 'im.' He did not look down at the dog at all. He lay back on his bunk and crossed his arms behind his head and stared at the ceiling.

From his pocket Carlson took a little leather thong. He stooped over and tied it around the old dog's neck. All the men except Candy watched him. 'Come, boy. Come on, boy,' he said gently. And he said apologetically to Candy: 'He won't even feel it.' Candy did not move nor answer him. He twitched the thong. 'Come on, boy.' The old dog got slowly and stiffly to his feet and followed the gently-pulling leash.

Slim said: 'Carlson.'

'Yeah?'

'You know what to do?'

'What ya mean, Slim?'

'Take a shovel,' said Slim shortly.

'Oh, sure! I get you.' He led the dog out into the darkness.

George followed to the door and shut the door and set the latch gently in its place. Candy lay rigidly on his bed staring at the ceiling.

Slim said loudly: 'One of my lead mules got a bad hoof. Got to get some tar on it.' His voice trailed off. It was silent outside. Carlson's footsteps died away. The silence came into the room. And the silence lasted.

George chuckled: 'I bet Lennie's right out there in the barn with his pup. He won't want to come in here no more now he's got a pup.'

Slim said: 'Candy, you can have any one of them pups you want.'

Candy did not answer. The silence fell on the room again. It came out of the night and invaded the room. George said: 'Anybody like to play a little euchre?'

'I'll play out a few with you,' said Whit.

They took places opposite each other at the table under the light, but George did not shuffle the cards. He rippled the edge of the deck nervously, and the little snapping noise drew the eyes of all the men in the room, so that he stopped doing it. The silence fell on the room again. A minute passed, and another minute. Candy lay still, staring at the ceiling. Slim gazed at him for a moment and then looked down at his hands; he subdued one hand with the other, and held it down. There came a little gnawing sound from under the floor and all the men looked down toward it gratefully. Only Candy continued to stare at the ceiling.

'Sounds like there was a rat under there,' said George. 'We ought to get a trap down there.'

Whit broke out: 'What the hell's takin' him so long. Lay out some cards, why don't you? We ain't going to get no euchre played this way.'

George brought the cards together tightly and studied the backs of them. The silence was in the room again.

A shot sounded in the distance. The men looked quickly at the old man. Every head turned toward him.

For a moment he continued to stare at the ceiling. Then he rolled slowly over and faced the wall and lay silent.

George shuffled the cards noisily and dealt them. Whit drew a scoring board to him and set the pegs to start. Whit said: 'I guess you guys really come here to work.'

'How do ya mean?' George asked.

Whit laughed. 'Well, ya come on a Friday. You got two days to work till Sunday.'

'I don't see how you figure,' said George.

Whit laughed again. 'You do if you been around these big ranches much. Guy that wants to look over a ranch comes in Sat'day afternoon. He gets Sat'day night supper an' three meals on Sunday, and he can quit Monday mornin' after breakfast without turning his hand. But you come to work Friday noon. You got to put in a day an' a half no matter how you figure.'

George looked at him levelly. 'We're gonna stick aroun' a while,' he said. 'Me an' Lennie's gonna roll up a stake.'

The door opened quietly and the stable buck put in his head; a lean negro head, lined with pain, the eye patient. 'Mr Slim.'

Slim took his eyes from old Candy. 'Huh? Oh! Hello, Crooks. What's 'a matter?'

'You told me to warm up tar for that mule's foot. I got it warm.'

'Oh! Sure, Crooks. I'll come right out an' put it on.'

'I can do it if you want, Mr Slim.'

'No. I'll come do it myself.' He stood up.

Crooks said: 'Mr Slim.'

'Yeah.'

'That big new guy's messin' around your pups out in the barn.'

'Well, he ain't doin' no harm. I give him one of them pups.'

'Just thought I'd tell ya,' said Crooks. 'He's takin' 'em outa nest and handlin' them. That won't do them no good.'

'He won't hurt 'em,' said Slim. 'I'll come along with you now.'

George looked up. 'If that crazy bastard's foolin' around too much, jus' kick him out, Slim.'

Slim followed the stable buck out of the room.

George dealt and Whit picked up his cards and examined them. 'Seen the new kid yet?' he asked.

'What kid?' George asked.

'Why, Curley's new wife.'

'Yeah, I see her.'

'Well, ain't she a looloo?'

'I ain't seen that much of her,' said George.

Whit laid down his cards impressively. 'Well, stick around an' keep your eyes open. You'll see plenty. She ain't concealin' nothing. I never seen nobody like her. She got the eye goin' all the time on everybody. I bet she even gives the stable buck the eye. I don't know what the hell she wants.'

George asked casually: 'Been any trouble since she got here?'

It was obvious that Whit was not interested in his cards. He laid his hand down and George scooped it in. George laid out his deliberate solitaire hand – seven cards, and six on top, and five on top of those.

Whit said: 'I see what you mean. No, they ain't been nothing yet. Curley's got yella-jackets in his drawers, but that's all so far. Ever' time the guys is around she shows up. She's lookin' for Curley, or she thought she lef' somethin' layin' around and she's lookin' for it. Seems like she can't keep away from guys. An' Curley's pants is just crawlin' with ants, but they ain't nothing come of it yet.'

George said: 'She's gonna make a mess. They's gonna be a bad mess about her. She's a jail bait all set on the trigger. That Curley got his work cut out for him. Ranch with a bunch of guys on it ain't no place for a girl, specially like her.'

Whit said: 'If you got idears, you ought to come in town with us guys tomorra night.'

'Why? What's doin'?'

'Jus' the usual thing. We go in to old Susy's place. Hell of a nice place. Old Susy's a laugh – always crackin' jokes. Like she says when we come up on the front porch las' Sat'day night. Susy opens the door and then she yells over her shoulder: "Get yor coats on, girls, here comes the sheriff." She never talks dirty, neither. Got five girls there.'

'What's it set you back?' George asked.

'Two an' a half. You can get a shot for two bits. Susy got nice chairs to set in, too. If a guy don't want a flop, why he can jest set in the chairs and have a couple or three shots and pass the time of day and Susy don't give a damn. She ain't rushin' guys through and kickin' 'em out of they don't want a flop.'

'Might go in and look the joint over,' said George.

'Sure. Come along. It's a hell of a lot of fun – her crackin' jokes all the time. Like she says one time, she says: "I've knew people that if they got a rag rug on the floor an' a kewpie doll lamp on the phonograph, they think they're running a parlour house." That's Clara's house she's talkin' about. An' Susy says: "I know what you boys want," she says. "My girls is clean," she says, "an' there ain't no water in my whisky," she says. "If any you guys wanta look at a kewpie doll lamp an' take your own chance gettin' burned, why you know where to go." An' she says: "There's guys around here walkin' bow-legged 'cause they like to look at a kewpie doll lamp."'

George asked: 'Clara runs the other house, huh?'

'Yeah,' said Whit. 'We don't never go there. Clara gets three bucks a crack and thirty-five cents a shot, and she don't crack no jokes. But Susy's place is clean and she got nice chairs. Don't let no goo-goos in, neither.'

'Me an' Lennie's rollin' up a stake,' said George. 'I might go in an' set and have a shot, but I ain't puttin' on no two and a half.'

'Well, a guy got to have some fun sometime,' said Whit.

The door opened and Lennie and Carlson came in together. Lennie crept to his bunk and sat down, trying not to attract attention. Carlson reached under his bunk and brought out his bag. He didn't look at old Candy, who still faced the wall. Carlson found a little cleaning rod in the bag and a can of oil. He laid them on his bed and then brought out the pistol, took out the magazine and snapped the loaded shell from the chamber. Then he fell to cleaning the barrel with the little rod. When the ejector snapped, Candy turned over and looked for a moment at the gun before he turned back to the wall again.

Carlson said casually: 'Curley been in yet?'

'No,' said Whit. 'What's eatin' on Curley?'

Carlson squinted down the barrel of his gun. 'Lookin' for his old lady. I seen him going round and round outside.'

Whit said sarcastically: 'He spends half his time lookin' for her, and the rest of the time she's lookin' for him.'

Curley burst into the room excitedly. 'Any you guys seen my wife?' he demanded.

'She ain't been here,' said Whit.

Curley looked threateningly about the room. 'Where's the hell's Slim?'

'Went out in the barn,' said George. 'He was gonna put some tar on a split hoof.'

Curley's shoulders dropped and squared. 'How long ago'd he go?'

'Five – ten minutes.'

Curley jumped out the door and banged it after him.

Whit stood up. 'I guess maybe I'd like to see this,' he said. 'Curley's just spoilin' or he wouldn't start for Slim. An' Curley's handy, God damn handy. Got in the finals for the Golden Gloves. He got newspaper clippings about it.' He considered. 'But jus' the same, he better leave Slim alone. Nobody knows what Slim can do.'

'Thinks Slim's with his wife, don't he?' said George.

'Looks like it,' Whit said. ''Course Slim ain't. Least I don't think Slim is. But I like to see the fuss if it comes off. Come on, let's go.'

George said: 'I'm stayin' right here. I don't want to get mixed up in nothing. Lennie and me got to make a stake.'

Carlson finished the cleaning of the gun and put it in the bag and pushed the bag under his bunk. 'I guess I'll go out and look her over,' he said. Old Candy lay still, and Lennie, from his bunk, watched George cautiously.

When Whit and Carlson were gone and the door closed after them, George turned to Lennie. 'What you got on your mind?'

'I ain't done nothing, George. Slim says I better not pet them pups so much for a while. Slim says it ain't good for them; so I come right in. I been good, George.'

'I coulda told you that,' said George.

'Well, I wasn't hurtin' 'em none. I jus' had mine in my lap pettin' it.'

George asked: 'Did you see Slim out in the barn?'

'Sure I did. He tol' me I better not pet that pup no more.'

'Did you see that girl?'

'You mean Curley's girl?'

'Yeah. Did she come in the barn?'

'No. Anyways I never seen her.'

'You never seen Slim talkin' to her?'

'Uh-uh. She ain't been in the barn.'

'O.K.,' said George. 'I guess them guys ain't gonna see no fight. If there's any fightin', Lennie, you keep out of it.'

'I don't want no fights,' said Lennie. He got up from his bunk and sat down at the table, across from George. Almost automatically George shuffled the cards and laid out his solitaire hand. He used a deliberate, thoughtful slowness.

Lennie reached for a face card and studied it, then turned it upside down and studied it. 'Both ends the same,' he said. 'George, why is it both end's the same?'

'I don't know,' said George. 'That's jus' the way they make 'em. What was Slim doin' in the barn when you seen him?'

'Slim?'

'Sure. You seen him in the barn, an' he tol' you not to pet the pups so much.'

'Oh, yeah. He had a can a' tar an' a paint brush. I don't know what for.'

'You sure that girl didn't come in like she come in here today?'

'No. She never come.'

George sighed. 'You give me a good whore-house every time,' he said. 'A guy can go in an' get drunk and get ever'-thing outa his system all at once, an' no messes. And he knows how much it's gonna set him back. These here jail baits is just set on the trigger of the hoosegow.'

Lennie followed his words admiringly, and moved his lips a little to keep up. George continued: 'You remember Andy Cushman, Lennie? Went to grammar school?'

'The one that his old lady used to make hot cakes for the kids?' Lennie asked.

'Yeah. That's the one. You can remember anything if there's anything to eat in it.' George looked carefully at the solitaire hand. He put an ace up on his scoring rack and piled a two, three and four of diamonds on it. 'Andy's in San Quentin right now on account of a tart,' said George.

Lennie drummed on the table with his fingers. 'George?'

'Huh?'

'George, how long's it gonna be till we get that little place an' live on the fatta the lan' – an' rabbits?'

'I don't know,' said George. 'We gotta get a big stake together. I know a little place we can get cheap, but they ain't givin' it away.'

Old Candy turned slowly over. His eyes were wide open. He watched George carefully.

Lennie said: 'Tell about that place, George.'

'I jus' tol' you, jus' las' night.'

'Go on – tell again, George.'

'Well, it's ten acres,' said George. 'Got a little win'mill. Got a little shack on it, an' a chicken run. Got a kitchen, orchard, cherries, apples, peaches, 'cots, nuts, got a few berries. They's a place for alfalfa and plenty water to flood it. They's a pig-pen . . .'

'An' rabbits, George.'

'No place for rabbits now, but I could easy build a few hutches and you could feed alfalfa to the rabbits.'

'Damn right, I could,' said Lennie. 'You God damn right I could.'

George's hands stopped working with the cards. His voice was growing warmer. 'An' we could have a few pigs. I could build a smoke-house like the one gran'pa had, an' when we kill a pig we can smoke the bacon and the hams, and make sausage an' all like that. An' when the salmon run up river we could catch a hundred of 'em an' salt 'em down or smoke 'em. We could have them for breakfast. They ain't nothing so nice as smoked salmon. When the fruit come in we could can it – and tomatoes, they're easy to can. Ever' Sunday we'd kill a chicken or a rabbit. Maybe, we'd have a cow or a goat, and the cream is so God damn thick you got to cut it with a knife and take it out with a spoon.'

Lennie watched him with wide eyes, and old Candy watched him too. Lennie said softly: 'We could live offa the fatta the lan'.'

'Sure,' said George. 'All kin's a vegetables in the garden, and if we want a little whisky we can sell a few eggs or something, or some milk. We'd jus' live there. We'd belong there. There wouldn't be no more runnin' round the country and gettin' fed by a Jap cook. No, sir, we'd have our own place where we belonged and not sleep in no bunkhouse.'

'Tell about the house, George,' Lennie begged.

'Sure, we'd have a little house an' a room to ourself. Little fat iron stove, an' in the winter we'd keep a fire goin' in it. It ain't enough land so we'd have to work too hard. Maybe six, seven hours a day. We wouldn't have to buck no barley eleven hours a day. An' when we put in a crop, why, we'd be there to take the crop up. We'd know what come of our planting.'

'An' rabbits,' Lennie said eagerly. 'An' I'd take care of 'em. Tell how I'd do that, George.'

'Sure, you'd go out in the alfalfa patch an' you'd have a sack. You'd fill up the sack and bring it in an' put in the rabbit cages.'

'They'd nibble an' they'd nibble," said Lennie, 'the way they do. I seen 'em.'

'Ever' six weeks or so,' George continued, 'them does would throw a litter, so we'd have plenty rabbits to eat an' to sell. An' we'd keep a few pigeons to go flyin' around the win'mill like they done when I was a kid.' He looked raptly at the wall over Lennie's head. 'An' it'd be our own, an' nobody could can us. If we don't like a guy we can say: "Get the hell out," and by God he's got to do it. An' if a fren' come along, why we'd have an extra bunk, an' we'd say: "Why don't you spen' the night," an' by God he would. We'd have a setter dog and a couple stripe cats, but you gotta watch out them cats don't get the little rabbits.'

Lennie breathed hard. 'You jus' let 'em try to get the rabbits. I'll break their God damn necks. I'll . . . I'll smash 'em with a stick.' He subsided, grumbling to himself, threatening the future cats which might dare to disturb the future rabbits.

George sat entranced with his own picture.

When Candy spoke they both jumped as though they had been caught doing something reprehensible. Candy said: 'You know where's a place like that?'

George was on guard immediately. 'S'pose I do,' he said. 'What's that to you?'

'You don't need to tell me where it's at. Might be any place.'

'Sure,' said George. 'That's right. You couldn't find it in a hundred years.'

Candy went on excitedly: 'How much they want for a place like that?'

George watched him suspiciously. 'Well – I could get it for six hundred bucks. The ol' people that owns it is flat bust an' the ol' lady needs an operation. Say – what's it to you? You got nothing to do with us.'

Candy said: 'I ain't much good with o'ny one hand. I lost my hand right here on this ranch. That's why they give me a job swampin'. An' they give me two hundred an' fifty dollars 'cause I los' my hand. An' I got fifty more saved up right in the bank, right now. Tha's three hundred, and I got fifty more comin' the enda the month. Tell you what . . .' He leaned forward eagerly. 'S'pose I went in with you guys. Tha's three hundred an' fifty bucks I'd put in. I ain't much good, but I could cook and tend the chickens and hoe the garden some. How'd that be?'

George half-closed his eyes. 'I gotta think about that. We was always gonna do it by ourselves.'

Candy interrupted him: 'I'd make a will an' leave my share to you guys in case I kick off, 'cause I ain't got no relatives nor nothing. You guys got any money? Maybe we could do her right now?'

George spat on the floor disgustedly. 'We got ten bucks between us.' Then he said thoughtfully: 'Look, if me an' Lennie work a month an' don't spen' nothing, we'll have a hundred bucks. That'd be four-fifty. I bet we could swing her for that. Then you an' Lennie could go get her started an' I'd get a job an' make up the res', an' you could sell eggs an' stuff like that.'

They fell into a silence. They looked at one another, amazed. This thing they had never really believed in was coming true. George said reverently: 'Jesus Christ! I bet we could swing her.' His eyes were full of wonder. 'I bet we could swing her,' he repeated softly.

Candy sat on the edge of his bunk. He scratched the stump of his wrist nervously. 'I got hurt four year ago,' he said. 'They'll can me purty soon. Jus' as soon as I can't swamp out no bunk-houses they'll put me on the county. Maybe if I give you guys my money, you'll let me hoe in the garden even after I ain't no good at it. An' I'll wash dishes an' little chicken stuff like that. But I'll be on our own place, an' I'll be let to work on our own place.' He said miserably: 'You seen what they done to my dog tonight? They says he wasn't no good to himself nor nobody else. When they can me here I wisht somebody'd shoot me. But they won't do nothing like that. I won't have no place to go, an' I can't get no more jobs. I'll have thirty dollars more comin', time you guys is ready to quit.'

George stood up. 'We'll do her,' he said. 'We'll fix up that little old place an' we'll go live there.' He sat down again.

They all sat still, all bemused by the beauty of the thing, each mind was popped into the future when this lovely thing should come about.

George said wanderingly: 'S'pose they was a carnival or a circus come to town, or a ball game, or any damn thing.' Old Candy nodded in appreciation of the idea. 'We'd just go to her,' George said. 'We wouldn't ask nobody if we could. Jus' say: "We'll go to her," an' we would. Jus' milk the cow and sling some grain to the chickens an' go to her.'

'An put some grass to the rabbits,' Lennie broke in. 'I wouldn't never forget to feed them. When we gon'ta do it, George?'

'In one month. Right squack in one month. Know what I'm gon'ta do. I'm gon'ta write to them old people that owns the place that we'll take it. An' Candy'll send a hunderd dollars to bind her.'

'Sure will,' said Candy. 'They got a good stove there?'

'Sure, got a nice stove, burns coal or wood.'

'I'm gonna take my pup,' said Lennie. 'I bet by Christ he likes it there, by Jesus.'

Voices were approaching from outside. George said quickly: 'Don't tell nobody about it. Jus' us three an' nobody else. They li'ble to can us we can't make no stake. Jus' go on like we was gonna buck barley the rest of our lives, then all of a sudden some day we'll go get our pay an' scram outa here.'

Lennie and Candy nodded, and they were grinning with delight. 'Don't tell nobody,' Lennie said to himself.

Candy said: 'George.'

'Huh?'

'I ought to of shot that dog myself, George. I shouldn't ought to of let no stranger shoot my dog.'

The door opened. Slim came in, followed by Curley and Carlson and Whit. Slim's hands were black with tar and he was scowling. Curley hung close to his elbow.

Curley said: 'Well, I didn't mean nothing, Slim. I just ast you.'

Slim said: 'Well, you been askin' me too often. I'm gettin'

God damn sick of it. If you can't look after your own God damn wife, what you expect me to do about it? You lay offa me.'

'I'm jus' tryin' to tell you I didn't mean nothing,' said Curley. 'I jus' thought you might of saw her.'

'Why'n't you tell her to stay the hell home where she belongs?' said Carlson. 'You let her hang around bunk-houses and pretty soon you're gonna have som'pin on your hands and you won't be able to do nothing about it.'

Curley whirled on Carlson. 'You keep outa this les' you wanta step outside.'

Carlson laughed. 'You God damn punk,' he said. 'You tried to throw a scare into Slim, an' you couldn't make it stick. Slim throwed a scare into you. You're yella as a frog belly. I don't care if you're the best welter in the country. You come for me, an' I'll kick your God damn head off.'

Candy joined the attack with joy. 'Glove fulla vaseline,' he said disgustedly. Curley glared at him. His eyes slipped on past and lighted on Lennie; and Lennie was still smiling with delight at the memory of the ranch.

Curley stepped over to Lennie like a terrier. 'What the hell you laughin' at?'

Lennie looked blankly at him. 'Huh?'

Then Curley's rage exploded. 'Come on, ya big bastard. Get up on your feet. No big son-of-a-bitch is gonna laugh at me. I'll show ya who's yella.'

Lennie looked helplessly at George, and then he got up and tried to retreat. Curley was balanced and poised. He slashed at Lennie with his left, and then smashed down his nose with a right. Lennie gave a cry of terror. Blood welled from his nose. 'George,' he cried. 'Make 'um let me alone, George.' He backed until he was against the wall, and Curley followed, slugging him in the face. Lennie's hands remained at his sides; he was too frightened to defend himself.

George was on his feet yelling: 'Get him, Lennie. Don't let him do it.'

Lennie covered his face with his huge paws and bleated with terror. He cried: 'Make 'um stop, George.' Then Curley attacked his stomach and cut off his wind.

Slim jumped up. 'The dirty little rat,' he cried, 'I'll get 'um myself.'

George put out his hand and grabbed Slim. 'Wait a minute,' he shouted. He cupped his hands around his mouth and yelled: 'Get 'im, Lennie!'

Lennie took his hands away from his face and looked about for George, and Curley slashed at his eyes. The big face was covered with blood. George yelled again: 'I said get him.'

Curley's fist was swinging when Lennie reached for it. The next minute Curley was flopping like a fish on a line, and his closed fist was lost in Lennie's big hand. George ran down the room. 'Leggo of him, Lennie. Let go.'

But Lennie watched in terror the flopping little man whom he held. Blood ran down Lennie's face, one of his eyes was cut and closed. George slapped him on the face again and again, and still Lennie held on to the closed fist. Curley was white and shrunken by now, and his struggling had become weak. He stood crying, his fist lost in Lennie's paw.

George shouted over and over: 'Leggo his hand, Lennie. Leggo. Slim, come help me while the guy got any hand left.'

Suddenly Lennie let go his hold. He crouched cowering against the wall. 'You tol' me to, George,' he said miserably.

Curley sat down on the floor, looking in wonder at his crushed hand. Slim and Carlson bent over him. Then Slim straightened up and regarded Lennie with horror. 'We got to get him in to a doctor,' he said. 'Looks to me like ever' bone in his han' is bust.'

'I didn't wanta,' Lennie cried. 'I didn't wanta hurt him.'

Slim said: 'Carlson, you get the candy wagon hitched up. We'll take 'um into Soledad an' get 'um fixed up.' Carlson hurried out. Slim turned to the whimpering Lennie. 'It ain't your fault,' he said. 'This punk sure had it comin' to him.

But – Jesus! He ain't hardly got no han' left.' Slim hurried out, and in a moment returned with a tin cup of water. He held it to Curley's lips.

George said: 'Slim, will we get canned now? We need the stake. Will Curley's old man can us now?'

Slim smiled wryly. He knelt down beside Curley. 'You got your senses in hand enough to listen?' he asked. Curley nodded. 'Well, then, listen,' Slim went on. 'I think you got your han' caught in a machine. If you don't tell nobody what happened, we ain't going to. But you jus' tell an' try to get this guy canned and we'll tell ever'body, an' then will you get the laugh.'

'I won't tell,' said Curley. He avoided looking at Lennie.

Buggy wheels sounded outside. Slim helped Curley up. 'Come on now. Carlson's gonna take you to a doctor.' He helped Curley out the door. The sound of wheels drew away. In a moment Slim came back into the bunk-house. He looked at Lennie, still crouched fearfully against the wall. 'Let's see your hands,' he asked.

Lennie stuck out his hands.

'Christ awmighty, I hate to have you mad at me,' Slim said.

George broke in: 'Lennie was jus' scairt,' he explained. 'He didn't know what to do. I told you nobody ought never to fight him. No, I guess it was Candy I told.'

Candy nodded solemnly. 'That's jus' what you done,' he said. 'Right this morning when Curley first lit intil your fren', you says: "He better not fool with Lennie if he knows what good for 'um." That's jus' what you says to me.'

George turned to Lennie. 'It ain't your fault,' he said. 'You don't need to be scairt no more. You done jus' what I tol' you to. Maybe you better go in the washroom an' clean up your face. You look like hell.'

Lennie smiled with his bruised mouth. 'I didn't want no trouble,' he said. He walked towards the door, but just before he came to it he turned back. 'George?'

'What you want?'

'I can still tend the rabbits, George?'

'Sure. You ain't done nothing wrong.'

'I didn't mean no harm, George.'
'Well, get the hell out and wash your face.'

*

CROOKS, the negro stable buck, had his bunk in the harness-room; a little shed that leaned off the wall of the barn. On one side of the little room there was a square four-paned window, and on the other, a narrow plank door leading into the barn. Crook's bunk was a long box filled with straw, on which his blankets were flung. On the wall by the window there were pegs on which hung broken harness in process of being mended, strips of new leather; and under the window itself a little bench for leather-working tools, curved knives and needles and balls of linen thread, and a small hand riveter. On pegs were also pieces of harness, a split collar with the horsehair stuffing sticking out, a broken hame, and a trace chain with its leather covering split. Crooks had his apple-box over his bunk, and in it a range of medicine bottles, both for himself and for the horses. There were cans of saddle soap and a drippy can of tar with its paint-brush sticking over the edge. And scattered about the floor were a number of personal possessions; for, being alone, Crooks could leave his things about, and being a stable buck and a cripple, he was more permanent than the other men, and he had accumulated more possessions than he could carry on his back.

Crooks possessed several pairs of shoes, a pair of rubber boots, a big alarm clock, and a single-barrelled shot-gun. And he had books, too; a tattered dictionary and a mauled copy of the California civil code for 1905. There were battered magazines and a few dirty books on a special shelf over his bunk. A pair of large gold-rimmed spectacles hung from a nail on the wall above his bed.

This room was swept and fairly neat, for Crooks was a proud, aloof man. He kept his distance and demanded that other people keep theirs. His body was bent over to the left by his crooked spine, and his eyes lay deep in his head, and because of their depth seemed to glitter with intensity. His lean face was lined with deep black wrinkles, and he had thin, pain-tightened lips which were lighter than his face.

It was Saturday night. Through the open door that led into the barn came the sound of moving horses, of feet stirring, of teeth champing on hay, of the rattle of halter chains. In the stable buck's room a small electric globe threw a meagre yellow light.

Crooks sat on his bunk. His shirt was out of his jeans at the back. In one hand he held a bottle of liniment, with the other he rubbed his spine. Now and then he poured a few drops of the liniment into his pink-palmed hand and reached up under his shirt to rub again. He flexed his muscles against his back and shivered.

Noiselessly, Lennie appeared in the open doorway and stood there looking in, his big shoulders nearly filling the opening. For a moment Crooks did not see him, but on raising his eyes he stiffened and a scowl came on his face. His hands came out from under his shirt.

Lennie smiled helplessly in an attempt to make friends.

Crooks said sharply: 'You got no right to come in my room. This here's my room. Nobody got any right in here but me.'

Lennie gulped and his smile grew more fawning. 'I ain't doing nothing,' he said. 'Just come to look at my puppy. And I seen your light,' he explained.

'Well, I got a right to have a light. You go on get outa my room. I ain't wanted in the bunk-house, and you ain't wanted in my room.'

'Why ain't you wanted?' Lennie asked.

''Cause I'm black. They play cards in there, but I can't play because I'm black. They say I stink. Well, I tell you, you all of you stink to me.'

Lennie flapped his big hands helplessly. 'Ever'body went into town,' he said. 'Slim an' George an' ever'body. George says I gotta stay here an' not get in no trouble. I seen your light.'

'Well, what do you want?'

'Nothing – I seen your light. I thought I could jus' come in an' set.'

Crooks stared at Lennie, and he reached behind him and took down the spectacles and adjusted them over his pink ears and stared again. 'I don't know what you're doin' in the barn anyway,' he complained. 'You ain't no skinner. They's no call for a bucker to come into the barn at all. You ain't no skinner. You ain't got nothing to do with the horses.'

'The pup,' Lennie repeated. 'I come to see my pup.'

'Well, go see your pup, then. Don't come in a place where you're not wanted.'

Lennie lost his smile. He advanced a step into the room, then remembered and backed to the door again. 'I looked at 'em a little. Slim says I ain't to pet 'em very much.'

Crooks said: 'Well, you been takin' 'em out of the nest all the time. I wonder the old lady don't move 'em someplace else.'

'Oh, she don't care. She lets me.' Lennie had moved into the room again.

Crooks scowled, but Lennie's disarming smile defeated him. 'Come on in and set a while,' Crooks said. ''Long as you won't get out and leave me alone, you might as well set down.' His tone was a little more friendly. 'All the boys gone into town, huh?'

'All but old Candy. He just sets in the bunk-house sharpening his pencil and sharpening and figuring.'

Crooks adjusted his glasses. 'Figuring? What's Candy figuring about?'

Lennie almost shouted: ''Bout the rabbits.'

'You're nuts,' said Crooks. 'You're crazy as a wedge. What rabbits you talkin' about?'

'The rabbits we're gonna get, and I get to tend 'em, cut grass an' give 'em water, an' like that.'

'Jus' nuts,' said Crooks. 'I don't blame the guy you travel with for keepin' you outa sight.'

Lennie said quietly: 'It ain't no lie. We're gonna do it. Gonna get a little place an' live on the fatta the lan'.'

Crooks settled himself more comfortably on his bunk. 'Set down,' he invited. 'Set down on the nail-keg.'

Lennie hunched down on the little barrel. 'You think it's

a lie,' Lennie said, 'but it ain't no lie. Ever' word's the truth, an' you can ast George.'

Crooks put his dark chin into his pink palm. 'You travel aroun' with George, don't ya?'

'Sure. Me an' him goes ever' place together.'

Crooks continued. 'Sometimes he talks, and you don't know what the hell he's talkin' about. Ain't that so?' He leaned forward, boring Lennie with his deep eyes. 'Ain't that so?'

'Yeah . . . sometimes.'

'Jus' talks on, an' you don't know what the hell it's all about?'

'Yeah . . . sometimes. But . . . not always.'

Crooks leaned forward over the edge of the bunk. 'I ain't a southern negro,' he said. 'I was born right here in California. My old man had a chicken ranch, 'bout ten acres. The white kids come to play at our place, an' sometimes I went to play with them, and some of them was pretty nice. My ol' man didn't like that. I never knew till long later why he didn't like that. But I know now.' He hesitated, and when he spoke again his voice was softer. 'There wasn't another coloured family for miles around. And now there ain't a coloured man on this ranch an' there's jus' one family in Soledad.' He laughed. 'If I say something, why it's just a nigger saying it.'

Lennie asked: 'How long you think it'll be before them pups will be old enough to pet?'

Crooks laughed again. 'A guy can talk to you an' be sure you won't go blabbin'. Couple of weeks' an' them pups'll be all right. George knows what he's about. Jus' talks, an' you don't understand nothing.' He leaned forward excitedly. 'This is just a nigger talkin', an' a busted-back nigger. So it don't mean nothing, see? You couldn't remember it anyways. I seen it over an' over an' over – a guy talkin' to another guy and it don't make no difference if he don't hear or understand. The thing is, they're talkin', or they're settin' still not talkin'. It don't make no difference, no difference.' His excitement had increased until he pounded his knee with his hand. 'George can tell you screwy things, and it don't matter. It's just the talking. It's just bein' with another guy. That's all.' He paused.

His voice grew soft and persuasive. 'S'pose George don't come back no more. S'pose he took a powder and just ain't coming back. What'll you do then?'

Lennie's attention came gradually to what had been said. 'What?' he demanded.

'I said s'pose George went into town tonight and you never heard of him no more.' Crooks pressed forward some kind of private victory. 'Just s'pose that,' he repeated.

'He won't do it,' Lennie cried. 'George wouldn't do nothing like that. I been with George a long time. He'll come back tonight . . .' But the doubt was too much for him. 'Don't you think he will?'

Crooks face lighted with pleasure in his torture. 'Nobody can't tell what a guy'll do,' he observed calmly. 'Le's say he wants to come back and can't. S'pose he gets killed or hurt so he can't come back.'

Lennie struggled to understand. 'George won't do nothing like that,' he repeated. 'George is careful. He won't get hurt. He ain't never been hurt, 'cause he's careful.'

'Well, s'pose, jus' s'pose he don't come back. What'll you do then?'

Lennie's face wrinkled with apprehension. 'I don' know. Say, what you doin' anyways?' he cried. 'This ain't true. George ain't got hurt.'

Crooks bored in on him. 'Want me ta tell ya what'll happen? They'll take ya to the booby hatch. They'll tie ya up with a collar, like a dog.'

Suddenly Lennie's eyes centred and grew quiet and mad. He stood up and walked dangerously towards Crooks. 'Who hurt George?' he demanded.

Crooks saw the danger as it approached him. He edged back on his bunk to get out of the way. 'I was just supposin',' he said. 'George ain't hurt. He's all right. He'll be back all right.'

Lennie stood over him. 'What you supposin' for? Ain't nobody goin' to suppose no hurt to George.'

Crooks removed his glasses and wiped his eyes with his fingers. 'Jus' set down,' he said. 'George ain't hurt.'

Lennie growled back to his seat on the nail-keg. 'Ain't nobody goin' to talk no hurt to George,' he grumbled.

Crooks said gently: 'Maybe you can see now. You got George. You *know* he's goin' to come back. S'pose you didn't have nobody. S'pose you couldn't go into the bunk-house and play rummy 'cause you was black. How'd you like that? S'pose you had to sit out here an' read books. Sure you could play horseshoes till it got dark, but then you got to read books. Books ain't no good. A guy needs somebody – to be near him.' He whined: 'A guy goes nuts if he ain't got nobody. Don't make no difference who the guy is, long's he's with you. I tell ya,' he cried, 'I tell ya a guy gets too lonely an' he gets sick.'

'George gonna come back,' Lennie reassured himself in a frightened voice. 'Maybe George come back already. Maybe I better go see.'

Crooks said: 'I didn't mean to scare you. He'll come back. I was talkin' about myself. A guy sets alone out here at night, maybe readin' books or thinkin' or stuff like that. Sometimes he gets thinkin', an' he got nothing to tell him what's so an' what ain't so. Maybe if he sees somethin', he don't know whether it's right or not. He can't turn to some other guy and ast him if he sees it too. He can't tell. He got nothing to measure by. I seen things out here. I wasn't drunk. I don't know if I was asleep. If some guy was with me, he could tell me I was asleep, an' then it would be all right. But I jus' don't know.' Crooks was looking across the room now, looking towards the window.

Lennie said miserably: 'George wun't go away and leave me. I know George wun't do that.'

The stable buck went on dreamily: 'I remember when I was a little kid on my old man's chicken ranch. Had two brothers. They was always near me, always there. Used to sleep right in the same room, right in the same bed – all three. Had a strawberry patch. Had an alfalfa patch. Used to turn the chickens out in the alfalfa on a sunny morning. My brothers'd set on a fence rail an' watch 'em – white chickens they was.'

Gradually Lennie's interest came around to what was

being said. 'George says we're gonna have alfalfa for the rabbits.'

'What rabbits?'

'We're gonna have rabbits an' a berry patch.'

'You're nuts.'

'We are too. You ast George.'

'You're nuts.' Crooks was scornful. 'I see hunderds of men come by on the road an' on the ranches with their bindles on their back an' that same damn thing in their heads. Hunderds of them. They come, an' they quit an' go on; an' every damn one of 'em's got a little piece of land in his head. An' never a God damn one of 'em ever gets it. Just like heaven. Ever'body wants a little piece of lan'. I read plenty of books out here. Nobody never gets to heaven, and nobody never gets no land. It's just in their head. They're all the time talkin' about it, but it's jus' in their head.' He paused and looked toward the open door, for the horses were moving restlessly and the halter chains clinked. A horse whinnied. 'I guess somebody's out there,' Crooks said. 'Maybe Slim. Slim comes in sometimes two, three times a night. Slim's a real skinner. He looks out for his team.' He pulled himself painfully upright and moved toward the door. 'That you, Slim?' he called.

Candy's voice answered. 'Slim went in town. Say, you seen Lennie?'

'Ya mean the big guy?'

'Yeah. Seen him around any place?'

'He's in here,' Crooks said shortly. He went back to his bunk and lay down.

Candy stood in the doorway scratching his bald wrist and looking blindly into the lighted room. He made no attempt to enter. 'Tell ya what, Lennie. I been figuring out about them rabbits.'

Crooks said irritably: 'You can come in if you want.'

Candy seemed embarrassed. 'I do' know. 'Course, if ya want me to.'

'Come on in. If ever'body's comin' in, you might just as well.' It was difficult for Crooks to conceal his pleasure with anger.

Candy came in, but he was still embarrassed. 'You got a nice cosy little place in here,' he said to Crooks. 'Must be nice to have a room all to yourself this way.'

'Sure,' said Crooks. 'And a manure pile under the window. Sure it's swell.'

Lennie broke in: 'You said about them rabbits.'

Candy leaned against the wall beside the broken collar while he scratched the wrist stump. 'I been here a long time,' he said. 'An' Crooks been here a long time. This's the first time I ever been in his room.'

Crooks said darkly: 'Guys don't come into a coloured man's room very much Nobody been here but Slim. Slim an' the boss.'

Candy quickly changed the subject. 'Slim's as good a skinner as I ever seen.'

Lennie leaned toward the old swamper. 'About them rabbits,' he insisted.

Candy smiled. 'I got it figured out. We can make some money on them rabbits if we go about it right.'

'But I get to tend 'em,' Lennie broke in. 'George says I get to tend 'em. He promised.'

Crooks interrupted brutally. 'You guys is just kiddin' yourself. You'll talk about it a hell of a lot, but you won't get no land. You'll be a swamper here till they take you out in a box. Hell, I seen too many guys. Lennie here'll quit an' be on the road in two, three weeks. Seems like ever' guy got land in his head.'

Candy rubbed his cheek angrily. 'You God damn right we're gonna do it. George says we are. We got the money right now.'

'Yeah?' said Crooks. 'An' where's George now? In town in a whore-house. That's where your money's goin'. Jesus, I seen it happen too many times. I seen too many guys with land in their head. They never get none under their hand.'

Candy cried: 'Sure they all want it. Everybody wants a little bit of land, not much. Jus' som'thin' that was his. Som'thin' he could live on and there couldn't nobody throw him off of it. I never had none. I planted crops for damn near ever'body in this state, but they wasn't my crops, and when I harvested 'em, it wasn't none of my harvest. But we gonna do it now, and don't you make no mistake about that. George ain't got the money in town. That money's in the bank. Me an' Lennie an' George. We gonna have a room to ourselves. We're gonna have a dog an' rabbits an' chickens. We're gonna have green corn an' maybe a cow or a goat.' He stopped, overwhelmed with his picture.

Crooks asked: 'You say you got the money?'

'Damn right. We got most of it. Just a little bit more to get. Have it all in one month. George got the land all picked out, too.'

Crooks reached around and explored his spine with his hand. 'I never seen a guy really do it,' he said. 'I seen guys nearly crazy with loneliness for land, but ever' time a whore-house or a blackjack game took what it takes.' He hesitated. '. . . If you . . . guys would want a hand to work for nothing – just his keep, why I'd come an' lend a hand. I ain't so crippled I can't work like a son-of-a-bitch if I want to.'

'Any you boys seen Curley?'

They swung their heads toward the door. Looking in was Curley's wife. Her face was heavily made up. Her lips were slightly parted. She breathed strongly, as though she had been running.

'Curley ain't been here,' Candy said sourly.

She stood still in the doorway, smiling a little at them, rubbing the nails of one hand with the thumb and fore-finger of the other. And her eyes travelled from one face to another. 'They left all the weak ones here,' she said finally. 'Think I don't know where they all went? Even Curley. I know where they all went.'

Lennie watched her fascinated; but Candy and Crooks were scowling down away from her eyes. Candy said: 'Then if you know, why you want to ast us where Curley is at?'

She regarded them amusedly. 'Funny thing,' she said. 'If I catch any one man, and he's alone, I get along fine with him. But just let two of the guys get together an' you won't talk. Jus' nothing but mad.' She dropped her fingers and put her hands on her hips. 'You're all scared of each other, that's what. Ever' one of you's scared the rest is goin' to get something on you.'

After a pause Crooks said: 'Maybe you better go along to your own house now. We don't want no trouble.'

'Well, I ain't giving you no trouble. Think I don't like to talk to somebody ever' once in a while? Think I like to stick in that house alla time?'

Candy laid the stump of his wrist on his knee and rubbed it gently with his hand. He said accusingly: 'You gotta husban'. You got no call foolin' aroun' with other guys, causin' trouble.'

The girl flared up. 'Sure I gotta husban'. You all seen him. Swell guy, ain't he? Spends all his time sayin' what he's gonna do to guys he don't like, and he don't like nobody. Think I'm gonna stay in that two-by-four house and listen how Curley's gonna lead with his left twice, and then bring in the ol' right cross? "One-two," he says. "Jus' the ol' one-two an' he'll go down."' She paused and her face lost its sullenness and grew interested. 'Say – what happened to Curley's han'?'

There was an embarrassed silence. Candy stole a look at Lennie. Then he coughed. 'Why . . . Curley . . . he got his han' caught in a machine, ma'am. Bust his han'.'

She watched for a moment, and then she laughed. 'Baloney? What you think you're sellin' me? Curley started somep'in he didn't finish. Caught in a machine – baloney! Why, he ain't give nobody the good ol' one-two since he got his han' bust. Who bust him?'

Candy repeated sullenly: 'Got it caught in a machine.'

'Awright,' she said contemptuously. 'Awright, cover 'im up if ya wanta. Whatta I care? You bindle bums think you're so damn good. Whatta ya think I am, a kid? I tell ya I could of went with shows. Not jus' one, neither. An' a guy tol' me he could put me in pitchers . . .' She was breathless with indignation. ' – Sat'iday night. Ever'body out doin' som'pin. Ever'body! An' what am I doin'? Standin' here talking to a bunch of bindle stiffs – a nigger an' a dum-dum and a lousy ol' sheep – an' likin' it because they ain't no-body else.'

Lennie watched her, his mouth half open. Crooks had re-tired into the terrible protective dignity of the negro. But a change came over old Candy. He stood up suddenly and knocked his nail-keg over backward. 'I had enough,' he said angrily. 'You ain't wanted here. We told you you ain't. An' I tell ya, you got floosy idears about what us guys amounts to. You ain't got sense enough in that chicken head to even see that we ain't stiffs. S'pose you get us canned. S'pose you do. You think we'll hit the highway an' look for another lousy two-bit job like this. You don't know that we got our own ranch to go to, an' our own house. We ain't got to stay here. We gotta house and chickens an' fruit trees an' a place a hunderd time prettier than this. An' we got frens, that's what we got. Maybe there was a time when we was scared of gettin' canned, but we ain't no more. We got our own lan', and it's ours, an' we c'n go to it.'

Curley's wife laughed at him. 'Baloney,' she said. 'I seen too many you guys. If you had two bits in the worl', why you'd be in gettin' two shots of corn with it and suckin' the bottom of the glass. I know you guys.'

Candy's face had grown redder and redder, but before she was done speaking, he had control of himself. He was the master of the situation. 'I might of knew,' he said gently. 'Maybe you just better go along an' roll your hoop. We ain't got nothing to say to you at all. We know what we got, and we don't care whether you know it or not. So maybe you better jus' scatter along now, 'cause Curley maybe ain't gonna like his wife out in the barn with us "bindle stiffs".'

She looked from one face to another, and they were all closed against her. And she looked longest at Lennie, until he dropped his eyes in embarrassment. Suddenly she said: 'Where'd you get them bruises on your face?'

Lennie looked up guiltily. 'Who – me?'

'Yeah, you.'

Lennie looked to Candy for help, and then he looked at his lap again. 'He got his han' caught in a machine,' he said.

Curley's wife laughed. 'O.K., Machine. I'll talk to you later. I like machines.'

Candy broke in. 'You let this guy alone. Don't you do no

messing aroun' with him. I'm gonna tell George what you
says. George won't have you messin' with Lennie.'

'Who's George?' she asked. 'The little guy you come
with?'

Lennie smiled happily. 'That's him,' he said. 'That's the
guy, an' he's gonna let me tend the rabbits.'

'Well, if that's all you want, I might get a couple rabbits
myself.'

Crooks stood up from his bunk and faced her. 'I had
enough,' he said coldly. 'You got no rights comin' in a
coloured man's room. You got no rights messing around in
here at all. Now you jus' get out, an' get out quick. If you
don't, I'm gonna ast the boss not to ever let you come in the
barn no more.'

She turned to him in scorn. 'Listen, Nigger,' she said.
'You know what I can do to you if you open your trap?'

Crooks stared hopelessly at her, and then he sat down on
his bunk and drew into himself.

She closed on him. 'You know what I could do?'

Crooks seemed to grow smaller, and he pressed himself
against the wall. 'Yes, ma'am.'

'Well, you keep your place then, Nigger. I could get you
strung up on a tree so easy it ain't even funny.'

Crooks had reduced himself to nothing. There was no
personality, no ego – nothing to arouse either like or dislike.
He said: 'Yes, ma'am,' and his voice was toneless.

For a moment she stood over him as though waiting for
him to move so that she could whip at him again; but
Crooks sat perfectly still, his eyes averted, everything that
might be hurt drawn in. She turned at last to the other two.

Old Candy was watching her, fascinated. 'If you was to
do that, we'd tell,' he said quietly. 'We'd tell about you
framin' Crooks.'

'Tell an' be damned,' she cried. 'Nobody'd listen to you,
an' you know it. Nobody'd listen to you.'

Candy subsided. 'No,' he agreed. ' – Nobody'd listen to
us.'

Lennie whined: 'I wisht George was here. I wisht George
was here.'

Candy stepped over to him. 'Don't you worry none,' he said. 'I jus' heard the guys comin' in. George'll be in the bunk-house right now, I bet.' He turned to Curley's wife. 'You better go home now,' he said quietly. 'If you go right now, we won't tell Curley you was here.'

She appraised him coolly. 'I ain't sure you heard nothing.'

'Better not take no chances,' he said. 'If you ain't sure you better take the safe way.'

She turned to Lennie. 'I'm glad you bust up Curley a little bit. He got it comin' to him. Sometimes I'd like to bust him myself.' She slipped out the door and disappeared into the dark barn. And while she went through the barn, the halter chains rattled, and some horses snorted and some stamped their feet.

Crooks seemed to come slowly out of the layers of protection he had put on. 'Was that the truth what you said about the guys come back?' he asked.

'Sure. I heard 'em.'

'Well, I didn't hear nothing.'

'The gate banged,' Candy said, and he went on, 'Jesus Christ, Curley's wife can move quiet. I guess she had a lot of practice though.'

Crooks avoided the whole subject now. 'Maybe you guys better go,' he said. 'I ain't sure I want you in here no more. A coloured man got to have some rights, even if he don't like 'em.'

Candy said: 'That bitch didn't ought to of said that to you.'

'It wasn't nothing,' Crooks said dully. 'You guys comin' in an' settin' made me forget. What she says is true.'

The horses snorted out in the barn and the chains rang and a voice called: 'Lennie. Oh, Lennie. You in the barn?'

'It's George,' Lennie cried. And he answered: 'Here, George. I'm right in here.'

In a second George stood framed in the door, and he looked disapprovingly about. 'What you doin' in Crooks's room. You hadn't ought to be here.'

Crooks nodded. 'I tol' 'em, but they come in anyways.'

'Well, why'n't you kick 'em out?'

'I di'n't care much,' said Crooks. 'Lennie's a nice fella.'

Now Candy aroused himself. 'Oh, George! I been figurin' and figurin'. I got it doped out how we can even make some money on them rabbits.'

George scowled. 'I thought I tol' you not to tell nobody about that.'

Candy was crestfallen. 'Didn't tell nobody but Crooks.'

George said: 'Well you guys get outa here. Jesus, seems like I can't go away for a minute.'

Candy and Lennie stood up and went toward the door. Crooks called: 'Candy!'

'Huh?'

''Member what I said about hoein' and doin' odd jobs?'

'Yeah,' said Candy. 'I remember.'

'Well, jus' forget it,' said Crooks. 'I didn' mean it. Jus' foolin'. I wouldn't want to go no place like that.'

'Well, O.K., if you feel like that. Good night.'

The three men went out of the door. As they went through the barn the horses snorted and the halter chains rattled.

Crooks sat on his bunk and looked at the door for a moment, and then he reached for the liniment bottle. He pulled out his shirt at the back, poured a little liniment in his pink palm, and, reaching around, he fell slowly to rubbing his back.

*

ONE end of the great barn was piled high with new hay and over the pile hung the four-taloned jackson fork suspended from its pulley. The hay came down like a mountain slope to the other end of the barn, and there was a level place as yet unfilled with the new crop. At the sides the feeding racks were visible, and between the slats the heads of horses could be seen.

It was Sunday afternoon. The resting horses nibbled the remaining wisps of hay, and they stamped their feet and they bit the wood of the mangers and rattled the halter chains. The afternoon sun sliced in through the cracks of the barn walls and lay in bright lines on the hay. There was the buzz of flies in the air, the lazy afternoon humming.

From outside came the clang of horseshoes on the playing peg and the shouts of men, playing, encouraging, jeering. But in the barn it was quiet and humming and lazy and warm.

Only Lennie was in the barn, and Lennie sat in the hay beside a packing-case under a manger in the end of the barn that had not been filled with hay. Lennie sat in the hay and looked at a little dead puppy that lay in front of him. Lennie looked at it for a long time, and then he put out his huge hand and stroked it, stroked it clear from one end to the other.

And Lennie said softly to the puppy: 'Why do you got to get killed? You ain't so little as mice. I didn't bounce you hard.' He bent the pup's head up and looked in its face, and he said to it: 'Now maybe George ain't gonna let me tend no rabbits, if he fin's out you got killed.'

He scooped a little hollow and laid the puppy in it and covered it over with hay, out of sight; but he continued to stare at the mound he had made. He said: 'This ain't no bad thing like I got to go hide in the brush. Oh! no. This ain't. I'll tell George I foun' it dead.'

He unburied the puppy and inspected it, and he stroked it from ears to tail. He went on sorrowfully: 'But he'll know. George always knows. He'll say: "You done it. Don't try to put nothing over on me." An' he'll say: "Now jus' for that you don't get to tend no rabbits!"'

Suddenly his anger rose. 'God damn you,' he cried. 'Why do you got to get killed? You ain't so little as mice.' He picked up the pup and hurled it from him. He turned his back on it. He sat bent over his knees and he whispered: 'Now I won't get to tend the rabbits. Now he won't let me.' He rocked himself back and forth in his sorrow.

From outside came the clang of horseshoes on the iron stake, and then a little chorus of cries. Lennie got up and brought the puppy back and laid it on the hay and sat down. He stroked the pup again. 'You wasn't big enough,' he said. 'They tol' me and tol' me you wasn't. I di'n't know you'd get killed so easy. He worked his fingers on the pup's limp ear. 'Maybe George won't care,' he said. 'This here God damn little son-of-a-bitch wasn't nothing to George.'

Curley's wife came around the end of the last stall. She came very quietly, so that Lennie didn't see her. She wore her bright cotton dress and the mules with the red ostrich feathers. Her face was made up and the little sausage curls were all in place. She was quite near to him before Lennie looked up and saw her.

In a panic he shovelled hay over the puppy with his fingers. He looked sullenly up at her.

She said: 'What you got there, sonny boy?'

Lennie glared at her. 'George says I ain't to have nothing to do with you – talk to you or nothing.'

She laughed. 'George giving you orders about everything?'

Lennie looked down at the hay. 'Says I can't tend no rabbits if I talk to you or anything.'

She said quietly: 'He's scared Curley'll get mad. Well, Curley got his arm in a sling – an' if Curley gets tough, you can break his other han'. You didn't put nothing over on me about gettin' it caught on no machine.'

But Lennie was not to be drawn. 'No, sir. I ain't gonna talk to you or nothing.'

She knelt in the hay beside him. 'Listen,' she said. 'All the guys got a horseshoe tenement goin' on. It's on'y about four o'clock. None of them guys is goin' to leave that tenement. Why can't I talk to you? I never get to talk to nobody. I get awful lonely.'

Lennie said: 'Well, I ain't supposed to talk to you or nothing.'

'I get lonely,' she said. 'You can talk to people, but I can't talk to nobody but Curley. Else he gets mad. How'd you like not to talk to anybody?'

Lennie said: 'Well, I ain't supposed to. George's scared I'll get in trouble.'

She changed the subject. 'What you got covered up there?'

Then all of Lennie's woe came back on him. 'Jus' my pup,' he said sadly. 'Jus' my little pup.' And he swept the hay from on top of it.

'Why, he's dead,' she cried.

'He was so little,' said Lennie. 'I was jus' playin' with him . . . an' he made like he's gonna bite me . . . an' I made like I was gonna smack him . . . an' . . . an' I done it. An' then he was dead.'

She consoled him. 'Don't you worry none. He was jus' a mutt. You can get another one easy. The whole country is fulla mutts.'

'It ain't that so much,' Lennie explained miserably. 'George ain't gonna let me tend no rabbits now.'

'Why don't he?'

'Well, he said if I done any more bad things he ain't gonna let me tend the rabbits.'

She moved closer to him and she spoke soothingly. 'Don't you worry about talkin' to me. Listen to the guys yell out there. They got four dollars bet in that tenement. None of them ain't gonna leave till it's over.'

'If George sees me talkin' to you he'll give me hell,' Lennie said cautiously. 'He tol' me so.'

Her face grew angry. 'What's the matter with me?' she cried. 'Ain't I got a right to talk to nobody? Whatta they think I am, anyways? You're a nice guy. I don't know why I can't talk to you. I ain't doin' no harm to you.'

'Well, George says you'll get us in a mess.'

'Aw, nuts!' she said. 'What kinda harm am I doin' to you? Seems like they ain't none of them cares how I gotta live. I tell you I ain't used to livin' like this. I coulda made somethin' of myself.' She said darkly: 'Maybe I will yet.' And then her words tumbled out in a passion of communication, as though she hurried before her listener could be taken away. 'I live right in Salinas,' she said. 'Come there when I was a kid. Well, a show come through, an' I met one of the actors. He says I could go with that show. But my ol' lady wouldn't let me. She says because I was on'y fifteen. But the guy says I coulda. If I'd went, I wouldn't be livin' like this, you bet.'

Lennie stroked the pup back and forth. 'We gonna have a little place – an' rabbits,' he explained.

She went on with her story quickly, before she should be interrupted. ''Nother time I met a guy, an' he was in pitchers. Went out to the Riverside Dance Palace with him. He says he was gonna put me in the movies. Says I was a natural. Soon's he got back to Hollywood he was gonna write to me about it.' She looked closely at Lennie to see whether she was impressing him. 'I never got that letter,' she said. 'I always thought my ol' lady stole it. Well, I wasn't gonna stay no place where I couldn't get nowhere or make something of myself, an' where they stole your letters. I ast her if she stole it, too, an' she says no. So I married Curley. Met him out to the Riverside Dance Palace that same night.' She demanded: 'You listenin'?'

'Me? Sure.'

'Well, I ain't told this to nobody before. Maybe I oughtn' to. I don' *like* Curley. He ain't a nice fella.' And because she had confided in him, she moved closer to Lennie and sat beside him. 'Coulda been in the movies, an' had nice clothes – all them nice clothes like they wear. An' I coulda sat in them big hotels, an' had pitchers took of me. When they had them previews I coulda went to them, an' spoke in the radio, an' it wouldn't cost me a cent because I was in the pitcher. An' all them nice clothes like they wear. Because this guy says I was a natural.' She looked up at Lennie, and she made a small grand gesture with her arm and hand to show that she could act. The fingers trailed after her leading wrist, and her little finger stuck out grandly from the rest.

Lennie sighed deeply. From outside came the clang of a horseshoe on metal, and then a chorus of cheers. 'Somebody made a ringer,' said Curley's wife.

Now the light was lifting as the sun went down, and the sun-streaks climbed up the wall and fell over the feeding-racks and over the heads of the horses.

Lennie said: 'Maybe if I took this pup out and throwed him away, George wouldn't never know. An' then I could tend the rabbits without no trouble.'

Curley's wife said angrily: 'Don't you think of nothing but rabbits?'

'We gonna have a little place,' Lennie explained patiently. 'We gonna have a house an' a garden and a place or alfalfa, an' that alfalfa is for the rabbits, an' I take a sack and get it all fulla alfalfa and then I take it to the rabbits.'

She asked: 'What makes you so nuts about rabbits?'

Lennie had to think carefully before he could come to a conclusion. He moved cautiously close to her, until he was right against her. 'I like to pet nice things. Once at a fair I seen some of them long-hair rabbits. An' they was nice, you bet. Sometimes I've even pet mice, but not when I could get nothing better.'

Curley's wife moved away from him a little. 'I think you're nuts,' she said.

'No, I ain't,' Lennie explained earnestly. 'George says I ain't. I like to pet nice things with my fingers, sof' things.'

She was a little bit reassured. 'Well, who don't?' she said. 'Ever'body likes that. I like to feel silk an' velvet. Do you like to feel velvet?'

Lennie chuckled with pleasure. 'You bet, by God,' he cried happily. 'An' I had some, too. A lady give me some, an' that lady was – my own Aunt Clara. She give it right to me – 'bout this big a piece. I wisht I had that velvet right now.' A frown came over his face. 'I lost it,' he said. 'I ain't seen it for a long time.'

Curley's wife laughed at him. 'You're nuts,' she said. 'But you're a kinda nice fella. Jus' like a big baby. But a person can see kinda what you mean. When I'm doin' my hair sometimes I jus' set an' stroke it 'cause it's so soft.' To show how she did it, she ran her fingers over the top of her head. 'Some people got kinda coarse hair,' she said complacently. 'Take Curley. His hair is jus' like wire. But mine is soft and fine. 'Course I brush it a lot. That makes it fine. Here – feel right here.' She took Lennie's hand and put it on her head. 'Feel right aroun' there an' see how soft it is.'

Lennie's big fingers fell to stroking her hair.

'Don't you muss it up,' she said.

Lennie said: 'Oh! That's nice,' and he stroked harder. 'Oh, that's nice.'

'Look out, now, you'll muss it.' And then she cried angrily: 'You stop it now, you'll mess it all up.' She jerked

her head sideways, and Lennie's fingers closed on her hair
and hung on. 'Let go,' she cried. 'You let go.'

Lennie was in a panic. His face was contorted. She
screamed then, and Lennie's other hand closed over her
mouth and nose. 'Please don't,' he begged. 'Oh! Please
don't do that. George'll be mad.'

She struggled violently under his hands. Her feet battered
on the hay and she writhed to be free; and from under Lennie's hand, came a muffled screaming. Lennie began to cry
with fright. 'Oh! Please don't do none of that,' he begged.
'George gonna say I done a bad thing. He ain't gonna let
me tend no rabbits.' He moved his hand a little and her
hoarse cry came out. Then Lennie grew angry. 'Now don't,'
he said. 'I don't want you to yell. You gonna get me in
trouble jus' like George says you will. Now don't you do
that.' And she continued to struggle, and her eyes were wild
with terror. He shook her then, and he was angry with her.
'Don't you go yellin',' he said, and he shook her; and her
body flopped like a fish. And then she was still, for Lennie
had broken her neck.

He looked down at her, and carefully he removed his
hand from over her mouth, and she lay still. 'I don't wanta hurt you,' he said, 'but George'll be mad if you yell.'
When she didn't answer nor move he bent closely over her.
He lifted her arm and let it drop. For a moment he seemed
bewildered. And then he whispered in fright: 'I done a bad
thing. I done another bad thing.'

He pawed up the hay until it partly covered her.

From outside the barn came a cry of men and the double
clang of shoes of metal. For the first time Lennie became
conscious of the outside. He crouched down in the hay and
listened. 'I done a real bad thing,' he said. 'I shouldn't of
did that. George'll be mad. An' . . . he said . . . an' hide in
the brush till he come. He's gonna be mad. In the brush till
he come. Tha's what he said.' Lennie went back and looked
at the dead girl. The puppy lay close to her. Lennie picked
it up. 'I'll throw him away,' he said. 'It's bad enough like it
is.' He put the pup under his coat, and he crept to the barn
wall and peered out between the cracks, toward the horse-

show game. And then he crept around the end of the last manger and disappeared.

The sun-streaks were high on the wall by now, and the light was growing soft in the barn. Curley's wife lay on her back, and she was half covered with hay.

It was very quiet in the barn, and the quiet of the afternoon was on the ranch. Even the clang of the pitched shoes, even the voices of the men in the game seemed to grow more quiet. The air in the barn was dusky in advance of the outside day. A pigeon flew in through the open hay door and circled and flew out again. Around the last stall came a shepherd bitch, lean and long, with heavy, hanging dugs. Half-way to the packing-box where the puppies were, she caught the dead scent of Curley's wife, and the hair arose along her spine. She whimpered and cringed to the packing-box, and jumped in among the puppies.

Curley's wife lay with a half-covering of yellow hay. And the meanness and the plannings and the discontent and the ache for attention were all gone from her face. She was very pretty and simple, and her face was sweet and young. Now her rouged cheeks and her reddened lips made her seem alive and sleeping very lightly. The curls, tiny little sausages, were spread on the hay behind her head, and her lips were parted.

As happens sometimes, a moment settled and hovered and remained for much more than a moment. And sound stopped and movement stopped for much, much more than a moment.

Then gradually time awakened again and moved sluggishly on. The horses stamped on the other side of the feeding-racks and the halter chains clinked. Outside, the men's voices became louder and clearer.

From around the end of the last stall old Candy's voice came. 'Lennie,' he called. 'Oh, Lennie! You in here? I been figuring some more. Tell you what we can do, Lennie.' Old Candy appeared around the end of the last stall. 'Oh, Lennie!' he called again; and then he stopped, and his body stiffened. He rubbed his smooth wrist on his white stubble whiskers. 'I di'n't know you was here,' he said to Curley's wife.

When she didn't answer, he stepped nearer. 'You oughten'
to sleep out here,' he said disapprovingly; and then he was
beside her and – 'Oh, Jesus Christ!' He looked about helplessly, and he rubbed his beard. And then he jumped up
and went quickly out of the barn.

But the barn was alive now. The horses stamped and
snorted, and they chewed the straw of their bedding and
they clashed the chains of their halters. In a moment Candy
came back, and George was with him.

George said: 'What was it you wanted to see me about?'

Candy pointed at Curley's wife. George stared. ' – What's
the matter with her?' he asked. He stepped closer, and then
he echoed Candy's words. 'Oh, Jesus Christ!' He was down
on his knees beside her. He put his hand over her heart. And
finally, when he stood up, slowly and stiffly, his face was as
hard and tight as wood, and his eyes were hard.

Candy said: 'What done it?'

George looked coldly at him. 'Ain't you got any idear?'
he asked. And Candy was silent. 'I should of knew,' George
said hopelessly. 'I guess maybe way back in my head I did.'

Candy asked: 'What we gonna do now, George. What
we gonna do now?'

George was a long time in answering. 'Guess . . . we gotta
tell the . . . guys. I guess we gotta get 'im an' lock 'im up.
We can't let 'im get away. Why, the poor bastard'd starve.'
And he tried to reassure himself. 'Maybe they'll lock 'im up
an' be nice to 'im.'

But Candy said excitedly: 'We oughtta let 'im get away.
You don't know that Curley. Curley go'n'ta wanta get 'im
lynched. Curley'll get 'im killed.'

George watched Candy's lips. 'Yeah,' he said at last,
'that's right, Curley will. An' the other guys will.' And he
looked back at Curley's wife.

Now Candy spoke his greatest fear. 'You an' me can get
that little place, can't we, George? You an' me can go there
an' live nice, can't we, George? Can't we?'

Before George answered, Candy dropped his head and
looked down at the hay. He knew.

George said softly: ' – I think I knowed from the very first.

I think I knowed we'd never do her. He usta like to hear about it so much I got to thinking maybe we would.'

'Then – it's all off?' Candy asked sulkily.

George didn't answer his question. George said: 'I'll work my month an' I'll take my fifty bucks an' I'll stay all night in some lousy cat-house. Or I'll set in some pool-room till ever'body goes home. An' then I'll come back an' work another month an' I'll have fifty bucks more.'

Candy said: 'He's such a nice fella. I didn' think he'd do nothing like this.'

George still stared at Curley's wife. 'Lennie never done it in meanness,' he said. 'All the time he done bad things but he never done one of 'em mean.' He straightened up and looked back at Candy. 'Now listen. We gotta tell the guys. They got to bring him in, I guess. They ain't no way out. Maybe they won't hurt 'im.' He said sharply: 'I ain't gonna let 'em hurt Lennie. Now you listen. The guys might think I was in on it. I'm gonna go in the bunk-house. Then in a minute you come out and tell the guys about her, and I'll come along and make like I never seen her. Will you do that? So the guys won't think I was on it?'

Candy said: 'Sure, George. Sure I'll do that.'

'O.K. Give me a couple minutes then, and you come runnin' out an' tell like you jus' found her. I'm going now.' George turned and went quickly out of the barn.

Old Candy watched him go. He looked helplessly back at Curley's wife, and gradually his sorrow and his anger grew into words. 'You God damn tramp,' he said viciously. 'You done it, di'n't you? I s'pose you're glad. Ever'body knowed you'd mess things up. You wasn't no good. You ain't no good now, you lousy tart.' He snivelled, and his voice shook. 'I could of hoed in the garden and washed dishes for them guys.' He paused, and then went on in a sing-song. And he repeated the old words: 'If they was a circus or a baseball game . . . we would of went to her . . . jus' said "ta hell with work", an' went to her. Never ast nobody's say so. An' they'd of been a pig and chickens . . . an' in the winter . . . the little fat stove . . . an' the rain comin' . . . an' us jus' settin' there.' His eyes blinded with

tears and he turned and went weakly out of the barn, and
he rubbed his bristly whiskers with his wrist stump.

Outside the noise of the game stopped. There was a rise
of voices in question, a drum of running feet, and the men
burst into the barn. Slim and Carlson and young White and
Curley, and Crooks keeping back out of attention range.
Candy came after them, and last of all came George. George
had put on his blue denim coat and buttoned it, and his
black hat was pulled down low over his eyes. The men raced
around the last stall. Their eyes found Curley's wife in the
gloom, they stopped and stood still and looked.

Then Slim went quietly over to her, and he felt her wrist.
One lean finger touched her cheek, and then his hand went
under her slightly twisted neck and his fingers explored her
neck. When he stood up the men crowded near and the spell
was broken.

Curley came suddenly to life. 'I know who done it,' he
cried. 'That big son-of-a-bitch done it. I know he done it.
Why – ever'body else was out there playin' horseshoes.' He
worked himself into a fury. 'I'm gonna get him. I'm going
for my shot-gun. I'll kill the big son-of-a-bitch myself. I'll
shoot 'im in the guts. Come on, you guys.' He ran furiously
out of the barn. Carlson said: 'I'll get my Luger,' and he
ran out, too.

Slim turned quietly to George. 'I guess Lennie done
it, all right,' he said. 'Her neck's bust. Lennie coulda did
that.'

George didn't answer, but he nodded slowly. His hat was
so far down on his forehead that his eyes were covered.

Slim went on: 'Maybe like that time in Weed you was
tellin' about.'

Again George nodded.

Slim sighed. 'Well, I guess we got to get him. Where you
think he might of went?'

It seemed to take George some time to free his words.
'He – would of went south,' he said. 'We come from north
so he would of went south.'

'I guess we gotta get 'im,' Slim repeated.

George stepped close. 'Couldn' we maybe bring him in

an' they'll lock him up? He's nuts, Slim. He never done this to be mean.'

Slim nodded. 'We might,' he said. 'If we could keep Curley in, we might. But Curley's gonna want to shoot 'im. Curley's still mad about his hand. An' s'pose they lock him up an' strap him down and put him in a cage. That ain't no good, George.'

'I know,' said George. 'I know.'

Carlson came running in. 'The bastard's stole my Luger,' he shouted. 'It ain't in my bag.' Curley followed him, and Curley carried a shot-gun in his good hand. Curley was cold now.

'All right, you guys,' he said. 'The nigger's got a shot-gun. You take it, Carlson. When you see 'um, don't give 'im no chance. Shoot for his guts. That'll double 'im over.'

Whit said excitedly: 'I ain't got a gun.'

Curley said: 'You go in Soledad an' get a cop. Get Al Wilts, he's deputy sheriff. Le's go now.' He turned suspiciously on George. 'You're comin' with us, fella.'

'Yeah,' said George. 'I'll come. But listen, Curley. The poor bastard's nuts. Don't shoot 'im. He di'n't know what he was doin'.'

'Don't shoot 'im?' Curley cried. 'He got Carlson's Luger. 'Course we'll shoot 'im.'

George said weakly: 'Maybe Carlson lost his gun.'

'I seen it this morning,' said Carlson. 'No, it's been took.'

Slim stood looking down at Curley's wife. He said: 'Curley – maybe you better stay here with your wife.'

Curley's face reddened. 'I'm goin',' he said. 'I'm gonna shoot the guts outa that big bastard myself, even if I only got one hand. I'm gonna get 'im.'

Slim turned to Candy. 'You stay here with her then, Candy. The rest of us better get goin'.'

They moved away. George stopped a moment beside Candy and they both looked down at the dead girl until Curley called: 'You, George! You stick with us so we don't think you had nothin' to do with this.'

George moved slowly after them, and his feet dragged heavily.

And when they were gone, Candy squatted down in the

hay and watched the face of Curley's wife. 'Poor bastard,' he said softly.

The sound of the men grew fainter. The barn was darkening gradually and, in their stalls, the horses shifted their feet and rattled the halter chains. Old Candy lay down in the hay and covered his eyes with his arm.

*

THE deep green pool of the Salinas River was still in the late afternoon. Already the sun had left the valley to go climbing up the slopes of the Gabilan mountains, and the hill-tops were rosy in the sun. But by the pool among the mottled sycamores, a pleasant shade had fallen.

A water-snake glided smoothly up the pool, twisting its periscope head from side to side; and it swam the length of the pool and came to the legs of a motionless heron that stood in the shallows. A silent head and beak lanced down and plucked it out by the head, and the beak swallowed the little snake while its tail waved frantically.

A far rush of wind sounded and a gust drove through the tops of the trees like a wave. The sycamore leaves turned up their silver sides, the brown, dry leaves on the ground scudded a few feet. And row on row of tiny wind-waves flowed up the pool's surface.

As quickly as it had come, the wind died, and the clearing was quiet again. The heron stood in the shallows, motionless and waiting. Another little water-snake swam up the pool, turning its periscope head from side to side.

Suddenly Lennie appeared out of the brush, and he came as silently as a creeping bear moves. The heron pounded the air with its wings, jacked itself clear of the water, and flew off down-river. The little snake slid in among the reeds at the pool's side.

Lennie came quietly to the pool's edge. He knelt down and drank, barely touching his lips to the water. When a little bird skittered over the dry leaves behind him, his head jerked up and he strained towards the sound with eyes and ears until he saw the bird, and then he dropped his head and drank again.

When he had finished, he sat down on the bank, with his side to the pool, so that he could watch the trail's entrance. He embraced his knees and laid his chin on his knees.

The light climbed on out of the valley, and as it went, the tops of the mountains seemed to blaze with increasing brightness.

Lennie said softly: 'I di'n't forget, you bet, God damn. Hide in the brush an' wait for George.' He pulled his hat down low over his eyes. 'George gonna give me hell,' he said. 'George gonna wish he was alone an' not have me botherin' him.' He turned his head and looked at the bright mountain-tops. 'I can go right off there an' find a cave,' he said. And he continued sadly: '– an' never have no ketchup – but I won't care. If George don't want me . . . I'll go away. I'll go away.'

And then from out of Lennie's head there came a little fat old woman. She wore thick bull's-eye glasses and she wore a huge gingham apron with pockets, and she was starched and clean. She stood in front of Lennie and put her hands on her hips, and she frowned disapprovingly at him.

And when she spoke, it was in Lennie's voice. 'I tol' you an' tol' you,' she said. 'I tol' you, "Min' George because he's such a nice fella an' good to you." But you don't never take no care. You do bad things.'

And Lennie answered her: 'I tried, Aunt Clara ma'am. I tried and tried. I couldn't help it.'

'You never give a thought to George,' she went on in Lennie's voice. 'He's been doin' nice things for you alla time. When he got a piece a pie you always got half or more'n half. An' if they was any ketchup, why, he'd give it all to you.'

'I know,' said Lennie miserably. 'I tried, Aunt Clara ma'am. I tried and tried.'

She interrupted him. 'All the time he coulda had such a good time if it wasn't for you. He woulda took his pay an' raised hell in a whore-house, and he coulda set in a pool-room an' played snooker. But he got to take care of you.'

Lennie moaned with grief. 'I know, Aunt Clara ma'am.

I'll go right off in the hills an' I'll fin' a cave an' I'll live there so I won't be no more trouble to George.'

'You jus' say that,' she said sharply. 'You're always sayin' that, an' you know son-of-a-bitching well you ain't never gonna do it. You'll jus' stick around an' stew the b'Jesus outa George all the time.'

Lennie said: 'I might jus' as well go away. George ain't gonna let me tend no rabbits now.'

Aunt Clara was gone, and from out of Lennie's head there came a gigantic rabbit. It sat on its haunches in front of him, and it waggled its ears and crinkled its nose at him. And it spoke in Lennie's voice, too.

'Tend rabbits,' it said scornfully. 'You crazy bastard. You ain't fit to lick the boots of no rabbit. You'd forget 'em and let 'em go hungry. That's what you'd do. An' then what would George think?'

'I would *not* forget,' Lennie said loudly.

'The hell you wouldn',' said the rabbit. 'You ain't worth a greased jack-pin to ram you into hell. Christ knows George done ever'thing he could to jack you outa the sewer, but it don't do no good. If you think George gonna let you tend rabbits, you're even crazier'n usual. He ain't. He's gonna beat hell outa you with a stick, that's what he's gonna do.'

Now Lennie retorted belligerently: 'He ain't neither. George won't do nothing like that. I've knew George since – I forget when – and he ain't never raised his han' to me with a stick. He's nice to me. He ain't gonna be mean.'

'Well, he's sick of you,' said the rabbit. 'He's gonna beat hell outa you an' then go away an' leave you.'

'He won't,' Lennie cried frantically. 'He won't do nothing like that. I know George. Me an' him travels together.'

But the rabbit repeated softly over and over: 'He gonna leave ya, ya crazy bastard. He gonna leave ya all alone. He gonna leave ya, crazy bastard.'

Lennie put his hands over his ears. 'He ain't, I tell ya he ain't.' And he cried: 'Oh! George – George – George!'

George came quietly out of the brush and the rabbit scuttled back into Lennie's brain.

George said quietly: 'What the hell you hellin' about?'

Lennie got up on his knees. 'You ain't gonna leave me, are ya, George? I know you ain't.'

George came stiffly near and sat down beside him. 'No.'

'I knowed it,' Lennie cried. 'You ain't that kind.'

George was silent.

Lennie said: 'George.'

'Yeah?'

'I done another bad thing.'

'It don't make no difference,' George said, and he fell silent again.

Only the topmost ridges were in the sun now. The shadow in the valley was blue and soft. From the distance came the sound of men shouting to one another. George turned his head and listened to the shouts.

Lennie said: 'George.'

'Yeah?'

'Ain't you gonna give me hell?'

'Give ya hell?'

'Sure, like you always done before. Like: "If I di'n't have you I'd take my fifty bucks . . ."'

'Jesus Christ, Lennie! You can't remember nothing that happens, but you remember ever' word I say.'

'Well, ain't you gonna say it?'

George shook himself. He said woodenly: 'If I was alone I could live so easy.' His voice was monotonous, had no emphasis. 'I could get a job an' not have no mess.' He stopped.

'Go on,' said Lennie. 'An' when the enda the month come . . .'

'An' when the end of the month come I could take my fifty bucks an' go to a . . . cat-house . . .' He stopped again.

Lennie looked eagerly at him. 'Go on, George. Ain't you gonna give me no more hell?'

'No,' said George.

'Well, I can go away,' said Lennie, 'I'll get right off in the hills an' find a cave if you don' want me.'

George shook himself again. 'No,' he said. 'I want you to stay with me here.'

Lennie said craftily: 'Tell me like you done before.'

'Tell you what?'

''Bout the other guys an' about us.'

George said: 'Guys like us got no fambly. They make a little stake an' then they blow it in. They ain't got nobody in the worl' that gives a hoot in hell about 'em . . .'

'*But not us*,' Lennie cried happily. 'Tell about us now.'

George was quiet for a moment. 'But not us,' he said.

'Because . . .'

'Because I got you an' . . .'

'An' I got you. We got each other, that's what, that gives a hoot in hell about us,' Lennie cried in triumph.

The little evening breeze blew over the clearing and the leaves rustled and the wind waves flowed up the green pool. And the shouts of men sounded again, this time much closer than before.

George took off his hat. He said shakily: 'Take off your hat, Lennie. The air feels fine.'

Lennie removed his hat dutifully and laid it on the ground in front of him. The shadow in the valley was bluer, and the evening came fast. On the wind the sound of crashing in the brush came to them.

Lennie said: 'Tell how it's gonna be.'

George had been listening to the distant sounds. For a moment he was business-like. 'Look acrost the river, Lennie, an' I'll tell you so you can almost see it.'

Lennie turned his head and looked off across the pool and up the darkening slopes of the Gabilans. 'We gonna get a little place,' George began. He reached in his side pocket and brought out Carlson's Luger; he snapped off the safety, and the hand and gun lay on the ground behind Lennie's back. He looked at the back of Lennie's head, at the place where the spine and skull were joined.

A man's voice called from up the river, and another man answered.

'Go on,' said Lennie.

George raised the gun and his hand shook, and he dropped his hand to the ground again.

'Go on,' said Lennie. 'How's it gonna be. We gonna get a little place.'

'We'll have a cow,' said George, 'An' we'll have maybe a pig an' chickens . . . an' down the flat we'll have a . . . little piece alfalfa . . .'

'For the rabbits,' Lennie shouted.

'For the rabbits,' George repeated.

'And I get to tend the rabbits.'

'An' you get to tend the rabbits.'

Lennie giggled with happiness. 'An' live on the fatta the lan'.'

'Yes.'

Lennie turned his head.

'No, Lennie. Look down there acrost the river, like you can almost see the place.'

Lennie obeyed him. George looked down at the gun.

There were crashing footsteps in the brush now. George turned and looked toward them.

'Go on, George. When we gonna do it?'

'Gonna do it soon.'

'Me an' you.'

'You . . . an' me. Ever'body gonna be nice to you. Ain't gonna be no more trouble. Nobody gonna hurt nobody nor steal from 'em.'

Lennie said: 'I thought you was mad at me, George.'

'No,' said George. 'No, Lennie. I ain't mad. I never been mad, an' I ain't now. That's a thing I want ya to know.'

The voices came close now. George raised the gun and listened to the voices.

Lennie begged: 'Le's to it now. Le's get that place now.'

'Sure, right now. I gotta. We gotta.'

And George raised the gun and steadied it, and he brought the muzzle of it close to the back of Lennie's head. The hand shook violently, but his face set and his hand steadied. He pulled the trigger. The crash of the shot rolled up the hills and rolled down again. Lennie jarred, and then settled slowly forward to the sand, and he lay without quivering.

George shivered and looked at the gun, and then he threw it from him, back up on the bank, near the pile of old ashes.

The brush seemed filled with cries and with the sound of

running feet. Slim's voice shouted: 'George. Where you at, George?'

But George sat stiffly on the bank and looked at his right hand that had thrown the gun away. The group burst into the clearing, and Curley was ahead. He saw Lennie lying on the sand. 'Got him, by God.' He went over and looked down at Lennie, and then he looked back at George. 'Right in the back of the head,' he said softly.

Slim came directly to George and sat down beside him, sat very close to him. 'Never you mind,' said Slim. 'A guy got to sometimes.'

But Carlson was standing over George. 'How'd you do it?' he asked.

'I just done it,' George said tiredly.

'Did he have my gun?'

'Yeah. He had your gun.'

'An' you got it away from him and you took it an' you killed him?'

'Yeah. Tha's how.' George's voice was almost a whisper. He looked steadily at his right hand that had held the gun.

Slim twitched George's elbow. 'Come on, George. Me an' you'll go in an' get a drink.'

George let himself be helped to his feet. 'Yah, a drink.'

Slim said: 'You hadda, George. I swear you hadda. Come on with me.' He led George into the entrance of the trail and up toward the highway.

Curley and Carlson looked after them. And Carlson said: 'Now what the hell ya suppose is eatin' them two guys?'

Cannery Row

CANNERY ROW

CANNERY ROW in Monterey in California is a poem, a stink, a grating noise, a quality of light, a tone, a habit, a nostalgia, a dream. Cannery Row is the gathered and scattered, tin and iron and rust and splintered wood, chipped pavement and weedy lots and junk heaps, sardine canneries or corrugated iron, honky-tonks, restaurants and whorehouses, and little crowded groceries, and laboratories and flop-houses. Its inhabitants are, as the man once said, 'whores, pimps, gamblers, and sons of bitches,' by which he meant Everybody. Had the man looked through another peep-hole he might have said: 'Saints and angels and martyrs and holy men,' and he would have meant the same thing.

In the morning when the sardine fleet had made a catch, the purse-seiners waddle heavily into the bay blowing their whistles. The deep-laden boats pull in against the coast where the canneries dip their tails into the bay. The figure is advisedly chosen, for if the canneries dipped their mouths into the bay the canned sardines which emerge from the other end would be metaphorically, at least, even more horrifying. Then cannery whistles scream and all over the town men and women scramble into their clothes and come running down to the Row to go to work. Then shining cars bring the upper classes down: superintendents, accountants, owners who disappear into offices. Then from the town pour Wops and Chinamen and Polaks, men and women in trousers and rubber coats and oilcloth aprons. They come running to clean and cut and pack and cook and can the fish. The whole street rumbles and groans and screams and rattles while the silver rivers of fish pour in out of the boats and the boats rise higher and higher in the water until they are empty. The canneries rumble and rattle and squeak until the last fish is cleaned and cut and cooked and canned and then the whistles scream again and the dripping, smelly, tired Wops and Chinamen and Polaks, men and women, straggle out and droop their ways up the hill into the town and Cannery Row becomes itself again – quiet and magical. Its normal life returns. The bums who retired in disgust under the black cypress-tree come out to sit on the rusty pipes in the vacant lot. The girls from Dora's emerge for a bit of sun if there is any. Doc strolls from the Western Biological Laboratory and crosses the street to Lee Chong's grocery for two quarts of beer. Henri the painter noses like an Airedale through the junk in the grass-grown lot for some part or piece of wood or metal he needs for the boat he is building. Then the darkness edges in and the street light comes on in front of Dora's – the lamp which makes perpetual moonlight in Cannery Row. Callers arrive at Western Biological to see Doc, and he crosses the street to Lee Chong's for five quarts of beer.

How can the poem and the stink and the grating noise – the quality of light, the tone, the habit and the dream – be set down alive? When you collect marine animals there are certain flat worms so delicate that they are almost impossible to capture whole, for they break and tatter under the touch. You must let them ooze and crawl of their own will on to a knife blade and then lift them gently into your bottle of sea water. And perhaps that might be the way to write this book – to open the page and to let the stories crawl in by themselves.

CHAPTER 1

LEE CHONG'S grocery, while not a model of neatness, was a miracle of supply. It was small and crowded but within its single room a man could find everything he needed or wanted to live and to be happy – clothes, food, both fresh and canned, liquor, tobacco, fishing equipment, machinery, boats, cordage, caps, pork-chops. You could buy at Lee Chong's a pair of slippers, a silk kimono, a quarter-pint of whisky, and a cigar. You could work out combinations to fit almost any mood. The one commodity Lee Chong did not keep could be had across the lot at Dora's.

The grocery opened at dawn and did not close until the last wandering vagrant dime had been spent or retired for the night. Not that Lee Chong was avaricious. He wasn't, but if one wanted to spend money, he was available. Lee's position in the community surprised him as much as he could be surprised. Over the course of the years everyone in Cannery Row owed him money. He never pressed his clients, but when the bill became too large, Lee cut off credit. Rather than walk into the town up the hill, the client usually paid or tried to.

Lee was round-faced and courteous. He spoke a stately English without ever using the letter R. When the tong wars were going on in California, it happened now and then that Lee found a price on his head. Then he would go secretly to San Francisco and enter a hospital until the trouble blew over. What he did with his money, no one ever knew. Perhaps he didn't get it. Maybe his wealth was entirely in unpaid bills. But he lived well and he had the respect of all his neighbours. He trusted his clients until further trust became ridiculous. Sometimes he made business errors, but even these he turned to advantage in good will if in no other way. It was that way with the Palace Flophouse and Grill. Anyone but Lee Chong would have considered the transaction a total loss.

Lee Chong's station in the grocery was behind the cigar

counter. The cash register was then on his left and the abacus on his right. Inside the glass case were the brown cigars, the cigarettes, the Bull Durham, the Duke's mixture, the Five Brothers, while behind him in racks on the wall were the pints, half-pints. and quarters of Old Green River, Old Town House, Old Colonel, and the favourite – Old Tennessee, a blended whisky guaranteed four months old, very cheap and known in the neighbourhood as Old Tennis Shoes. Lee Chong did not stand between the whisky and the customer without reason. Some very practical minds had on occasion tried to divert his attention to another part of the store. Cousins, nephews, sons, and daughters-in-law waited on the rest of the store, but Lee never left the cigar counter. The top of the glass was his desk. His fat delicate hands rested on the glass, the fingers moving like small restless sausages. A broad golden wedding-ring on the middle finger of his left hand was his only jewellery and with it he silently tapped on the rubber change mat from which the little rubber tits had long been worn. Lee's mouth was full and benevolent and the flash of gold when he smiled was rich and warm. He wore half-glasses and since he looked at everything through them, he had to tilt his head back to see the distance. Interest and discounts, addition, subtraction he worked out on the abacus with his little restless sausage fingers, and his brown friendly eyes roved over the grocery and his teeth flashed at the customers.

On an evening when he stood in his place on a pad of newspaper to keep his feet warm, he contemplated with humour and sadness a business deal that had been consummated that afternoon and reconsummated later the same afternoon. When you leave the grocery, if you walk catty-cornered across the grass-grown lot, threading your way among the great rusty pipes thrown out of the canneries, you will see a path worn in the weeds. Follow it past the cypress-tree, across the railroad track, up a chicken-walk with cleats, and you will come to a long low building which for a long time was used as a storage place for fish meal. It was just a great big roofed room and it belonged to a worried gentleman named Horace Abbeville. Horace had two wives and six children, and over a period of years he had managed through pleading and persuasion to build a grocery debt second to none in Monterey. That afternoon he had come into the grocery and his sensitive tired face had flinched at the shadow of sternness that crossed Lee's face. Lee's fat finger tapped the rubber mat. Horace laid his hands palm up on the cigar counter. 'I guess I owe you plenty dough,' he said simply.

Lee's teeth flashed up in appreciation of an approach so different from any he had ever heard. He nodded gravely, but he waited for the trick to develop.

Horace wet his lips with his tongue, a good job from corner to corner. 'I hate to have my kids with that hanging over them,' he said. 'Why, I bet you wouldn't let them have a pack of spearmint now.'

Lee Chong's face agreed with this conclusion. 'Plenty dough,' he said.

Horace continued: 'You know that place of mine across the track up there where the fish meal is.'

Lee Chong nodded. It was his fish meal.

Horace said earnestly: 'If I was to give you that place – would it clear me up with you?'

Lee Chong tilted his head back and stared at Horace through his half-glasses while his mind flicked among accounts and his right hand moved restlessly to the abacus. He considered the construction which was flimsy and the lot which might be valuable if a cannery ever wanted to expand. 'Shu,' said Lee Chong.

'Well, get out the accounts and I'll make you a bill of sale on that place.' Horace seemed in a hurry.

'No need papers,' said Lee. 'I make paid-in-full paper.'

They finished the deal with dignity and Lee Chong threw in a quarter-pint of Old Tennis Shoes. And then Horace Abbeville walking very straight went across the lot and past the cypress-tree and across the track and up the chicken-walk and into the building that had been his, and he shot himself on a heap of fish meal. And although it has nothing to do with this story, no Abbeville child, no matter who its mother was, knew the lack of a stick of spearmint ever afterward.

But to get back to the evening. Horace was on the trestle with the embalming needles in him, and his two wives were sitting on the steps of his house with their arms about each other (they were good friends until after the funeral, and then they divided up the children and never spoke to each other again). Lee Chong stood behind the cigar counter and his nice brown eyes were turned inward on a calm and eternal Chinese sorrow. He knew he could not have helped it, but he wished he might have known and perhaps tried to help. It was deeply a part of Lee's kindness and understanding that man's right to kill himself is inviolable, but sometimes a friend can make it unnecessary. Lee had already underwritten the funeral and sent a wash-basket of groceries to the stricken families.

Now Lee Chong owned the Abbeville building – a good roof, a good floor, two windows and a door. True it was piled high with fish meal and the smell of it was delicate and penetrating. Lee Chong considered it as a storehouse for groceries, as a kind of warehouse, but he gave that up on second thought. It was too far away and anyone can go in through a window. He was tapping the rubber mat with his gold ring and considering the problem when the door opened and Mack came in. Mack was the elder, leader, mentor, and to a small extent the exploiter of a little group of men who had in common no families, no money, and no ambitions beyond food, drink, and contentment. But whereas most men in their search for contentment destroy themselves and fall wearily short of their targets, Mack and his friends approached contentment casually, quietly, and absorbed it gently. Mack and Hazel, a young man of great strength, Eddie who filled in as a bar-tender at La Ida, Hughie and Jones who occasionally collected frogs and cats for Western Biological, were currently living in those large rusty pipes in the lot next to Lee Chong's. That is, they lived in the pipes when it was damp, but in fine weather they lived in the shadow of the black cypress-tree at the top of the lot. The limbs folded down and made a canopy under which a man could lie and look out at the flow and vitality of Cannery Row.

Lee Chong stiffened ever so slightly when Mack came in and his eyes glanced quickly about the store to make sure that Eddie or Hazel or Hughie or Jones had not come in too and drifted away among the groceries.

Mack laid out his cards with a winning honesty. 'Lee,' he said, 'I and Eddie and the rest heard you own the Abbeville place.'

Lee Chong nodded and waited.

'I and my friends thought we'd ast you if we could move in there. We'll keep up the property,' he added quickly. 'Wouldn't let anybody break in or hurt anything. Kids might knock out the windows, you know . . .' Mack suggested. 'Place might burn down if somebody don't keep an eye on it.'

Lee tilted his head back and looked into Mack's eyes through the half-glasses and Lee's tapping finger slowed its tempo as he thought deeply. In Mack's eyes there was good will and good fellowship and a desire to make everyone happy. Why then did Lee Chong feel slightly surrounded? Why did his mind pick its way as delicately as a cat through cactus? It had been sweetly done, almost in a spirit of philanthropy. Lee's mind leaped ahead at the possibilities – no, they were probabilities, and his finger tapping slowed still further. He saw himself refusing Mack's request and he saw the broken glass from the windows. Then Mack would offer a second time to watch over and preserve Lee's property and at the second refusal, Lee could smell the smoke, could see the little flames creeping up the walls. Mack and his friends would try to help to put it out. Lee's finger came to a gentle rest on the change-mat. He was beaten. He knew that. There was left to him only the possibility of saving face, and Mack was likely to be very generous about that. Lee said: 'You like pay lent my place? You like live there same hotel?'

Mack smiled broadly and he was generous. 'Say . . .' he cried. 'That's an idear. Sure. How much?'

Lee considered. He knew it didn't matter what he charged. He wasn't going to get it, anyway. He might just as well make it a really sturdy face-saving sum. 'Fi' dolla' week,' said Lee.

T—D

Mack played it through to the end. 'I'll have to talk to the boys about it,' he said dubiously. 'Couldn't you make that four dollars a week?'

'Fi' dolla,' said Lee firmly.

'Well, I'll see what the boys say,' said Mack.

And that was the way it was. Everyone was happy about it. And if it be thought that Lee Chong suffered a total loss, at least his mind did not work that way. The windows were not broken. Fire did not break out, and while no rent was ever paid, if the tenants ever had any money, and quite often they did have, it never occurred to them to spend it anywhere except at Lee Chong's grocery. What he had was a little group of active and potential customers under wraps. But it went further than that. If a drunk caused trouble in the grocery, if the kids swarmed down from New Monterey intent on plunder, Lee Chong had only to call and his tenants rushed to his aid. One further bond it established – you cannot steal from your benefactor. The saving to Lee Chong in cans of beans and tomatoes and milk and watermelons more than paid the rent. And if there was a sudden and increased leakage among the groceries in New Monterey that was none of Lee Chong's affair.

The boys moved in and the fish-meal moved out. No one knows who named the house that has been known ever after as the Palace Flophouse Grill. In the pipes and under the cypress-tree there had been no room for furniture and the little niceties which are not only the diagnoses but the boundaries of our civilization. Once in the Palace Flophouse, the boys set about furnishing it. A chair appeared and a cot and another chair. A hardware store supplied a can of red paint not reluctantly because it never knew about it, and as a new table or footstool appeared it was painted, which not only made it very pretty but also disguised it to a certain extent in case a former owner looked in. And the Palace Flophouse Grill began to function. The boys could sit in front of their door and look down across the track and across the lot and across the street right into the front windows of Western Biological. They could hear the music from the laboratory at night. And their eyes followed Doc across the street when he went to Lee Chong's for beer. And Mack said: 'That Doc is a fine fellow. We ought to do something for him.'

CHAPTER II

THE word is a symbol and a delight which sucks up men and scenes, trees, plants, factories, and Pekinese. Then the Thing becomes the Word and back to Thing again, but warped and woven into a fantastic pattern. The Word sucks up Cannery Row, digests it, and spews it out, and the Row has taken the shimmer of the green world and the sky-reflecting seas. Lee Chong is more than a Chinese grocer. He must be. Perhaps he is evil balanced and held suspended by good – an Asiatic planet held to its orbit by the pull of Lao Tze and held away from Lao Tze by the centrifugality of abacus and cash register – Lee Chong suspended, spinning, whirling among groceries and ghosts. A hard man with a can of beans – a soft man with the bones of his grandfather. For Lee Chong dug into the grave on China Point and found the yellow bones, the skull with grey ropy hair still sticking to it. And Lee carefully packed the bones, femurs, and tibias really straight, skull in the middle, with pelvis and clavicle surrounding it and ribs curving on either side. Then Lee Chong sent his boxed and brittle grandfather over the western sea to lie at last in ground made holy by his ancestors.

Mack and the boys, too, spinning in their orbits. They are the Virtues, the Graces, the Beauties of the hurried mangled craziness of Monterey and the cosmic Monterey where men in fear and hunger destroy their stomachs in the fight to secure certain food, where men hungering for love destroy everything lovable about them. Mack and the boys are the Beauties, the Virtues, the Graces. In the world ruled by tigers with ulcers, rutted by strictured bulls, scavenged by blind jackals, Mack and the boys dine delicately with the tigers, fondle the frantic heifers, and wrap up the crumbs to feed the sea-gulls of Cannery Row. What can it profit a man to gain the whole world and to come to his property with a gastric ulcer, a blown prostate, and bifocals? Mack and the boys avoid the trap, walk around the poison, step over the noose while a generation of trapped, poisoned, and trussed-up men scream at them and call them no-goods, come-to-bad-ends, blots-on-the-town, thieves, rascals, bums. Our Father who art in nature, who has given the gift of survival to the coyote, the common brown rat, the English sparrow, the house-fly, and the moth, must have a great and overwhelming love for no-goods and blots-on-the-town and bums, and Mack and the boys. Virtues and graces and laziness and zest. Our Father who art in nature.

CHAPTER III

LEE CHONG's is to the right of the vacant lot (although why it is called vacant when it is piled high with old boilers, with rusting pipes, with great square timbers, and stacks of five-gallon cans, no one can say). In the rear of the vacant lot is the railroad track and the Palace Flophouse. But on the left-hand boundary of the lot is the stern and stately whore-house of Dora Flood; a decent, clean, honest, old-fashioned sporting house where a man can take a glass of beer among friends. This is no fly-by-night cheap clip-joint, but a sturdy, virtuous club, built, maintained, and disci-plined by Dora, who, madam and girl for fifty years, has through the exercise of special gifts of tact and honesty, charity and a certain realism, made herself respected by the intelligent, the learned, and the kind. And by the same token she is hated by the twisted and lascivious sisterhood of mar-ried spinsters whose husbands respect the home but don't like it very much.

Dora is a great woman, a great big woman with flaming orange hair and a taste for Nile-green evening dresses. She keeps an honest, one-price house, sells no hard liquor, and permits no loud or vulgar talk in her house. Of her girls some are fairly inactive, due to age and infirmities, but Dora never puts them aside, although, as she says, some of them don't turn three tricks a month, but they go right on eating three meals a day. In a moment of local love Dora named her place the Bear Flag Restaurant and the stories are many of people who have gone in for a sandwich. There are normally twelve girls in the house, counting the old ones, a Greek cook, and a man who is known as a watchman, but who undertakes all manner of delicate and dangerous tasks. He stops fights, ejects drunks, soothes hysteria, cures headaches, and tends bar. He bandages cuts and bruises, passes the time of day with cops, and since a good half of the girls are Christian Scientists, reads aloud his share of *Science and Health* on a Sunday morning. His predecessor, being a less well-balanced man, came to an evil end as shall be reported, but Alfred has triumphed over his environment and has brought his environment up with him. He knows what men should be there and what men shouldn't be there. He knows more about the home life of Monterey citizens than anyone in town.

As for Dora – she leads a ticklish existence. Being against the law, at least against its letter, she must be twice as law-abiding as anyone else. There must be no drunks, no fighting, no vulgarity, or they close Dora up. Also being illegal Dora must be especially philanthropic. Everyone puts the bite on her. If the police give a dance for their pension fund and everyone else gives a dollar, Dora has to give fifty dollars. When the Chamber of Commerce improved its gardens, the merchants each gave five dollars, but Dora was asked for and gave a hundred. With everyone else it is the same, Red Cross, Community Chest, Boy Scouts, Dora's unsung, unpublicized, shameless dirty wages of sin lead the list of donations. But during the depression she was hardest hit. In addition to the usual charities, Dora saw the hungry children of Cannery Row and the jobless fathers and the worried women, and Dora paid grocery bills right and left for two years and very nearly went broke in the process. Dora's girls are well trained and pleasant. They never speak to a man on the street although he may have been in the night before.

Before Alfy, the present watchman, took over, there was a tragedy in the Bear Flag Restaurant which saddened everyone. The previous watchman was named William, and he was a dark and lonesome-looking man. In the day-time when his duties were few he would grow tired of female company. Through the windows he could see Mack and the boys sitting on the pipes in the vacant lot, dangling their feet in the mallow weeds and take the sun while they discoursed slowly and philosophically of matters of interest but of no importance. Now and then as he watched them he saw them take out a pint of Old Tennis Shoes and wiping the neck of the bottle on a sleeve, raise the pint one after another. And William began to wish he could join that good group. He walked out one day and sat on the pipe. Conversation stopped and an uneasy and hostile silence fell on the group. After a while William went disconsolately back to the Bear Flag, and through the window he saw the conversation spring up again, and it saddened him. He had a dark and ugly face and a mouth twisted with brooding.

The next day he went again, and this time he took a pint of whisky. Mack and the boys drank the whisky, after all they weren't crazy, but all the talking they did was 'Good luck', and 'Lookin' at you'.

After a while William went back to the Bear Flag and he watched them through the window, and he heard Mack raise his voice saying: 'But God damn it, I hate a pimp!' Now this was obviously untrue, although William didn't know that. Mack and the boys just didn't like William.

Now William's heart broke. The bums would not receive him socially. They felt that he was too far beneath them. William had always been introspective and self-accusing. He put on his hat and walked out along the sea, clear out to the Lighthouse. And he stood in the pretty little cemetery where you can hear the waves drumming always. William thought dark and broody thoughts. No one loved him. No one cared about him. They might call him a watchman, but he was a pimp – a dirty pimp, the lowest thing in the world. And then he thought how he had a right to live and be happy just like anyone else, by God he had. He walked back angrily, but his anger went away when he came to the Bear Flag and climbed the steps. It was evening and the juke-box was playing *Harvest Moon* and William remembered that the first hooker who ever gaffed for him used to like that song before she ran away and got married and disappeared. The song made him awfully sad. Dora was in the back parlour having a cup of tea when William came in. She said: 'What's the matter, you sick?'

'No,' said William. 'But what's the percentage? I feel lousy. I think I'll bump myself off.'

Dora had handled plenty of neurotics in her time. Kid 'em out of it was her motto. 'Well, do it on your own time and don't mess up the rugs,' she said.

A grey damp cloud folded over William's heart and he walked slowly out and down the hall and knocked on Eva Flanegan's door. She had red hair and went to confession every week. Eva was quite a spiritual girl with a big family of brothers and sisters, but she was an unpredictable drunk. She was painting her nails and messing them pretty badly when William went in and he knew she was bagged and Dora wouldn't let a bagged girl work. Her fingers were nail polish to the first joint and she was angry. 'What's eating you?' she said. William grew angry too. 'I'm going to bump myself off,' he said fiercely.

Eva screeched at him. 'That's a dirty, lousy, stinking sin,' she cried, and then: 'Wouldn't it be like you to get the joint pinched just when I got almost enough kick to take a trip to East St Louis. You're a no-good bastard.' She was still screaming at him when William shut her door after him and went to the kitchen. He was very tired of women. The Greek would be restful after women.

The Greek, big apron, sleeves rolled up, was frying pork-chops in two big skillets, turning them over with an ice-pick, 'Hello, Kits. How is going things?' The pork-chops hissed and swished in the pan.

'I don't know, Lou,' said William. 'Sometimes I think the best thing to do would be – kluck!' He drew his finger across his throat.

The Greek laid the ice-pick on the stove and rolled his sleeves higher. 'I tell you what I hear, Kits,' he said. 'I hear like the fella talks about it don't never do it.' William's hand went out for the ice-pick and he held it easily in his hand.

His eyes looked deeply into the Greek's dark eyes, and he saw disbelief and amusement, and then as he stared the Greek's eyes grew troubled and then worried. And William saw the change, saw first how the Greek knew he could do it and then the Greek knew he would do it. As soon as he saw that in the Greek's eyes William knew he had to do it. He was sad because now it seemed silly. His hand rose and the ice-pick snapped into his heart. It was amazing how easily it went in. William was the watchman before Alfred came. Everyone liked Alfred. He could sit on the pipes with Mack and the boys any time. He could even visit up at the Palace Flophouse.

CHAPTER IV

IN the evening just at dusk, a curious thing happened on Cannery Row. It happened in the time between sunset and the lighting of the street light. There is a small quiet grey period then. Down the hill, past the Palace Flophouse, down the chicken-walk, and through the vacant lot came an old Chinaman. He wore an ancient flat straw hat, blue jeans, both coat and trousers, and heavy shoes of which one sole was loose so that it slapped the ground when he walked. In his hand he carried a covered wicker-basket. His face was lean and brown and corded as jerky and his old eyes were brown, even the whites were brown and deep-set so that they looked out of holes. He came by just at dusk and crossed the street and went through the opening between Western Biological and the Hediondo Cannery. Then he crossed the little beach and disappeared among the piles and steel posts which support the piers. No one saw him again until dawn.

But in the dawn, during that time when the street light has been turned off and the daylight has not come, the old Chinaman crept out from among the piles, crossed the beach and the street. His wicker-basket was heavy and wet and dropping now. His loose sole flap-flapped on the street. He went up the hill to the second street, went through a gate in a high board fence, and was not seen again until evening.

People, sleeping, heard his flapping shoe go by and they awakened for a moment. It had been happening for years, but no one ever got used to him. Some people thought he was God and very old people thought he was Death and children thought he was a very funny old Chinaman, as children always think anything old and strange is funny. But the children did not taunt him or shout at him as they should, for he carried a little cloud of fear about with him.

Only one brave and beautiful boy of ten named Andy from Salinas ever crossed the old Chinaman. Andy was visiting in Monterey and he saw the old man and knew he must shout at him if only to keep his self-respect, but even Andy, brave as he was, felt the little cloud of fear. Andy watched him go by evening after evening, while his duty and his terror wrestled. And then one evening Andy braced himself and marched behind the old man singing in a shrill falsetto: 'Ching-Chong Chinaman sitting on a rail – 'Long came a white man an' chopped off his tail.'

The old man stopped and turned. Andy stopped. The deep-brown eyes looked at Andy and the thin corded lips moved. What happened then Andy was never able either to explain or to forget. For the eyes spread out until there was no Chinaman. And then it was one eye – one huge brown eye as big as a church door. Andy looked through the shiny transparent brown door and through it he saw a lonely countryside, flat for miles but ending against a row of fantastic mountains shaped like cows' and dogs' heads and tents and mushrooms. There was low coarse grass on the plain and here and there a little mound. And a small animal like a woodchuck sat on each mound. And the loneliness – the desolate cold aloneness of the landscape made Andy whimper because there wasn't anybody at all in the world and he was left. Andy shut his eyes so he wouldn't have to see it any more and when he opened them, he was in Cannery Row and the old Chinaman was just flip-flapping between Western Biological and the Hediondo Cannery. Andy was the only boy who ever did that and he never did it again.

CHAPTER V

WESTERN BIOLOGICAL was right across the street and facing the vacant lot. Lee Chong's grocery was on its catty corner right and Dora's Bear Flag Restaurant was on it catty-corner left. Western Biological deals in strange and beautiful wares. It sells the lovely animals of the sea, the sponges, tunicates, anemones, the stars and buttlestars, and sun stars, the bivalves, barnacles, the worm and shells, the fabulous and multiform little brothers, the living moving flowers of the sea, nudibranchs and ectibranchs, the spiked and nobbed and needy urchins, the crabs and demi-crabs the little dragoons, the snapping shrimps, and ghost shrimp so transparent that they hardly throw a shadow. And Western Biological sells bugs and snails and spiders, and rattlesnakes, and rats, and honey bees and gila monsters These are all for sale. Then there are little unborn humans some whole and others sliced thin and mounted on slides And for students there are sharks with the blood drained out and yellow and blue colour substituted in veins and arteries, so that you may follow the systems with a scalpel And there are cats with coloured veins and arteries, and frogs the same. You can order anything living from Western Biological and sooner or later you will get it.

It is a low building facing the street. The basement is the store-room with shelves, shelves clear to the ceiling, loaded with jars of preserved animals. And in the basement is a sink and instrument for embalming and for injecting. Then you go through the backyard to a covered shed on piles over the ocean and here are the tanks for the larger animals, the sharks and rays and octopi, each in their concrete tanks. There is a stairway up the front of the building and a door that opens into an office where there is a desk piled high with unopened mail, filing cabinets, and a safe with the door propped open. Once the safe got locked by mistake and no one knew the combination. And in the safe was an open can of sardines and a piece of Roquefort cheese.

Before the combination could be sent by the maker of the lock, there was trouble in the safe. It was then that Doc devised a method for getting revenge on a bank if anyone should ever want to. 'Rent a safety-deposit box,' he said, 'then deposit in it one whole fresh salmon and go away for six months.' After the trouble with the safe, it was not permitted to keep food there any more. It is kept in the filing cabinets. Behind the office is a room where in aquaria are many living animals; there are also the microscopes and the slides and the drug cabinets, the cases of laboratory glass, the work benches and little motors, the chemicals. From this room comes smells – formaline, and dry starfish, and sea water and menthol, carbolic acid and acetic acid, smell of brown wrapping-paper and straw and rope, smell of chloroform and ether, smell of ozone from the motors, smell of fine steel and thin lubricant from the microscopes, smell of banana oil and rubber tubing, smell of drying wool socks and boots, sharp pungent smell of rattlesnakes, and musty frightening smell of rats. And through the back door comes the smell of kelp and barnacles when the tide is out and the smell of salt and spray when the tide is in.

To the left the office opens into a library. The walls are bookcases to the ceiling, boxes of pamphlets and separates, books of all kinds, dictionaries, encyclopaedias, poetry, plays. A great phonograph stands against the wall with hundreds of records lined up beside it. Under the window is a red-wood bed and on the walls and to the bookcases are pinned reproductions of Daumiers, and Graham, Titian, and Leonardo and Picasso, Dali and George Grosz, pinned here and there at eye level, so that you can look at them if you want to. There are chairs and benches in this little room and of course, the bed. As many as forty people have been here at one time.

Behind this library or music-room, or whatever you want to call it, is the kitchen, a narrow chamber with a gas-stove, a water-heater, and a sink. But whereas some food is kept in the filing cabinets in the office, dishes and cooking fat and vegetables are kept in glass-fronted sectional bookcases in the kitchen. No whimsy dictated this. It just happened.

From the ceiling of the kitchen hang pieces of bacon, and salami, and black bêche-de-mer. Behind the kitchen is a toilet and a shower. The toilet leaked for five years until a clever and handsome guest fixed it with a piece of chewing-gum.

Doc is the owner and operator of the Western Biological Laboratory. Doc is rather small, deceptively small, for he is wiry and very strong and when passionate anger comes on him he can be very fierce. He wears a beard and his face is half Christ and half satyr and his face tells the truth. It is said that he has helped many a girl out of one trouble and into another. Doc has the hands of a brain surgeon, and a cool warm mind. Doc tips his hat to dogs as he drives by and the dogs look up and smile at him. He can kill anything for need, but he could not even hurt a feeling for pleasure. He has one great fear – that of getting his head wet, so that summer or winter he ordinarily wears a rain hat. He will wade in a tide pool up to the chest without feeling damp, but a drop of rain water on his head makes him panicky.

Over a period of years Doc dug himself into Cannery Row to an extent not even he suspected. He became the fountain of philosophy and science and art. In the laboratory the girls from Dora's heard the Plain Songs and Gregorian music for the first time. Lee Chong listened while Li Po was read to him in English. Henri the painter heard for the first time the Book of the Dead and was so moved that he changed his medium. Henri had been painting with glue, iron rust, and coloured chicken feathers, but he changed and his next four paintings were done entirely with different kinds of nutshells. Doc would listen to any kind of nonsense and change it for you to a kind of wisdom. His mind had no horizon – and his sympathy had no warp. He could talk to children, telling them very profound things so that they understood. He lived in a world of wonders, of excitement. He was concupiscent as a rabbit and gentle as hell. Everyone who knew him was indebted to him. And everyone who thought of him thought next: 'I really must do something nice for Doc.'

CHAPTER VI

DOC was collecting marine animals in the Great Tide Pool on the tip of the Peninsula. It is a fabulous place; when the tide is in, a wave-churned basin, creamy with foam, whipped by the combers that roll in from the whistling buoy on the reef. But when the tide goes out the little water world becomes quiet and lovely. The sea is very clear and the bottom becomes fantastic with hurrying, fighting, feeding, breeding animals. Crabs rush from frond to frond of the waving algae. Starfish squat over mussels and limpets, attach their million little suckers and then slowly lift with incredible power until the prey is broken from the rock. And then the starfish stomach comes out and envelops its food. Orange and speckled and fluted nudibranchs slide gracefully over the rocks, their skirts waving like the dresses of Spanish dancers. And black eels poke their heads out of crevices and wait for prey. The snapping shrimps with their trigger claws pop loudly. The lovely, coloured world is glassed over. Hermit crabs like frantic children scamper on the bottom sand. And now one, finding an empty snail shell he likes better than his own, creeps out, exposing his soft body to the enemy for a moment, and then pops into the new shell. A wave breaks over the barrier, and churns the glassy water for a moment and mixes bubbles into the pool, and then it clears and is tranquil and lovely and murderous again. Here a crab tears a leg from his brother. The anemones expand like soft and brilliant flowers, inviting any tired and perplexed animal to lie for a moment in their arms, and when some small crab or little tide-pool Johnnie accepts the green and purple invitation, the petals whip in, the stinging cells shoot tiny narcotic needles into the prey and it grows weak and perhaps sleepy while the searing caustic digestive acids melt its body down.

Then the creeping murderer, the octopus, steals out, slowly, softly, moving like a grey mist, pretending now to be a bit of weed, now a rock, now a lump of decaying meat,

while its evil goat eyes watch coldly. It oozes and flow
toward a feeding crab, and as it comes close its yellow eye
burn and its body turns rosy with the pulsing colour c
anticipation and rage. Then suddenly it runs lightly on th
tip of its arms, as ferociously as a charging cat. It leap
savagely on the crab, there is a puff of black fluid, and th
struggling mass is obscured in the sepia cloud while th
octopus murders the crab. On the exposed rocks out c
water, the barnacles bubble behind their closed doors an
the limpets dry out. And down to the rocks come the blac
flies to eat anything they can find. The sharp smell of iodin
from the algae, and the lime smell of calcareous bodies an
the smell of powerful protean, smell of sperm and ova fil
the air. On the exposed rocks the starfish emit semen an
eggs from between their rays. The smells of life and rich
ness, of death and digestion, of decay and birth, burden th
air. And salt spray blows in from the barrier where th
ocean waits for its rising-tide strength to permit it back int
the Great Tide Pool again. And on the roof the whistlin
buoy bellows like a sad and patient bull.

In the pool Doc and Hazel worked together. Hazel live
in the Palace Flophouse with Mack and the boys. Hazel go
his name in as haphazard a way as his life was ever after
ward. His worried mother had had seven children in eigh
years. Hazel was the eighth, and his mother became con
fused about his sex when he was born. She was tired an
run down anyway from trying to feed and clothe seven
children and their father. She had tried every possible way
of making money – paper flowers, mushrooms at home, rab
bits for meat and fur – while her husband from a canvas
chair gave her every help his advice and reasoning and
criticism could offer. She had a great aunt named Haze
who was reputed to carry life insurance. The eighth child
was named Hazel before the mother got it through her head
that Hazel was a boy and by that time she was used to the
name and never bothered to change it. Hazel grew up – did
four years in grammar school, four years in reform school
and didn't learn anything in either place. Reform school
are supposed to teach viciousness and criminality, but Hazel

didn't pay enough attention. He came out of reform school as innocent of viciousness as he was of fractions and long division. Hazel loved to hear conversation but he didn't listen to words – just to the tone of conversation. He asked questions, not to hear the answers but simply to continue the flow. He was twenty-six – dark-haired and pleasant, strong, willing, and loyal. Quite often he went collecting with Doc and he was very good at it once he knew what was wanted. His fingers would creep like an octopus, could grab and hold like an anemone. He was sure-footed on the slippery rocks and he loved the hunt. Doc wore his rain hat and high rubber-boots as he worked, but Hazel sloshed about in tennis-shoes and blue jeans. They were collecting starfish. Doc had an order for three hundred.

Hazel picked a nobby purplish starfish from the bottom of the pool and popped it into his nearly-full gunny sack. 'I wonder what they do with them,' he said.

'Do with what?' Doc asked.

'The starfish,' said Hazel. 'You sell 'em. You'll send out a barrel of 'em. What do the guys do with 'em? You can't eat 'em.'

'They study them,' said Doc patiently and he remembered that he had answered this question for Hazel dozens of times before. But Doc had one mental habit he could not get over. When anyone asked a question, Doc thought he wanted to know the answer. That was the way with Doc. *He* never asked unless he wanted to know and he could not conceive of the brain that would ask without wanting to know. But Hazel, who simply wanted to hear talk, had developed a system of making the answer to one question the basis of another. It kept conversation going.

'What do they find to study?' Hazel continued. 'They're just starfish. There's millions of 'em around. I could get you a million of 'em.'

'They're complicated and interesting animals,' Doc said a little defensively. 'Besides, these are going to the Middle West to Northwestern University.'

Hazel used his trick. 'They got no starfish there?'

'They got no ocean there,' said Doc.

'Oh!' said Hazel and he cast frantically about for a peg to hang a new question on. He hated to have a conversation die out like this. He wasn't quick enough. While he was looking for a question Doc asked one. Hazel hated that, it meant casting about in his mind for an answer and casting about in Hazel's mind was like wandering alone in a deserted museum. Hazel's mind was choked with uncatalogued exhibits. He never forgot anything, but he never bothered to arrange his memories. Everything was thrown together like fishing-tackle in the bottom of a rowboat, hooks and sinkers and line and lures and gaffs all snarled up.

Doc asked: 'How are things going up at the Palace?'

Hazel ran his fingers through his dark hair and he peered into the clutter of his mind. 'Pretty good,' he said. 'That fellow Gay is moving in with us, I guess. His wife hits him pretty bad. He don't mind that when he's awake, but she waits 'til he gets to sleep and then hits him. He hates that. He has to wake up and beat her up and then when he goes back to sleep she hits him again. He don't get any rest, so he's moving in with us.'

'That's a new one,' said Doc. 'She used to swear out a warrant and put him in jail.'

'Yeah!' said Hazel. 'But that was before they built the new jail in Salinas. Used to be thirty days and Gay was pretty hot to get out, but this new jail – radio in the tank and good bunks and the sheriff's a nice fellow. Gay gets in there and he don't want to come out. He likes it so much his wife won't get him arrested any more. So she figured out this hitting him while he's asleep. It's nerve racking, he says. And you know as good as me – Gay never did take any pleasure in beating her up. He only done it to keep his self-respect. But he gets tired of it. I guess he'll be with us now.'

Doc straightened up. The waves were beginning to break over the barrier of the Great Tide Pool. The tide was coming in and little rivers from the sea had begun to flow over the rocks. The wind blew freshly in from the whistling buoy and the barking sea-lions came from around the point. Doc pushed his rain hat on the back of his head. 'We've got enough starfish,' he said and then went on: 'Look, Hazel,

I know you've got six or seven undersized abalones in the bottom of your sack. If we get stopped by a game warden, you're going to say they're mine, on my permit – aren't you?'

'Well – hell,' said Hazel.

'Look,' Doc said kindly. 'Suppose I get an order for abalones and maybe the game warden thinks I'm using my collecting permit too often. Suppose he thinks I'm eating them.'

'Well – hell,' said Hazel.

'It's like the industrial alcohol board. They've got suspicious minds. They always think I'm drinking the alcohol. They think that about everyone.'

'Well, ain't you?'

'Not much of it,' said Doc. 'That stuff they put in it tastes terrible and it's a big job to re-distil it.'

'That stuff ain't so bad,' said Hazel. 'Me and Mack had a snort at it the other day. What is it they put in?'

Doc was about to answer when he saw it was Hazel's trick again. 'Let's get moving,' he said. He hoisted his sack of starfish on his shoulder. And he had forgotten the illegal abalones in the bottom of Hazel's sack.

Hazel followed him up out of the tide pool and up the slippery trail to solid ground. The little crabs scampered and skittered out of their way. Hazel felt that he had better cement the grave over the topic of the abalones.

'That painter guy came back to the Palace,' he offered.

'Yes?' said Doc.

'Yeah! You see, he done all our pictures in chicken-feathers and now he says he got to do them all over again with nut-shells. He says he changed his – his med – medium.'

Doc chuckled. 'He still building his boat?'

'Sure,' said Hazel. 'He's got it all changed around. New kind of a boat. I guess he'll take it apart and change it. Doc – is he nuts?'

Doc swung his heavy sack of starfish to the ground and stood panting a little. 'Nuts?' he asked. 'Oh, yes, I guess so. Nuts about the same amount we are, only in a different way.'

Such a thing had never occurred to Hazel. He looked

upon himself as a crystal pool of clarity and on his life as a troubled glass of misunderstood virtue. Doc's last statement had outraged him a little. 'But the boat . . .' he cried. 'He's been building that boat for seven years that I know of. The blocks rotted out and he made concrete blocks. Every time he gets it nearly finished he changes it and starts over again. I think he's nuts. Seven years on a boat.'

Doc was sitting on the ground pulling off his rubber boots. 'You don't understand,' he said gently. 'Henri loves boats, but he's afraid of the ocean.'

'What's he want a boat for then?' Hazel demanded.

'He likes boats,' said Doc. 'But suppose he finishes his boat. Once it's finished people will say: "Why don't you put it in the water?" Then if he puts it in the water, he'll have to go out in it, and he hates the water. So you see, he never finishes the boat – so he doesn't ever have to launch it.'

Hazel had followed this reasoning to a certain point, but he abandoned it before it was resolved, not only abandoned it but searched for some way to change the subject. 'I think he's nuts,' he said lamely.

On the black earth on which the ice-plants bloomed hundreds of black stink bugs crawled. And many of them stuck their tails up in the air. 'Look at all them stink bugs,' Hazel remarked, grateful to the bugs for being there.

'They're interesting,' said Doc.

'Well, what they got their asses up in the air for?'

Doc rolled up his wool socks and put them in the rubber-boots and from his pocket he brought out dry socks and a pair of thin moccasins. 'I don't know why,' he said. 'I looked them up recently – they're very common animals and one of the commonest things they do is put their tails up in the air. And in all the books there isn't one mention of the fact that they put their tails up in the air or why.'

Hazel turned one of the stink bugs over with the toe of his wet tennis-shoe and the shining black beetle strove madly with floundering legs to get upright again. 'Well, why do *you* think they do it?'

'I think they're praying,' said Doc.

'What!' Hazel was shocked.

'The remarkable thing,' said Doc, 'isn't that they put their tails up in the air – the really incredibly remarkable thing is that we find it remarkable. We can only use ourselves as yardsticks. If we did something as inexplicable and strange we'd probably be praying – so maybe they're praying.'

'Let's get the hell out of here,' said Hazel.

CHAPTER VII

THE Palace Flophouse was no sudden development. Indeed when Mack and Hazel and Eddie and Hughie and Jones moved into it, they looked upon it as little more than shelter from the wind and the rain, as a place to go when everything else had closed or when their welcome was thin and sere with over-use. Then the Palace was only a long bare room, lit dimly by two small windows, walled with unpainted wood smelling strongly of fish meal. They had not loved it then. But Mack knew that some kind of organization was necessary, particularly among such a group of ravening individualists.

A training army which has not been equipped with guns and artillery and tanks uses artificial guns and masquerading trucks to simulate its destructive panoply – and its toughening soldiers get used to field-guns by handling logs on wheels.

Mack, with a piece of chalk, drew five oblongs on the floor, each seven feet long and four feet wide, and in each square he wrote a name. These were the simulated beds. Each man had property rights inviolable in his space. He could legally fight a man who encroached on his square. The rest of the room was property common to all. That was in the first days when Mack and the boys sat on the floor, played cards hunkered down, and slept on the hard boards. Perhaps, save for an accident of weather, they might always have lived that way. However, an unprecedented rainfall which went on for over a month changed all that. House-ridden, the boys grew tired of squatting on the floor. Their eyes became outraged by the bare board walls. Because it sheltered them the house grew dear to them. And it had the charm of never knowing the entrance of an outraged landlord. For Lee Chong never came near it. Then one afternoon Hughie came in with an army cot which had a torn canvas. He spent two hours sewing up the rip with fishingline. And that night the others lying on the floor in their squares watched Hughie ooze gracefully into his cot – they heard him sigh with abysmal comfort and he was asleep and snoring before anyone else.

The next day Mack puffed up the hill carrying a rusty set of springs he had found on a scrap-iron dump. The apathy was broken then. The boys outdid one another in beautifying the Palace Flophouse until after a few months it was, if anything, over-furnished. There were old carpets on the floor, chairs with and without seats. Mack had a wicker chaise-longue painted bright red. There were tables, a grandfather clock without dial face or works. The walls were whitewashed, which made it almost light and airy. Pictures began to appear – mostly calendars showing improbable luscious blondes holding bottles of Coca-Cola. Henri had contributed two pieces from his chicken-feather period. A bundle of gilded cat-tails stood in one corner and a sheaf of peacock-feathers was nailed to the wall beside the grandfather clock.

They were some time acquiring a stove and when they did find what they wanted, a silver-scrolled monster with floriated warming ovens and a front like a nickel-plated tulip garden, they had trouble getting it. It was too big to steal and its owner refused to part with it to the sick widow with eight children whom Mack invented and patronized in the same moment. The owner wanted a dollar and a half and didn't come down to eighty cents for three days. The boys closed at eighty cents and gave him an IOU, which he probably still has. This transaction took place in Seaside and the stove weighed three hundred pounds. Mack and Hughie exhausted every possibility of haulage for ten days and only when they realized that no one was going to take this stove home for them did they begin to carry it. It took them three days to carry it to Cannery Row, a distance of five miles, and they camped beside it at night. But once installed in the Palace Flophouse it was the glory and the heart and the centre. Its nickel flowers and foliage shone with a cheery light. It was the gold tooth of the Palace. Fired up, it warmed the big room. Its oven was wonderful and you could fry an egg on its shiny black lids.

With the great stove came pride, and with pride, the Palace became home. Eddie planted morning glories to run over the door and Hazel acquired some rather rare fuchsia-bushes planted in five-gallon cans which made the entrance formal and a little cluttered. Mack and the boys loved the Palace and they even cleaned it a little sometimes. In their minds they sneered at unsettled people who had no house to go to and occasionally in their pride they brought a guest home for a day or two.

Eddie was understudy bar-tender at 'La Ida'. He filled in when Whitey the regular bar-tender was sick, which was as often as Whitey could get away with it. Every time Eddie filled in, a few bottles disappeared, so he couldn't fill in too often. But Whitey liked to have Eddie take his place because he was convinced, and correctly, that Eddie was one man who wouldn't try to keep his job permanently. Almost anyone could have trusted Eddie to this extent. Eddie didn't have to remove much liquor. He kept a gallon jug under the bar and in the mouth of the jug there was a funnel. Anything left in the glasses Eddie poured into the funnel before he washed the glasses. If an argument or a song were going on at 'La Ida', or late at night when good fellowship had reached its logical conclusion, Eddie poured glasses half- or two-thirds full into the funnel. The resulting punch which he took back to the Palace was always interesting and sometimes surprising. The mixture of rye, beer, bourbon, Scotch, wine, rum, and gin was fairly constant, but now and then some effete customer would order a stinger or an anisette or a curaçao and these little touches gave a distinct character to the punch. It was Eddie's habit always to shake a little Angostura into the jug before he left. On a good night Eddie got three-quarters of a gallon. It was a source of satisfaction to him that nobody was out anything. He had observed that a man got just as drunk on half a glass as on a whole one, that is, if he was in the mood to get drunk at all.

Eddie was a very desirable inhabitant of the Palace Flophouse. The others never asked him to help with the house-cleaning and once Hazel washed four pairs of Eddie's socks.

Now on the afternoon when Hazel was out collecting with Doc in the Great Tide Pool, the boys were sitting around in the Palace sipping the result of Eddie's latest contribution. Gay was there too, the latest member of the group. Eddie sipped speculatively from his glass and smacked his lips. 'It's funny how you get a run,' he said. 'Take last night. There was at least ten guys ordered Manhattans. Sometimes maybe you don't get two calls for a Manhattan in a month. It's the grenadine gives the stuff that taste.'

Mack tasted his – a big taste – and refilled his glass. 'Yes,' he said sombrely, 'it's little things make the difference.' He looked about to see how this gem had set with the others.

Only Gay got the full impact. 'Sure is,' he said. 'Does . . .'

'Where's Hazel today?' Mack asked.

Jones said: 'Hazel went out with Doc to get some starfish.'

Mack nodded his head soberly. 'That Doc is a hell of a nice fella,' he said. 'He'll give you a quarter any time. When I cut myself he put on a new bandage every day. A hell of a nice fella.'

The others nodded in profound agreement.

'I been wondering for a long time,' Mack continued, 'what we could do for him – something nice. Something he'd like.'

'He'd like a dame,' said Hughie.

'He's got three four dames,' said Jones. 'You can always tell – when he pulls them front curtains closed and when he plays that kind of church music on the phonograph.'

Mack said reprovingly to Hughie: 'Just because he doesn't run no dame naked through the streets in the day-time, you think Doc's celebrate.'

'What's celebrate?' Eddie asked.

'That's when you can't get no dame,' said Mack.

'I thought it was a kind of party,' said Jones.

A silence fell on the room. Mack shifted in his chaise-longue. Hughie let the front legs of his chair down on the floor. They looked into space and then they all looked at Mack. Mack said: 'Hum!'

Eddie said: 'What kind of a party you think Doc'd like?'

'What other kind is there?' said Jones.

Mack mused: 'Doc wouldn't like this stuff from the winin' jug.'

'How do you know?' Hughie demanded. 'You never offered him none.'

'Oh, I know,' said Mack. 'He's been to college. Once I seen a dame in a fur coat go in there. Never did see her come out. It was two o'clock the last I looked – and that church music goin'. No – you couldn't offer him none of this.' He filled his glass again.

'This tastes pretty nice after the third glass,' Hughie said loyally.

'No,' said Mack. 'Not for Doc. Have to be whisky – the real thing.'

'He likes beer,' said Jones. 'He's all the time going over to Lee's for beer – sometimes in the middle of the night.'

Mack said: 'I figure when you buy beer, you're buying too much tare. Take 8 per cent beer – why you're spending your dough for 92 per cent water and colour and hops and stuff like that. Eddie,' he added, 'you think you could get four five bottles of whisky at "La Ida" next time Whitey's sick?'

'Sure,' said Eddie. 'Sure I could get it, but that'd be the end – no more golden eggs. I think Johnnie's suspicious anyways. Other day he says: "I smell a mouse named Eddie." I was gonna lay low and only bring the jug for a while.'

'Yeah!' said Jones. 'Don't you lose that job. If something happened to Whitey, you could fall right in there for a week or so 'til they got somebody else. I guess if we're goin' to give a party for Doc, we got to buy the whisky. How much is whisky a gallon?'

'I don't know,' said Hughie. 'I never get more than a half-pint at a time myself – at one time that is. I figure you get a quart and right away you got friends. But you get a half-pint and you can drink it in the lot before – well before you got a lot of folks around.'

'It's going to take dough to give Doc a party,' said Mack. 'If we're going to give him a party at all it ought to be a good one. Should have a big cake. I wonder when is his birthday?'

'Don't need a birthday for a party,' said Jones.

'No – but it's nice,' said Mack. 'I figure it would take ten or twelve bucks to give Doc a party you wouldn't be ashamed of.'

They looked at one another speculatively. Hughie suggested: 'The Hediondo Cannery is hiring guys.'

'No,' said Mack quickly. 'We got good reputations and we don't want to spoil them. Every one of us keeps a job for a month or more when we take one. That's why we can always get a job when we need one. S'pose we take a job for a day or so – why we'll lose our reputation for sticking. Then if we needed a job there wouldn't nobody have us.' The rest nodded quick agreement.

'I figure I'm gonna work a couple of months – November and part of December,' said Jones. 'Makes it nice to have money around Christmas. We could cook a turkey this year.'

'By God, we could,' said Mack. 'I know a place up Carmel Valley where there's fifteen hundred in one flock.'

'Valley,' said Hughie. 'You know I used to collect stuff up the Valley for Doc, turtles and crayfish and frogs. Got a nickel apiece for frogs.'

'Me, too,' said Gay. 'I got five hundred frogs one time."

'If Doc needs frogs it's a set-up,' said Mack. 'We could go up the Carmel River and have a little outing and we wouldn't tell Doc what it was for and then we'd give him one hell of a party.'

A quiet excitement grew in the Palace Flophouse. 'Gay,' said Mack, 'take a look out the door and see if Doc's car is in front of his place.'

Gay set down his glass and looked out. 'Not yet,' he said.

'Well, he ought to be back any minute,' said Mack. 'Now here's how we'll go about it . . .'

CHAPTER VIII

IN April 1932, the boiler at the Hediondo Cannery blew a tube for the third time in two weeks and the board of directors, consisting of Mr Randolph and a stenographer, decided that it would be cheaper to buy a new boiler than to have to shut down so often. In time the new boiler arrived and the old one was moved into the vacant lot between Lee Chong's and the Bear Flag Restaurant, where it was set on blocks to await an inspiration on Mr Randolph's part on how to make some money out of it. Gradually, the plant engineer removed the tubing to use to patch other out-worn equipment at the Hediondo. The boiler looked like an old-fashioned locomotive without wheels. It had a big door in the centre of its nose and a low fire door. Gradually, it became red and soft with rust and gradually the mallow weeds grew up around it and the flaking rust fed the weeds. Flowering myrtle crept up its sides and the wild anise perfumed the air about it. Then someone threw out a datura root and the thick fleshy tree grew up and the great white bells hung over the boiler door and at night the flowers smelled of love and excitement, an incredibly sweet and moving odour.

In 1935 Mr and Mrs Sam Malloy moved into the boiler. The tubing was all gone now and it was a roomy, dry and safe apartment. True, if you came in through the fire door you had to get down on your hands and knees, but once in there was head room in the middle and you couldn't want a dryer, warmer place to stay. They shagged a mattress through the fire door and settled down. Mr Malloy was happy and contented there and for quite a long time so was Mrs Malloy.

Below the boiler on the hill there were numbers of large pipes also abandoned by the Hediondo. Toward the end of 1937 there was a great catch of fish and the canneries were working full time and a housing shortage occurred. Then it was that Mr Malloy took to renting the larger pipes as sleeping-quarters for single men at a very nominal fee. With a piece of tar paper over one end and a square of carpet over the other, they made comfortable bedrooms, although men used to sleeping curled up had to change their habits or move out. There were those too who claimed that their snores echoing back from the pipes woke them up. But on the whole Mr Malloy did a steady small business and was happy.

Mrs Malloy had been contented until her husband became a landlord and then she began to change. First it was a rug, then a wash-tub, then a lamp with a coloured silk shade. Finally, she came into the boiler on her hands and knees one day and she stood up and said a little breathlessly: 'Holman's are having a sale of curtains. Real lace curtains and edges of blue and pink — $1.98 a set with curtain rods thrown in.'

Mr Malloy sat up on the mattress. 'Curtains?' he demanded. 'What in God's name do you want curtains for?'

'I like things nice,' said Mrs Malloy. 'I always did like to have things nice for you,' and her lower lip began to tremble.

'But, darling,' Sam Malloy cried, 'I got nothing against curtains. I like curtains.'

'Only $1.98,' Mrs Malloy quavered, 'and you begrutch me $1.98,' and she sniffled and her chest heaved.

'I don't begrutch you,' said Mr Malloy. 'But, darling — for Christ's sake what are we going to do with curtains? We got no windows.'

Mrs Malloy cried and cried and Sam held her in his arms and comforted her.

'Men just don't understand how a woman feels,' she sobbed. 'Men just never try to put themselves in a woman's place.'

And Sam lay beside her and rubbed her back for a long time before she went to sleep.

CHAPTER IX

WHEN Doc's car came back to the laboratory, Mack and the boys secretly watched Hazel help to carry in the sacks of starfish. In a few minutes Hazel came damply up the chicken-walk to the Palace. His jeans were wet with sea water to the thighs and where it was drying the white salt rings were forming. He sat heavily in the patient rocker that was his and shucked off his wet tennis shoes.

Mack asked: 'How is Doc feeling?'

'Fine,' said Hazel. 'You can't understand a word he says. Know what he said about stink bugs? No – I better not tell you.'

'He seem in a nice friendly mood?' Mack asked.

'Sure,' said Hazel. 'We got two three hundred starfish. He's all right.'

'I wonder if we better all go over?' Mack asked himself and he answered himself: 'No, I guess it would be better if one went alone. It might get him mixed up if we all went.'

'What is this?' Hazel asked.

'We got plans,' said Mack. 'I'll go myself so as not to startle him. You guys stay here and wait. I'll come back in a few minutes.'

Mack went out and he teetered down the chicken-walk and across the track. Mr Malloy was sitting on a brick in front of his boiler.

'How are you, Sam?' Mack asked.

'Pretty good.'

'How's the missus?'

'Pretty good,' said Mr Malloy. 'You know any kind of glue that you can stick cloth to iron?'

Ordinarily, Mack would have thrown himself headlong into this problem, but now he was not to be deflected. 'No,' he said.

He went across the vacant lot, crossed the street, and entered the basement of the laboratory.

Doc had his hat off now, since there was practically no

chance of getting his head wet unless a pipe broke. He was busy removing the starfish from the wet sacks and arranging them on the cool concrete floor. The starfish were twisted and knotted up, for a starfish loves to hang on to something and for an hour these had found only each other. Doc arranged them in long lines and very slowly they straightened out until they lay in symmetrical stars on the concrete floor. Doc's pointed brown beard was damp with perspiration as he worked. He looked up a little nervously as Mack entered. It was not that trouble always came in with Mack, but something always entered with him.

'Hiya, Doc?' said Mack.

'All right,' said Doc uneasily.

'Hear about Phyllis Mae over at the Bear Flag? She hit a drunk and got his tooth in her fist and it's infected clear to the elbow. She showed me the tooth. It was out of a plate. Is a false-tooth poison, Doc?'

'I guess everything that comes out the human mouth is of poison,' said Doc warningfully. 'Has she got a doctor?'

'The bouncer fixed her up,' said Mack.

'I'll take her some sulfa,' said Doc, and he waited for the storm to break. He knew Mack had come for something and Mack knew he knew it.

Mack said: 'Doc, you got any need for any kind of animals now?'

Doc sighed with relief. 'Why?' he asked guardedly.

Mack became open and confidential. 'I'll tell you, Doc. I and the boys got to get some dough – we simply got to. It's for a good purpose, you might say a worthy cause.'

'Phyllis Mae's arm?'

Mack saw the chance, weighed it, and gave it up. 'Well – no,' he said. 'It's more important than that. You can't kill a whore. No – this is different. I and the boys thought if you needed something why we'd get it for you and that way we could make a little piece of change.'

It seemed simple and innocent. Doc laid down four more starfish in lines. 'I could use three or four hundred frogs,' he said. 'I'd get them myself, but I've got to go down to La

Jolla tonight. There's a good tide tomorrow and I have to get some octopi.'

'Same price for frogs?' Mack asked. 'Five cents apiece.'

'Same price,' said Doc.

Mack was jovial. 'Don't you worry about frogs, Doc,' he said. 'We'll get you all the frogs you want. You just rest easy about frogs. Why we can get them right up Carmel River. I know a place.'

'Good,' said Doc. 'I'll take all you get, but I need about three hundred.'

'Just you rest easy, Doc. Don't you lose no sleep about it. You'll get your frogs, maybe seven eight hundred.' He put the Doc at his ease about frogs and then a little cloud crossed Mack's face. 'Doc,' he said, 'any chance of using your car to go up the Valley?'

'No,' said Doc. 'I told you. I have to drive to La Jolla tonight to make tomorrow's tide.'

'Oh,' said Mack dispiritedly. 'Oh. Well, don't you worry about it, Doc. Maybe we can get Lee Chong's old truck.' And then his face fell a little further. 'Doc,' he said, 'on a business deal like this, would you advance two or three bucks for petrol? I know Lee Chong won't give us petrol.'

'No,' said Doc. He had fallen into this before. Once he had financed Gay to go for turtles. He financed him for two weeks and at the end of that time Gay was in jail on his wife's charge and he never did go for turtles.

'Well, maybe we can't go then,' said Mack sadly.

Now Doc really needed the frogs. He tried to work out some method which was business and not philanthropy. 'I'll tell you what I'll do,' he said. 'I'll give you a note to my petrol station so you can get ten gallons of petrol. How will that be?'

Mack smiled. 'Fine,' he said. 'That will work out just fine. I and the boys will get an early start tomorrow. Time you get back from the south, we'll have more damn frogs than you ever seen in your life.'

Doc went to the labelling desk and wrote a note to Red Williams at the petrol station, authorizing the issue of ten gallons of petrol to Mack. 'Here you are,' he said.

Mack was smiling broadly. 'Doc,' he said, 'you can get to sleep tonight and not even give frogs a thought. We'll have piss-pots full of them by the time you get back.'

Doc watched him go a little uneasily. Doc's dealings with Mack and the boys had always been interesting, but rarely had they been profitable to Doc. He remembered ruefully the time Mack sold him fifteen tom-cats and by night the owners came and got every one. 'Mack,' he had asked, 'why all tom-cats?'

Mack said: 'Doc, it's my own invention, but I'll tell you because you're a good friend. You make a big wire trap and then you don't use bait. You use – well – you use a lady cat. Catch every God-damn tom-cat in the country that way.'

From the laboratory Mack crossed the street and went through the swinging screen doors into Lee Chong's grocery. Mrs Lee was cutting bacon on the big butcher's block. A Lee cousin primped up slightly wilted heads of lettuce the way a girl primps a loose finger wave. A cat lay asleep on a big pile of oranges. Lee Chong stood in his usual place behind the cigar counter and in front of the liquor shelves. His tapping finger on the change mat speeded up a little when Mack came in.

Mack wasted no time in sparring. 'Lee,' he said, 'Doc over there's got a problem. He's got a big order for frogs from the New York Museum. Means a lot to Doc. Besides the dough there's a lot of credit getting an order like that. Doc's got to go south and I and the boys said we'd help him out. I think a guy's friends ought to help him out of a hole when they can, especially a nice guy like Doc. Why I bet he spends sixty seventy dollars a month with you.'

Lee Chong remained silent and watchful. His fat finger barely moved on the change mat, but it flicked slightly like a tense cat's tail.

Mack plunged into his thesis. 'Will you let us take your old truck to go up Carmel Valley for frogs for Doc – for good old Doc?'

Lee Chong smiled in triumph. 'Tluck no good,' he said. 'Bloke down.'

This staggered Mack for a moment, but he recovered. He

spread the order for petrol on the cigar counter. 'Look!' he said. 'Doc needs them frogs. He give me this order for petrol to get them. I can't let Doc down. Now Gay is a good mechanic. If he fixes your truck and puts it in good shape, will you let us take it?'

Lee put back his head so that he could see Mack through his half-glasses. There didn't seem to be anything wrong with the proposition. The truck really wouldn't run. Gay really was a good mechanic and the order for petrol was definite evidence of good faith.

'How long you be gone?' Lee asked.

'Maybe half a day, maybe a whole day. Just 'til we get the frogs.'

Lee was worried, but he couldn't see any way out. The dangers were all there and Lee knew all of them. 'Okay,' said Lee.

'Good,' said Mack. 'I knew Doc could depend on you. I'll get Gay right to work on that truck.' He turned about to leave. 'By the way,' he said. 'Doc's paying us five cents apiece for those frogs. We're going to get seven or eight hundred. How about taking a pint of Old Tennis Shoes just 'til we can get back with the frogs?'

'No!' said Lee Chong.

CHAPTER X

FRANKIE began coming to Western Biological when he was eleven years old. For a week or so he just stood outside the basement door and looked in. Then one day he stood inside the door. Ten days later he was in the basement. He had very large eyes and his hair was a dark, wiry, dirty shock. His hands were filthy. He picked up a piece of excelsior and put it in a garbage can and then he looked at Doc where he worked labelling specimen bottles containing purple Velella. Finally Frankie got to the work-bench and he put his dirty fingers on the bench. It took Frankie three weeks to get that far, and he was ready to bolt every instant of the time.

Finally one day Doc spoke to him. 'What's your name, son?'

'Frankie.'

'Where do you live?'

'Up there,' a gesture up the hill.

'Why aren't you in school?'

'I don't go to school.'

'Why not?'

'They don't want me there.'

'Your hands are dirty. Don't you ever wash?'

Frankie looked stricken and then he went to the sink and scrubbed his hands, and always afterwards he scrubbed his hands almost raw every day.

And he came to the laboratory every day. It was an association without much talk. Doc by a telephone call established that what Frankie said was true. They didn't want him in school. He couldn't learn and there was something a little wrong with his co-ordination. There was no place for him. He wasn't an idiot, he wasn't dangerous, his parents, or parent, would not pay for his keep on an institution. Frankie didn't often sleep at the laboratory, but he spent his days there. And sometimes he crawled in the excelsior crate and slept. That was probably when there was a crisis at home.

Doc asked: 'Why do you come here?'

'You don't hit me or give me a nickel,' said Frankie.

'Do they hit you at home?'

'There's uncles around all the time at home. Some of them hit me and tell me to get out and some of them give me a nickel and tell me to get out.'

'Where's your father?'

'Dead,' said Frankie vaguely.

'Where's your mother?'

'With the uncles.'

Doc clipped Frankie's hair and got rid of the lice. At Lee Chong's he got him a new pair of overalls and a striped sweater and Frankie became his slave.

'I love you,' he said one afternoon. 'Oh, I love you.'

He wanted to work in the laboratory. He swept out every day, but there was something a little wrong. He couldn't get a floor quite clean. He tried to help with grading crayfish for size. There they were in a bucket, all sizes. They were to be grouped in the big pans – laid out – all the three-inch ones together and all the four-inch ones, and so forth. Frankie tried and the perspiration stood on his forehead, but he couldn't do it. Size relationships just didn't get through to him.

'No,' Doc would say. 'Look, Frankie. Put them beside your finger like this so you'll know which ones are this long. See? This one goes from the tip of your finger to the base of your thumb. Now you just pick out another one that goes from the tip of your finger down to the same place and it will be right.' Frankie tried and he couldn't do it. When Doc went upstairs Frankie crawled in the excelsior box and didn't come out all afternoon.

But Frankie was a nice, good, kind boy. He learned to light Doc's cigars and he wanted Doc to smoke all the time so he could light the cigars.

Better than anything else Frankie loved it when there were parties upstairs in the laboratory. When girls and men gathered to sit and talk, when the great phonograph played music that throbbed in his stomach and made beautiful and huge pictures form vaguely in his head. Frankie loved it. Then he crouched down in a corner behind a chair where he was hidden and could watch and listen. When there was laughter at a joke he didn't understand Frankie laughed delightedly behind his chair, and when the conversation dealt with abstractions his brow furrowed and he became intent and serious.

One afternoon he did a desperate thing. There was a small party in the laboratory. Doc was in the kitchen pouring beer when Frankie appeared beside him. Frankie grabbed a glass of beer and rushed it through the door and gave it to a girl sitting in a big chair.

She took the glass and said: 'Why, thank you,' and she smiled at him.

And Doc coming through the door said: 'Yes, Frankie is a great help to me.'

Frankie couldn't forget that. He did the thing in his mind over and over, just how he had taken the glass and just how the girl sat and then her voice – 'Why, thank you,' and Doc '– a great help to me – Frankie is a great help to me – sure Frankie is a great help – Frankie,' and Oh, my God!

He knew a big party was coming because Doc bought steaks and a great deal of beer and Doc let him help clean out all the upstairs. But that was nothing, for a great plan had formed in Frankie's mind and he could see just how it would be. He went over it again and again. It was beautiful. It was perfect.

Then the party started and people came and sat in the front room, girls and young women and men.

Frankie had to wait until he had the kitchen to himself, and the door closed. And it was some time before he had it so. But at last he was alone and the door was shut. He could hear the chatter of conversation and the music from the great phonograph. He worked very quietly – first the tray – then get out the glasses without breaking any. Now fill them with beer and let the foam settle a little and then fill again.

Now he was ready. He took a great breath and opened the door. The music and the talk roared around him. Frankie picked up the tray of beer and walked through the door. He knew how. He went straight toward the same young woman who had thanked him before. And then right in front of her, the thing happened, and co-ordination failed, the hands fumbled, the muscles panicked, the nerves tele-graphed to a dead operator, the responses did not come back. Tray and beer collapsed forward into the young woman's lap. For a moment Frankie stood still. And then he turned and ran.

The room was quiet. They could hear him run downstairs and go into the cellar. They heard a hollow scrabbling sound – and then silence.

Doc walked quietly down the stairs and into the cellar. Frankie was in the excelsior box burrowed down clear to the bottom, with the pile of excelsior on top of him. Doc could hear him whimpering there. Doc waited for a moment and then he went quietly back upstairs.

There wasn't a thing in the world he could do.

CHAPTER XI

THE Model T Ford truck of Lee Chong had a dignified history. In 1923 it had been a passenger car belonging to Dr W. T. Waters. He used it for five years and sold it to an insurance man named Rattle. Mr Rattle was not a careful man. The car he got in clean nice condition he drove like fury. Mr Rattle drank on Saturday nights and the car suffered. The fenders were broken and bent. He was a pedal rider too and the bands had to be changed often. When Mr Rattle embezzled a client's money and ran away to San Jose, he was caught with a high-hair blonde and sent up within ten days.

The body of the car was so battered that its next owner cut it in two and added a little truck bed.

The next owner took off the front of the cab and the windshield. He used it to haul squids and he liked a fresh breeze to blow in his face. His name was Francis Almones, and he had a sad life, for he always made just a fraction less than he needed to live. His father had left him a little money, but year by year and month by month, no matter how hard Francis worked or how careful he was, his money grew less until he just dried up and blew away.

Lee Chong got the truck in payment of a grocery bill.

By this time the truck was little more than four wheels and an engine, and the engine was so crotchety and sullen and senile that it required expert care and consideration. Lee Chong did not give it these things, with the result that the truck stood in the tall grass back of the grocery most of the time with the mallows growing between its spokes. It had solid tyres on its back wheels and blocks held its front wheels off the ground.

Probably any one of the boys from the Palace Flophouse could have made the truck run, for they were all competent practical mechanics, but Gay was an inspired mechanic. There is no term comparable to green thumbs to apply to such a mechanic, but there should be. For there are men who can look, listen, tap, make an adjustment, and a machine works. Indeed there are men near whom a car runs better. And such a one was Gay. His fingers on a timer or a carburettor adjustment screw were gentle and wise and sure. He could fix the delicate electric motors in the laboratory. He could have worked in the canneries all the time had he wished, for in that industry, which complains bitterly when it does not make back its total investment every year in profits, the machinery is much less important than the fiscal statement. Indeed, if you could can sardines with ledgers, the owners would have been very happy. As it was they used decrepit, struggling old horrors of machines that needed the constant attention of a man like Gay.

Mack got the boys up early. They had their coffee and immediately moved over to the truck where it lay among the weeds. Gay was in charge. He kicked the blocked-up front wheels. 'Go borrow a pump and get those pumped up,' he said. Then he put a stick in the petrol-tank under the board which served as a seat. By some miracle there was a half-inch of petrol in the tank. Now Gay went over the most probable difficulties. He took out the coil boxes, scraped the points, adjusted the gap, and put them back. He opened the carburettor to see that petrol came through. He pushed on the crank to see that the whole shaft wasn't frozen and the pistons rusted in their cylinders.

Meanwhile the pump arrived and Eddie and Jones spelled each other on the tyres.

Gay hummed: 'Dum tiddy – dum tiddy,' as he worked. He removed the spark-plugs and scraped the points and bored the carbon out. Then Gay drained a little petrol into a can and poured some into each cylinder before he put the spark-plugs back. He straightened up. 'We're going to need a couple of dry cells,' he said. 'See if Lee Chong will let us have a couple.'

Mack departed and returned almost immediately with a universal No which was designed by Lee Chong to cover all future requests.

Gay thought deeply. 'I know where's a couple – pretty good ones too, but I won't go get them.'

'Where?' asked Mack.

'Down cellar at my house,' said Gay. 'They run the front-door bell. If one of you fellas wants to kind of edge into my cellar without my wife seeing you, they're on top of the side stringer on the left-hand side as you go in. But for God's sake, don't let my wife catch you.'

A conference elected Eddie to go and he departed.

'If you get caught don't mention me,' Gay called out after him. Meanwhile Gay tested the bands. The low-high pedal didn't quite touch the floor, so he knew there was a little band left. The brake pedal did touch the floor, so there was no brake, but the reverse pedal had lots of band left. On a Model T Ford the reverse is your margin of safety. When your brake is gone, you can use reverse as a brake. And when the low gear band is worn too thin to pull up a steep hill, why, you can turn round and back up it. Gay found there was plenty of reverse and he knew everything was all right.

It was a good omen that Eddie came back with the dry cells without trouble. Mrs Gay had been in the kitchen. Eddie could hear her walking about, but she didn't hear Eddie. He was very good at such things.

Gay connected the dry cells and he advanced the petrol and retarded the spark-lever. 'Twist her tail,' he said.

He was such a wonder, Gay was – the little mechanic of God, the St Francis of all things that turn and twist and explode, the St Francis of coils and armatures and gears. And if at some time all the heaps of cars, cut-down Dusenbergs, Buicks, De Sotos and Plymouths, American Austins and Isotta-Fraschinis praise God in a great chorus – it will be largely due to Gay and his brotherhood.

One twist – one little twist and the engine caught and laboured and faltered and caught again. Gay advanced the spark and reduced the petrol. He switched over to the magneto and the Ford of Lee Chong chuckled and jiggled and clattered happily as though it knew it was working for a man who loved and understood it.

There were two small technical legal difficulties with the truck – it had no recent licence plates and it had no lights. But the boys hung a rag permanently and accidentally on the rear plate to conceal its vintage and they dabbed the front plate with good thick mud. The equipment of the expedition was slight: some long-handled frog-nets and some gunny-sacks. City hunters going out for sport load themselves with food and liquor, but not Mack. He presumed rightly that the country was where food came from. Two loaves of bread and what was left of Eddie's wining jug was all the supply. The party clambered on the truck. Gay drove and Mack sat beside him; they bumped round the corner of Lee Chong's and down through the lot, threading among the pipes. Mr Malloy waved at them from his seat by the boiler. Gay eased across the pavement and down off the kerb gently because the front tyres showed fabric all the way around. With all their alacrity, it was afternoon when they got started.

The truck eased into Red Williams' service station. Mack got out and gave his paper to Red. He said: 'Doc was a little short of change. So if you'll put five gallons in and just give us a buck instead of the other five gallons, why, that's what Doc wants. He had to go south, you know. Had a big deal down there.'

Red smiled good-naturedly. 'You know, Mack,' he said, 'Doc got to figuring if there was some kind of loop-hole, and he put his finger on the same one you did. Doc's a pretty bright fellow. So he phoned me last night.'

'Put in the whole ten gallons,' said Mack. 'No – wait. It'll slop around and spill. Put in five and give us five in a can – one of them sealed cans.'

Red smiled happily. 'Doc kind of figured that one too,' he said.

'Put in ten gallons,' said Mack. 'And don't go leaving none in the hose.'

The little expedition did not go through the centre of Monterey. A delicacy about the licence plates and the lights made Gay choose back streets. There would be the time when they would go up Carmel Hill and down into the Valley, a good four miles on a main highway, exposed to any passing cop until they turned up the fairly unfrequented Carmel Valley road. Gay chose a back street that brought them out on the main highway at Peter's Gate just before the steep Carmel Hill starts. Gay took a good noisy clattering run at the hill and in fifty yards he put the pedal down too low. He knew it wouldn't work, the band was worn too thin. On the level it was all right, but not on a hill. He stopped, let the truck back round and aimed it down the hill. Then he gave it the petrol and the reverse pedal. And the reverse was not worn. The truck crawled steadily and slowly but backward up Carmel Hill.

And they very nearly made it. The radiator boiled, of course, but most Model T experts believed that it wasn't working well if it wasn't boiling.

Someone should write an erudite essay on the moral, physical, and aesthetic effect of the Model T Ford on the American nation. Two generations of Americans knew more about the Ford coil than the clitoris, about the planetary system of gears than the solar system of stars. With the Model T, part of the concept of private property disappeared. Pliers ceased to be privately owned and a tyre-pump belonged to the last man who had picked it up. Most of the babies of the period were conceived in Model T Fords and not a few were born in them. The theory of the Anglo-Saxon home became so warped that it never quite recovered.

The truck backed sturdily up Carmel Hill and it got past the Jack's Peak road and was just going into the last and steepest pull when the motor's breathing thickened, gulped, and strangled. It seemed very quiet when the motor was still. Gay, who was heading down-hill, anyway, ran down the hill fifty feet and turned into the Jack's Peak road entrance.

'What is it?' Mack asked.

'Carburettor, I think,' said Gay. The engine sizzled and creaked with heat and the jet of steam that blew down the overflow-pipe sounded like the hiss of an alligator.

The carburettor of a Model T is not complicated, but it needs all of its parts to function. There is a needle valve, and the point must be on the needle and must sit in its hole or the carburettor does not work.

Gay held the needle in his hand and the point was broken off. 'How in hell you s'pose that happened?' he asked.

'Magic,' said Mack, 'just pure magic. Can you fix it?'

'Hell, no,' said Gay. 'Got to get another one.'

'How much they cost?'

'About a buck if you buy one new – quarter at a wrecker's.'

'You got a buck?' Mack asked.

'Yeah, but I won't need it.'

'Well, get back as soon as you can, will you? We'll just stay right here.'

'Anyways, you won't go running off without a needle valve,' said Gay. He stepped out to the road. He thumbed three cars before one stopped for him. The boys watched him climb in and start down the hill. They didn't see him again for one hundred and eighty days.

Oh, the infinity of possibility! How could it happen that the car that picked up Gay broke down before it got into Monterey? If Gay had not been a mechanic, he would not have fixed the car. If he had not fixed it the owner wouldn't have taken him to Jimmy Brucia's for a drink. And why was it Jimmy's birthday? Out of all the possibilities in the world – the millions of them – only events occurred that lead to the Salinas jail. Sparky Enea and Tiny Colletti had made up a quarrel and were helping Jimmy to celebrate his birthday. The blonde came in. The musical argument in front of the juke-box. Gay's new friend who knew a judo hold and tried to show it to Sparky and got his wrist broken when the hold went wrong. The policeman with a bad stomach – all unrelated, irrelevant details and yet all running in one direction. Fate just didn't intend Gay to go on that frog-hunt, and Fate took a hell of a lot of trouble and people and accidents to keep him from it. When the final climax came with the front of Holman's bootery broken out and the party trying on the shoes in the display window only Gay didn't hear the fire whistle. Only Gay didn't go to the fire, and when the police came they found him sitting all alone in Holman's window wearing one brown Oxford and one patent leather dress shoe with a grey cloth top.

Back at the truck the boys built a little fire when it got dark and the chill crept up from the ocean. The pines above them soughed in the fresh sea wind. The boys lay in the pine-needles and looked at the lonely sky through the pine branches. For a while they spoke of the difficulties Gay must be having getting a needle valve, and then gradually as the time passed they didn't mention him any more.

'Somebody should of gone with him,' said Mack.

About ten o'clock Eddie got up. 'There's a construction camp a piece up the hill,' he said. 'I think I'll go up and see if they got any Model T's.'

CHAPTER XII

MONTEREY is a city with a long and brilliant literary tradition. It remembers with pleasure and some glory that Robert Louis Stevenson lived there. Treasure Island certainly has the topography and the coastal plan of Pt Lobos. More recently in Carmel there have been a great number of literary men about, but there is not the old flavour, the old dignity of the true *belles-lettres*. Once the town was greatly outraged over what the citizens considered a slight to an author. It had to do with the death of Josh Billings, the great humorist.

Where the new post office is, there used to be a deep gulch with water flowing in it and a little foot-bridge over it. On one side of the gulch was a fine old adobe and on the other the house of the doctor who handled all the sickness, birth, and death in the town. He worked with animals too and, having studied in France, he even dabbled in the new practice of embalming bodies before they were buried. Some of the old-timers considered this sentimental and some thought it wasteful, and to some it was sacrilegious since there was no provision for it in any sacred volume. But the better and richer families were coming to it, and it looked to become a fad.

One morning elderly Mr Carriaga was walking from his house on the hill down toward Alvarado Street. He was just crossing the foot-bridge when his attention was drawn to a small boy and a dog struggling up out of the gulch. The boy carried a liver while the dog dragged yards of intestine at the end of which a stomach dangled. Mr Carriaga paused and addressed the little boy politely: 'Good morning.'

In those days little boys were courteous. 'Good morning, sir.'

'Where are you going with the liver?'

'I'm going to make some chum and catch some mackerel.'

Mr Carriaga smiled. 'And the dog, will he catch mackerel too?'

'The dog found that. It's his, sir. We found them in the gulch.'

Mr Carriaga smiled and strolled on and then his mind began to work. That isn't a beef liver, it's too small. And it isn't a calf's liver, it's too red. It isn't a sheep's liver . . . Now his mind was alert. At the corner he met Mr Ryan.

'Anyone die in Monterey last night?' he asked.

'Not that I know of,' said Mr Ryan.

'Anyone killed?'

'No.'

They walked on together and Mr Carriaga told about the little boy and the dog.

At the 'Adobe Bar' a number of citizens were gathered for their morning conversation. There Mr Carriaga told his story again, and he had just finished when the constable came into the 'Adobe'. He should know if anyone had died. 'No one died in Monterey,' he said. 'But Josh Billings died out at the Hotel del Monte.'

The men in the bar were silent. And the same thought went through all their minds. Josh Billings was a great man, a great writer. He had honoured Monterey by dying there and he had been degraded. Without much discussion a committee formed made up of everyone there. The stern men walked quickly to the gulch and across the foot-bridge and they hammered on the door of the doctor who had studied in France.

He had worked late. The knocking got him out of bed and brought him tousled of hair and beard to the door in his nightgown. Mr Carriaga addressed him sternly: 'Did you embalm Josh Billings?'

'Why – yes.'

'What did you do with his "inards"?'

'Why – I threw them in the gulch where I always do.'

They made him dress quickly then and they hurried down to the beach. If the little boy had gone quickly about his business, it would have been too late. He was just getting into a boat when the committee arrived. The intestine was in the sand where the dog had abandoned it.

Then the French doctor was made to collect the parts. He was forced to wash them reverently and pick out as much sand as possible. The doctor himself had to stand the expense of the leaden box which went into the coffin of Josh Billings. For Monterey was not a town to let dishonour come to a literary man.

CHAPTER XIII

MACK and the boys slept peacefully on the pine-needles. Some time before dawn Eddie came back. He had gone a long way before he found a Model T. And then when he did, he wondered whether or not it would be a good idea to take the needle out of its seat. It might not fit. So he took the whole carburettor. The boys didn't wake up when he got back. He lay down beside them and slept under the pine-trees. There was one nice thing about Model T's. The parts were not only interchangeable, they were unidentifiable.

There is a beautiful view from the Carmel grade, the curving bay with the waves creaming on the sand, the dune country around Seaside and right at the bottom of the hill, the warm intimacy of the town.

Mack got up in the dawn and hustled his pants where they bound him and he stood looking down on the bay. He could see some of the purse-seiners coming in. A tanker stood over against Seaside, taking on oil. Behind him the rabbits stirred in the bush. Then the sun came up and shook the night chill out of the air the way you'd shake a rug. When he felt the first sun warmth, Mack shivered.

The boys ate a little bread while Eddie installed the new carburettor. And when it was ready, they didn't bother to crank it. They pushed it out to the highway and coasted in gear until it started. And then, Eddie driving, they backed up over the rise, over the top and turned and headed forward and down past Hatton Fields. In Carmel Valley the artichoke plants stood grey-green, and the willows were lush along the river. They turned left up the valley. Luck blossomed from the first. A dusty Rhode Island red rooster who had wandered too far from his own farmyard crossed the road and Eddie hit him without running too far off the road. Sitting in the back of the truck, Hazel picked him as they went and let the feathers fly from his hand, the most widely distributed evidence on record, for there was a little breeze in the morning blowing down from Jamesburg and some of the red chicken feathers were deposited on Pt Lobos and some even blew out to sea.

The Carmel is a lovely little river. It isn't very long, but in its course it has everything a river should have. It rises in the mountains, and tumbles down a while, runs through shallows, is dammed to make a lake, spills over the dam, crackles among round boulders, wanders lazily under sycamores, spills into pools where trout live, drops in against banks where crayfish live. In the winter it becomes a torrent, a mean little fierce river, and in the summer it is a place for children to wade in and for fishermen to wander in. Frogs blink from its banks and the deep ferns grow beside it. Deer and foxes come to drink from it, secretly in the morning and evening, and now and then a mountain lion crouched flat laps its water. The farms of the rich little valley back up to the river and take its water for the orchards and the vegetables. The quail call beside it and the wild doves come whistling in at dusk. Raccoons pace its edges looking for frogs. It's everything a river should be.

A few miles up the valley the river cuts in under a high cliff from which vines and ferns hang down. At the base of this cliff there is a pool, green and deep, and on the other side of the pool there is a little sandy place where it is good to sit and to cook your dinner.

Mack and the boys came down to this place happily. It was perfect. If frogs were available, they would be here. It was a place to relax, a place to be happy. On the way out they had thriven. In addition to the big red chicken there was a sack of carrots which had fallen from a vegetable truck, half a dozen onions which had not. Mack had a bag of coffee in his pocket. In the truck there was a five-gallon can with the top cut off. The wining-jug was nearly half full. Such things as salt and pepper had been brought. Mack and the boys would have thought anyone who travelled without salt, pepper, and coffee very silly indeed.

Without effort, confusion, or much thought, four round stones were rolled together on the little beach. The rooster who had challenged the sunrise of this very day lay dismembered and clean in water in the five-gallon can with peeled onions about him, while a little fire of dead willow sticks sputtered between the stones, a very little fire. Only fools build big fires. It would take a long time to cook this rooster, for it had taken him a long time to achieve his size and muscularity. But as the water began to boil gently about him, he smelled good from the beginning.

Mack gave them a pep talk. 'The best time for frogs is at night,' he said, 'so I guess we'll just lay around 'til it gets dark.' They sat in the shade and gradually one by one they stretched out and slept.

Mack was right. Frogs do not move around much in the day-time; they hide under ferns and they look secretly out of holes under rocks. The way to catch frogs is with a flashlight at night. The men slept knowing they might have a very active night. Only Hazel stayed awake to replenish the little fire under the cooking chicken.

There is no golden afternoon next to the cliff. When the sun went over it at about two o'clock a whispering shade came to the beach. The sycamores rustled in the afternoon breeze. Little water-snakes slipped down to the rocks and then gently entered the water and swam along through the pool, their heads held up like little periscopes and a tiny wake spreading behind them. A big trout jumped in the pool. The gnats and mosquitoes which avoid the sun came out and buzzed over the water. All of the sun bugs, the flies, the dragonflies, the wasps, the hornets, went home. And as the shadow came to the beach, as the first quail began to call, Mack and the boys awakened. The smell of the chicken stew was heart-breaking. Hazel had picked a fresh bay-leaf from a tree by the river and he had dropped it in. The carrots were in now. Coffee in its own can was simmering on its own rock, far enough from the flame so that it did not boil too hard. Mack awakened, started up, stretched, staggered to the pool, washed his face with cupped hands, hacked, spat, washed out his mouth, broke wind, tightened his belt, scratched his legs, combed his wet hair with his fingers, drank from the jug, belched, and sat down by the fire. 'By God that smells good,' he said.

Men all do about the same things when they wake up. Mack's process was loosely the one all of them followed. And soon they had all come to the fire and complimented Hazel. Hazel stuck his pocket-knife into the muscles of the chicken.

'He ain't going to be what you'd call tender,' said Hazel. 'You'd have to cook him about two weeks to get him tender. How old about do you judge he was, Mack?'

'I'm forty-eight and I ain't as tough as he is,' said Mack.

Eddie said: 'How old can a chicken get, do you think – that's if nobody pushed him around or he don't get sick?'

'That's something nobody isn't ever going to find out,' said Jones.

It was a pleasant time. The jug went around and warmed them.

Jones said: 'Eddie, I don't mean to complain none. I was just thinkin'. S'pose you had two or three jugs back of the bar. S'pose you put all the whisky in one and all the wine in another and all the beer in another . . .'

A slightly shocked silence followed the suggestion. 'I didn't mean nothing,' said Jones quickly. 'I like it this way . . .' Jones talked too much then because he knew he had made a social blunder and he wasn't able to stop. 'What I like about it this way is you never know what kind of a drunk you're going to get out of it,' he said. 'You take whisky,' he said hurriedly. 'You more or less know what you'll do. A fightin' guy fights and a cryin' guy cries, but this' – he said magnanimously – 'why, you don't know whether it'll run you up a pine-tree or start you swimming to Santa Cruz. I's more fun that way,' he said weakly.

'Speaking of swimming,' said Mack to fill in the indelicate place in the conversation and to shut Jones up. 'I wonder whatever happened to that guy McKinley Moran. Remember that deep-sea diver?'

'I remember him,' said Hughie. 'I and him used to hang around together. He just didn't get much work and then he got to drinking. It's kind of tough on you divin' and drinkin'. Got to worryin' too. Finally he sold his suit and helmet and pump and went on a hell of a drunk and then he left town. I don't know where he went. He wasn't no good after he went down after that Wop that got took down with the anchor from the *Twelve Brothers*. McKinley just dove down. Bust his ear-drums, and he wasn't no good after that. Didn't hurt the Wop a bit.'

Mack sampled the jug again. 'He used to make a lot of dough during Prohibition,' Mack said. 'Used to get twenty-five bucks a day from the government to dive lookin' for liquor on the bottom and he got three dollars a case from Louie for not findin' it. Had it worked out so he brought up one case a day to keep the government happy. Louie didn't mind that none. Made it so they didn't get in no new divers. McKinley made a lot of dough.'

'Yeah,' said Hughie. 'But he's like everybody else – gets some dough and he wants to get married. He got married three times before his dough run out. I could always tell. He'd buy a white fox piece and bang! – next thing you'd know, he's married.'

'I wonder what happened to Gay,' Eddie asked. It was the first time they had spoken of him.

'Same thing, I guess,' said Mack. 'You just can't trust a married guy. No matter how much he hates his old lady why he'll go back to her. Get to thinkin' and broodin' and back he'll go. You can't trust him no more. Take Gay,' said Mack. 'His old lady hits him. But I bet you when Gay's away from her three days, he gets it figured out that it's his fault and he goes back to make it up to her.'

They ate long and daintily, spearing out pieces of chicken,

holding the dripping pieces until they cooled, and then gnawing the muscled meat from the bone. They speared the carrots on pointed willow switches and finally they passed the can and drank the juice. And around them the evening crept in as delicately as music. The quail called each other down to the water. The trout jumped in the pool. And the moths came down and fluttered about the pool as the daylight mixed into the darkness. They passed the coffee-can about and they were warm and fed and silent. At last Mack said: 'God damn it. I hate a liar.'

'Who's been lyin' to you?' Eddie asked.

'Oh, I don't mind a guy that tells a little one to get along or to hop up a conversation, but I hate a guy that lies to himself.'

'Who done that?' Eddie asked.

'Me,' said Mack. 'And maybe you guys. Here we are,' he said earnestly, ' the whole God damned shabby lot of us. We worked it out that we wanted to give Doc a party. So we come out here and have a hell of a lot of fun. Then we'll go back and get the dough from Doc. There's five of us, so we'll drink five times as much liquor as he will. And I ain't sure we're doin' it for Doc. I ain't sure we ain't doin' it for ourselves. And Doc's too nice a fella to do that to. Doc is the nicest fella I ever knew. I don't want to be the kind of a guy that would take advantage of him. You know one time I put the bee on him for a buck. I give him a hell of a story. Right in the middle I seen he knew God damn well the story was so much malarky. So right in the middle I says: "Doc, that's a fuggin' lie!" And he put his hand in his pocket and brought out a buck. "Mack," he says, "I figure a guy that needs it bad enough to make up a lie to get it, really needs it," and he give me the buck. I paid him that buck back the next day. I never did spend it. Just kept it overnight and then give it back to him.'

Hazel said: 'There ain't nobody likes a party better than Doc. We're givin' him the party. What the hell is the beef?'

'I don't know,' said Mack, 'I'd like just to give him something when I didn't get most of it back.'

'How about a present?' Hughie suggested. 'S'pose we

just bought the whisky and give it to him and let him do what he wants.'

'Now you're talkin',' said Mack. 'That's just what we'll do. We'll just give him the whisky and fade out.'

'You know what'll happen,' said Eddie. 'Henri and them people from Carmel will smell that whisky out and then instead of only five of us there'll be twenty. Doc told me one time himself they can smell him fryin' a steak from Cannery Row clear down to Point Sur. I don't see the percentage. He'd come out better if we give him the party ourselves.'

Mack considered this reasoning. 'Maybe you're right,' he said at last. 'But s'pose we give him something except whisky, maybe cuff-links with his initials.'

'Oh, horse shit,' said Hazel. 'Doc don't want stuff like that.'

The night was in by now and the stars were white in the sky. Hazel fed the fire and it put a little room of light on the beach. Over the hill a fox was barking sharply. And now in the night the smell of sage came down from the hills. The water chuckled on the stones where it went out of the deep pool.

Mack was mulling over the last piece of reasoning when the sound of footsteps on the ground made them turn. A man dark and large stalked near and he had a shot-gun over his arm and a pointer walked shyly and delicately at his heel.

'What the hell are you doing here?' he asked.

'Nothing,' said Mack.

'The land's posted. No fishing, hunting, fires, camping. Now you just pack up and put that fire out and get off this land.'

Mack stood up humbly. 'I didn't know, Captain,' he said. 'Honest we never seen the sign, Captain.'

'There's signs all over. You couldn't have missed them.'

'Look, Captain, we made a mistake and we're sorry,' said Mack. He paused and looked closely at the slouching figure. 'You are a military man, aren't you, sir? I can always tell. Military man don't carry his shoulders the same as ordinary people. I was in the army so long, I can always tell.'

Imperceptibly the shoulders of the man straightened, nothing obvious, but he held himself differently.

'I don't allow fires on my place,' he said.

'Well, we're sorry,' said Mack. 'We'll get right out, Captain. You see, we're workin' for some scientists. We're goin' to get some frogs. They're working on cancer and we're helpin' out getting some frogs.'

The man hesitated for a moment. 'What do they do with the frogs?' he asked.

'Well, sir,' said Mack, 'they give cancer to the frogs and then they can study and experiment and they got it nearly licked if they can just get some frogs. But if you don't want us on your land, Captain, we'll get right out. Never would of come in if we knew.' Suddenly Mack seemed to see the pointer for the first time. 'By God that's a fine-lookin' bitch,' he said enthusiastically. 'She looks like Nola that win the field trials in Virginia last year. She a Virginia dog, Captain?'

The captain hesitated and then he lied. 'Yes,' he said shortly. 'She's lame. Tick got her right on her shoulder.'

Mack was instantly solicitous. 'Mind if I look, Captain? Come, girl. Come on, girl.' The pointer looked up at her master and then sidled up to Mack. 'Pile on some twigs so I can see,' he said to Hazel.

'It's up where she can't lick it,' said the captain, and he leaned over Mack's shoulder to look.

Mack pressed some pus out of the evil-looking crater on the dog's shoulder. 'I had a dog once had a thing like this and it went right in and killed him. She just had pups, didn't she?'

'Yes,' said the captain, 'six. I put iodine on that place.'

'No,' said Mack, 'that won't draw. You got any Epsom salts up at your place?'

'Yes – there's a big bottle.'

'Well, you make a hot poultice of Epsom salts and put it on there. She's weak, you know, from the pups. Be a shame if she got sick now. You'd lose the pups too.' The pointer looked deep into Mack's eyes and then she licked his hand.

'Tell you what I'll do, Captain. I'll look after her myself. Epsom salt'll do the trick. That's the best thing.'

The captain stroked the dog's head. 'You know, I've got a pond up by the house that's so full of frogs I can't sleep nights. Why don't you look up there? They bellow all night. I'd be glad to get rid of them.'

'That's mighty nice of you,' said Mack. 'I'll bet those docs would thank you for that. But I'd like to get a poultice on this dog.' He turned to the others. 'You put out this fire,' he said. 'Make sure there ain't a spark left and clean up around. You don't want to leave no mess. I and the captain will go and take care of Nola here. You fellows follow along when you get cleared up.' Mack and the captain walked away together.

Hazel kicked sand on the fire. 'I bet Mack could of been president of the U.S. if he wanted,' he said.

'What could he do with it if he had it?' Jones asked. 'There wouldn't be no fun in that.'

CHAPTER XIV

EARLY morning is a time of magic in Cannery Row. In the grey time after the light has come and before the sun has risen, the Row seems to hang suspended out of time in a silvery light. The street lights go out, and the weeds are a brilliant green. The corrugated iron of the canneries glows with the pearly lucence of platinum or old pewter. No automobiles are running then. The street is silent of progress and business. And the rush and drag of the waves can be heard as they splash in among the piles of the canneries. It is a time of great peace, a deserted time, a little era of rest. Cats drip over the fences and slither like syrup over the ground to look for fish-heads. Silent early-morning dogs parade majestically, picking and choosing judiciously whereon to pee. The sea-gulls come flapping in to sit on the cannery roofs to await the day of refuse. They sit on the roof peaks shoulder to shoulder. From the rocks near the Hopkins Marine Station comes the barking of sea-lions like the baying of hounds. The air is cool and fresh. In the back gardens the gophers push up the morning mounds of fresh damp earth and they creep out and drag flowers into their holes. Very few people are about, just enough to make it seem more deserted than it is. One of Dora's girls comes home from a call on a patron too wealthy or too sick to visit the Bear Flag. Her make-up is a little sticky and her feet are tired. Lee Chong brings the garbage cans out and stands them on the kerb. The old Chinaman comes out of the sea and flap-flaps across the street and up past the Palace. The cannery watchmen look out and blink at the morning light. The bouncer at the Bear Flag steps out on the porch in his shirt-sleeves and stretches and yawns and scratches his stomach. The snores of Mr Malloy's tenants in the pipes have a deep tunnelly quality. It is the hour of the pearl – the interval between day and night when time stops and examines itself.

On such a morning and in such a light two soldiers and two girls strolled easily along the street. They had come out of 'La Ida' and they were very tired and very happy. The girls were hefty, big-breasted, and strong and their blonde hair was in slight disarray. They wore printed rayon party dresses, wrinkled now and clinging to their convexities. And each girl wore a soldier's cap, one far back on her head and the other with the visor down almost on her nose. They were full-lipped, broad-nosed, hippy girls and they were very tired.

The soldiers' tunics were unbuttoned and their belts were threaded through their epaulettes. The ties were pulled down a little so the shirt-collars could be unbuttoned. And the soldiers wore the girls' hats, one a tiny yellow straw boater with a bunch of daisies on the crown, the other a white knitted half-hat to which medallions of blue cellophane adhered. They walked holding hands, swinging their hands rhythmically. The soldier on the outside had a large brown paper bag filled with cold canned beer. They strolled softly in the pearly light. They had had a hell of a time and they felt good. They smiled delicately like weary children remembering a party. They looked at one another and

smiled and they swung their hands. Past the Bear Flag they
went and said 'Hiya' to the bouncer who was scratching his
stomach. They listened to the snores from the pipes and
laughed a little. At Lee Chong's they stopped and looked
into the messy display window where tools and clothes and
food crowded for attention. Swinging their hands and scuf-
fing their feet, they came to the end of Cannery Row and
turned up to the railroad track. The girls climbed on the
rails and walked along on them and the soldiers put their
arms around the plump waists to keep them from falling.
Then they went past the boat-works and turned down into
the park-like property of the Hopkins Marine Station.
There is a tiny curved beach in front of the station, a minia-
ture beach between little reefs. The gentle morning waves
licked up the beach and whispered softly. The fine smell of
seaweed came from the exposed rocks. As the four came to
the beach a sliver of the sun broke over Tom Work's land
across the head of the bay and it gilded the water and made
the rocks yellow. The girls sat formally down in the sand and
straightened their skirts over their knees. One of the soldiers
punched holes in four cans of beer and handed them round.
And then the men lay down and put their heads in the girls'
laps and looked up into their faces. And they smiled at each
other, a tired and peaceful and wonderful secret.

From up near the station came the barking of a dog – the
watchman, a dark and surly man, had seen them and his
black and surly cocker spaniel had seen them. He shouted
at them, and when they did not move he came down on the
beach and his dog barked monotonously. 'Don't you know
you can't lay around here? You got to get off. This is private
property!'

The soldiers did not even seem to hear him. They smiled
on and the girls were stroking their hair over the temples.
At last in slow motion one of the soldiers turned his head so
that his cheek was cradled between the girl's legs. He smiled
benevolently at the caretaker. 'Why don't you take a flying
fuggut the moon?' he said kindly, and he turned back to
look at the girl.

The sun lighted her blonde hair and she scratched him

over one ear. They didn't even see the caretaker go back to his house.

CHAPTER XV

By the time the boys got up to the farm-house Mack was in the kitchen. The pointer bitch lay on her side, and Mack held a cloth saturated with Epsom salts against her tick-bite. Among her legs the big fat wiener pups nuzzled and bumped for milk and the bitch looked patiently up into Mack's face saying: 'You see how it is? I try to tell him, but he doesn't understand.'

The captain held a lamp and looked down on Mack.

'I'm glad to know about that,' he said.

Mack said: 'I don't want to tell you about your business, sir, but these pups ought to be weaned. She ain't got a hell of a lot of milk left and them pups are chewin' her to pieces.'

'I know,' said the captain. 'I s'pose I should have drowned them all but one. I've been so busy trying to keep the place going. People don't take the interest in bird dogs they used to. It's all poodles and boxers and Dobermans.'

'I know,' said Mack. 'And there ain't no dog like a pointer for a man. I don't know what's come over people. But you wouldn't of drowned them, would you, sir?'

'Well,' said the captain, 'since my wife went into politics, I'm just running crazy. She got elected to the Assembly for this district and when the Legislature isn't in session, she's off making speeches. And when she's home she's studying all the time and writing bills.'

'Must be lousy in – I mean it must be pretty lonely,' said Mack. 'Now if I had a pup like this' – he picked up a squirming puzz-faced pup – 'why, I bet I'd have a real bird dog in three years. I'd take a bitch every time.'

'Would you like to have one?' the captain asked.

Mack looked up. 'You mean you'd let me have one? Oh! Jesus Christ yes.'

'Take your pick,' said the Captain. 'Nobody seems to understand bird dogs any more.'

The boys stood in the kitchen and gathered quick impressions. It was obvious that the wife was away – the opened cans, the frying-pan with lace from fried egg still sticking to it, the crumbs on the kitchen table, the open box of shotgun shells on the bread-box all shrieked of the lack of a woman, while the white curtains and the papers on the dish shelves and the too small towels on the rack told them a woman had been there. And they were unconsciously glad she wasn't there. The kind of women who put papers on shelves and had little towels like that instinctively distrusted and disliked Mack and the boys. Such women knew that they were the worst threats to a home, for they offered ease and thought and companionship as opposed to neatness, order, and properness. They were glad she was away.

Now the captain seemed to feel that they were doing him a favour. He didn't want them to leave. He said hesitantly: 'S'pose you boys would like a little something to warm you up before you go out for the frogs?'

The others looked at Mack. Mack was frowning as though he was thinking it through. 'When we're out doin' scientific stuff, we make it a kind of a rule not to touch nothin',' he said, and then quickly, as though he might have gone too far: 'But seein' as how you been so nice to us – well, I wouldn't mind a short one myself. I don't know about the boys.'

The boys agreed that they wouldn't mind a short one either. The captain got a flashlight and went down in the cellar. They could hear him moving lumber and boxes about, and he came back upstairs with a five-gallon oak keg in his arms. He set it on the table. 'During Prohibition I got some corn whisky and laid it away. I just got to thinking I'd like to see how it is. It's pretty old now. I'd almost forgot it. You see – my wife . . .' he let it go at that because it was apparent that they understood. The captain knocked out the oak plug from the end of the keg and got glasses down from the shelf that had scallop-edged paper laid on it. It is a hard job to pour a small drink from a five-gallon keg. Each of them got half a water-glass of the clear brown liquor. They waited ceremoniously for the captain and then they said: 'Over the river,' and tossed it back. They swallowed, tasted their tongues, sucked their lips, and there was a far-away look in their eyes.

Mack peered into his empty glass as though some holy message was written in the bottom. And then he raised his eyes. 'You can't say nothin' about that,' he said. 'They don't put that in bottles.' He breathed in deeply and sucked his breath as it came out. 'I don't think I ever tasted nothin' as good as that,' he said.

The captain looked pleased. His glance wandered back to the keg. 'It is good,' he said. 'You think we might have another little one?'

Mack stared into his glass again. 'Maybe a short one,' he agreed. 'Wouldn't it be easier to pour out some in a pitcher? You're liable to spill it that way.'

Two hours later they recalled what they had come for.

The frog pool was square – fifty feet wide and seventy feet long and four feet deep. Lush soft grass grew about its edge and a little ditch brought the water from the river to it and from it little ditches went out to the orchards. There were frogs there all right, thousands of them. Their voices beat the night, they boomed and barked and croaked and rattled. They sang to the stars, to the waning moon, to the waving grasses. They bellowed love songs and challenges. The men crept through the darkness towards the pool. The captain carried a nearly-filled pitcher of whisky and every man had his own glass. The captain had found them flash-lights that worked. Hughie and Jones carried gunny-sacks. As they drew quietly near, the frogs heard them coming. The night had been roaring with frog song and then suddenly it was silent. Mack and the boys and the captain sat down on the ground to have one last short one and to map their campaign. And the plan was bold.

During the millennia that frogs and men have lived in the same world, it is probable that men have hunted frogs. And during that time a pattern of hunt and parry has developed. The man with net or bow or lance or gun creeps noiselessly, as he thinks, toward the frog. The pattern requires that the frog sit still, sit very still and wait. The rules of the game require the frog to wait until the final flicker of a second, when the net is descending, when the lance is in the air, when the finger squeezes the trigger, then the frog jumps, plops into the water, swims to the bottom, and waits until the man goes away. That is the way it is done, the way it has always been done. Frogs have every right to expect it will always be done that way. Now and then the net is too quick, the lance pierces, the gun flicks, and that frog is gone, but it is all fair and in the frame-work. Frogs don't resent that. But how could they have anticipated Mack's new method? How could they have foreseen the horror that followed? The sudden flashing of lights, the shouting and squealing of men, the rush of feet. Every frog leaped, plopped into the pool, and swam frantically to the bottom. Then into the pool plunged the line of men, stamping, churning, moving in a crazy line up the pool, flinging their feet about. Hysterically the frogs, displaced from their placid spots, swam ahead of the crazy thrashing feet and the feet came on. Frogs are good swimmers, but they haven't much endurance. Down the pool they went until finally they were bunched and crowded against the ends. And the feet and wildly-plunging bodies followed them. A few frogs lost their heads and floundered among the feet and got through and these were saved. But the majority decided to leave this pool for ever, to find a new home in a new country where this kind of thing didn't happen. A wave of frantic, frustrated frogs, big ones, little ones, brown ones, green ones, men frogs and women frogs, a wave of them broke over the bank, crawled, leaped, scrambled. They clambered up the grass, they clutched at each other, little ones rode on big ones. And then – horror on horror – the flashlights found them. Two men gathered them like berries. The line came out of the water and closed in on their rear and gathered them like potatoes. Tens and fifties of them were flung into the gunny-sacks and the sacks filled with tired, frightened, and disillusioned frogs, with dripping, whimpering frogs. Some got away, of course, and some had been saved in the pool. But never in frog history had such an execution taken place. Frogs by the pound, by the fifty pounds. They weren't counted, but there must have been six or seven hundred. Then happily Mack tied up the necks of the sacks. They were soaking, dripping wet and the air was cool. They had a short one in the grass before they went back to the house, so they wouldn't catch cold.

It is doubtful whether the captain had ever had so much fun. He was indebted to Mack and the boys. Later when the curtains caught fire and were put out with the little towels, the captain told the boys not to mind it. He felt it was an honour to have them burn his house clear down, if they wanted to. 'My wife is a wonderful woman,' he said in a kind of peroration. 'Most wonderful woman. Ought to of been a man. If she was a man I wouldn' of married her.' He laughed a long time over that and repeated it three or four times and resolved to remember it, so he could tell it to a lot of other people. He filled a jug with whisky and gave it to Mack. He wanted to go to live with them in the Palace Flophouse. He decided that his wife would like Mack and the boys if she only knew them. Finally, he went to sleep on the floor with his head among the puppies. Mack and the boys poured themselves a short one and regarded him seriously.

Mack said: 'He give me that jug of whisky, didn't he? You heard him?'

'Sure he did,' said Eddie. 'I heard him.'

'And he give me a pup?'

'Sure, pick of the litter. We all heard him. Why?'

'I never did roll a drunk and I ain't gonna start now,' said Mack. 'We got to get out of here. He's gonna wake up feelin' lousy and it's goin' to be all our fault. I just don't want to be here.' Mack glanced at the burned curtains, at the floor glistening with whisky and puppy dirt, at the bacon grease that was coagulating on the stove front. He went to the pups, looked them over carefully, felt bone and frame, looked in eyes, and regarded jaws, and he picked out a beautifully-spotted bitch with a liver-coloured nose and a fine dark-yellow eye. 'Come on, darling,' he said.

They blew out the lamp because of the danger of fire. It was just turning dawn as they left the house.

'I don't think I ever had such a fine trip,' said Mack. 'But

I got to thinkin' about his wife comin' back and it gave me the shivers.' The pup whined in his arms and he put it under his coat. 'He's a real nice fella,' said Mack. 'After you get him feelin' easy, that is.' He strode on toward the place where they had parked the Ford. 'We shouldn't go forgettin' we're doin' all this for Doc,' he said. 'From the way things are pannin' out, it looks like Doc is a pretty lucky guy.'

CHAPTER XVI

PROBABLY the busiest time the girls of the Bear Flag ever had was the March of the big sardine catch. It wasn't only that the fish ran in silvery billions and money ran almost as freely. A new regiment moved into the Presidio and a new bunch of soldiers always shop around a good deal before they settle down. Dora was short-handed just at that time too, for Eva Flanagan had gone to East St Louis on a vacation, Phyllis Mae had broken her leg getting out of the roller coaster in Santa Cruz, and Elsie Doublebottom had made a novena and wasn't much good for anything else. The men from the sardine fleet, loaded with dough, were in and out all afternoon. They sail at dark and fish all night, so they must play in the afternoon. In the evening the soldiers of the new regiment came down and stood around playing the musical-box and drinking Coca-Cola and sizing up the girls for the time when they would be paid. Dora was having trouble with her income-tax, for she was entangled in that curious enigma which said the business was illegal and then taxed her for it. In addition to everything else there were the regulars – the steady customers who had been coming down for years, the labourers from the gravel-pits, the riders from the ranches, the railroad men who came in the front door, and the city officials and prominent business men who came in the rear entrance by the tracks and who had little chintz sitting-rooms assigned to them.

All in all it was a terrific month and right in the middle of it the influenza epidemic had to break out. It came to the whole town. Mrs Talbot and her daughter of the San

Carlos Hotel had it. Tom Work had it. Benjamin Peabody and his wife had it. Excelentisima Maria Antonia Field had it. The whole Gross family came down with it.

The doctors of Monterey – and there were enough of them to take care of the ordinary diseases, accidents, and neuroses – were running crazy. They had more business than they could do among clients who, if they didn't pay their bills, at least had the money to pay them. Cannery Row, which produces a tougher breed than the rest of the town, was late in contracting it, but finally it got them too. The schools were closed. There wasn't a house that hadn't feverish children and sick parents. It was not a deadly disease, as it was in 1917, but with children it had a tendency to go into the mastoids. The medical profession was very busy, and besides, Cannery Row was not considered a very good financial risk.

Now Doc of the Western Biological Laboratory had no right to practise medicine. It was not his fault that everyone in the Row came to him for medical advice. Before he knew it he found himself running from shanty to shanty taking temperatures, giving physics, borrowing and delivering blankets, and even taking food from house to house where mothers looked at him with inflamed eyes from their beds, and thanked him and put the full responsibility for their children's recovery on him. When a case got really out of hand he phoned a local doctor and sometimes one came, if it seemed to be an emergency. But to the families it was all emergency. Doc didn't get much sleep. He lived on beer and canned sardines. In Lee Chong's where he went to get beer he met Dora, who was there to buy a pair of nail clippers.

'You look done in,' Dora said.

'I am,' Doc admitted. 'I haven't had any sleep for about a week.'

'I know,' said Dora. 'I hear it's bad. Comes at a bad time too.'

'Well, we haven't lost anybody yet,' said Doc. 'But there are some awful sick kids. The Ransel kids have all developed mastoiditis.'

'Is there anything I can do?' Dora asked.

Doc said: 'You know there is. People get so scared and

helpless. Take the Ransels – they're scared to death and they're scared to be alone. If you, or some of the girls, could just sit with them.'

Dora, who was soft as a mouse's belly, could be as hard as carborundum. She went back to the Bear Flag and organized it for service. It was a bad time for her, but she did it. The Greek cook made a ten-gallon cauldron of strong soup and kept it full and kept it strong. The girls tried to keep up their business, but they went in shifts to sit with the families, and they carried pots of soup when they went. Doc was in almost constant demand. Dora consulted him and detailed the girls where he suggested. And all the time the business at the Bear Flag was booming. The musical-box never stopped playing. The men of the fishing fleet and the soldiers stood in line. And the girls did their work and then they took their pots of soup and went to sit with the Ransels, with the McCarthys, with the Ferrias. The girls slipped out the back door, and sometimes staying with the sleeping children the girls dropped to sleep in their chairs. They didn't use make-up for work any more. They didn't have to. Dora herself said she could have used the total membership of the old ladies' home. It was the busiest time the girls at the Bear Flag could remember. Everyone was glad when it was over.

CHAPTER XVII

IN spite of his friendliness and his friends Doc was a lonely and a set-apart man. Mack probably noticed it more than anybody. In a group, Doc seemed always alone. When the lights were on and the curtains drawn, and the Gregorian music played on the great phonograph, Mack used to look down on the laboratory from the Palace Flophouse. He knew Doc had a girl in there, but Mack used to get a dreadful feeling of loneliness out of it. Even in the dear close contact with a girl Mack felt that Doc would be lonely. Doc was a night crawler. The lights were on in the lab all night and yet he seemed to be up in the daytime too. And the great shrouds of music came out of the lab at any time of the day or night. Sometimes when it was all dark and when it seemed that sleep had come at last, the diamond-true child voices of the Sistine Choir would come from the windows of the laboratory.

Doc had to keep up his collecting. He tried to get to the good tides along the coast. The sea rocks and the beaches were his stock pile. He knew where everything was when he wanted it. All the articles of his trade were filed away on the coast, sea cradles here, octopi here, tubs worms in another place, sea pansies in another. He knew where to get them, but he could not go for them exactly when he wanted. For Nature locked up the items and released them only occasionally. Doc had to know not only the tides, but when a particular low tide was good in a particular place. When such a low tide occurred, he packed his collecting tools in his car, he packed his jars, his bottles, his plates and preservatives and he went to the beach or reef or rock ledge where the animals he needed were stored.

Now he had an order for small octopi and the nearest place to get them was the boulder-strewn inter-tidal zone at La Jolla, between Los Angeles and San Diego. It meant a five-hundred-mile drive each way and his arrival had to coincide with the retreating waters.

The little octopi live among the boulders embedded in sand. Being timid and young, they prefer a bottom on which there are many caves and little crevices and lumps of mud where they may hide from predators and protect themselves from the waves. But on the same flat there are millions of sea cradles. While filling a definite order for octopi, Doc could replenish his stock of the cradles.

Low tide was 5.17 a.m. on a Thursday. If Doc left Monterey on Wednesday morning he could be there easily in time for the tide on Thursday. He would have taken someone with him for company, but quite by accident everyone was away or was busy. Mack and the boys were up Carmel Valley collecting frogs. Three young women he knew and would have enjoyed as companions had jobs and couldn't get away in the middle of the week. Henri the painter was occupied, for Holman's Department Store had employed not a flag-pole sitter, but a flag-pole skater. On a tall mast on top of the store he had a little round platform and there he was on skates going round and round. He had been there three days and three nights. He was out to set a new record for being on skates on a platform. The previous record was 127 hours, so he had some time to go. Henri had taken up his post across the street at Red Williams' petrol station. Henri was fascinated. He thought of doing a huge abstraction called Substratum Dream of a Flag-pole Skater. Henri couldn't leave town while the skater was up there. He protested that there were philosophic implications in flag-pole skating that no one had touched. Henri sat in a chair, leaned back against the lattice which concealed the door of the men's toilet at Red Williams'. He kept his eye on the eyrie skating platform and obviously he couldn't go with Doc to La Jolla. Doc had to go alone because the tide would not wait.

Early in the morning he got his things together. Personal things went in a small satchel. Another satchel held instruments and syringes. Having packed, he combed and trimmed his brown beard, saw that his pencils were in his shirt pocket, and his magnifying glass attached to his lapel. He packed the trays, bottles, glass plates, preservatives, rubberboots, and a blanket into the back of his car. He worked through the pearly time, washed three days' dishes, put the garbage into the surf. He closed the doors, but did not lock them, and by nine o'clock was on his way.

It took Doc longer to go places than other people. He didn't drive fast and he stopped and ate hamburgers very often. Driving up to Lighthouse Avenue he waved at a dog that looked round and smiled at him. In Monterey before he even started, he felt hungry and stopped at Herman's for a hamburger and beer. While he ate his sandwich and sipped his beer, a lot of conversation came back to him. Blaisedell, the poet, had said to him: 'You love beer so much. I'll bet some day you'll go in and order a beer milkshake.' It was a simple piece of foolery, but it had bothered Doc ever since. He wondered what a beer milk-shake would taste like. The idea gagged him, but he couldn't let it alone.

It cropped up every time he had a glass of beer. Would it curdle the milk? Would you add sugar? It was like a shrimp ice-cream. Once the thing got into your head you couldn't forget it. He finished his sandwich and paid Herman. He purposely didn't look at the milk-shake machines lined up so shiny against the back wall. If a man ordered a beer milk-shake, he thought, he'd better do it in a town where he wasn't known. But then, a man with a beard, ordering a beer milk-shake in a town where he wasn't known – they might call the police. A man with a beard was always a little suspect anyway. You couldn't say you wore a beard because you like a beard. People didn't like you for telling the truth. You had to say you had a scar, so you couldn't shave. Once when Doc was at the University of Chicago he had loved trouble and he had worked too hard. He thought it would be nice to take a very long walk. He put on a little knapsack and he walked through Indiana and Kentucky and North Carolina and Georgia, clear to Florida. He walked among farmers and mountain people, among the swamp people and fishermen. And everywhere people asked him why he was walking through the country.

Because he loved true things he tried to explain. He said he was nervous and besides he wanted to see the country, smell the ground and look at grass and birds and trees, to savour the country, and there was no other way to do it save on foot. And people didn't like him for telling the truth. They scowled, or shook and tapped their heads, they laughed as though they knew it was a lie and they appreciated a liar. And some, afraid for their daughters or their pigs, told him to move on, to get along, just not to stop near their place if he knew what was good for him.

And so he stopped trying to tell the truth. He said he was doing it on a bet – that he stood to win a hundred dollars. Everyone liked him then and believed him. They asked him in to dinner and gave him a bed and they put lunches up for him and wished him good luck and thought he was a hell of a fine fellow. Doc still loved true things, but he knew it was not a general love and it could be a very dangerous mistress.

Doc didn't stop in Salinas for a hamburger. But he

stopped in Gonzales, in King City, and in Paso Robles. He had hamburger and beer at Santa Maria – two in Santa Maria, because it was a long pull from there to Santa Barbara. In Santa Barbara he had soup, lettuce and string-bean salad, pot roast and mashed potatoes, pineapple-pie and blue cheese and coffee, and after that he filled the petrol tank and went to the toilet. While the service station checked his oil and tyres, Doc washed his face and combed his beard and when he came back to the car a number of potential hitch-hikers were waiting.

'Going south, Mister?'

Doc travelled on the highways a good deal. He was an old hand. You have to pick your hitch-hikers very carefully. It's best to get an experienced one, for he relapses into silence. But the new ones try to pay for their ride by being interesting. Doc had had a leg talked off by some of these. Then after you have made up your mind about the one you want to take, you protect yourself by saying you aren't going far. If your man turns out too much for you, you can drop him. On the other hand, you may be just lucky and get a man very much worth knowing. Doc made a quick survey of the line and chose his company, a thin-faced salesman-like man in a blue suit. He had deep lines beside his mouth and dark brooding eyes.

He looked at Doc with dislike. 'Going south, Mister?'

'Yes,' said Doc, 'a little way.'

'Mind taking me along?'

'Get in!' said Doc.

When they got to Ventura it was pretty soon after the heavy dinner, so Doc only stopped for beer. The hitch-hiker hadn't spoken once. Doc pulled up at a roadside stand.

'Want some beer?'

'No,' said the hitch-hiker. 'And I don't mind saying I think it's not a very good idea to drive under the influence of alcohol. It's none of my business what you do with your own life, but in this case you've got an automobile, and that can be a murderous weapon in the hands of a drunken driver.'

T—F

At the beginning Doc had been slightly startled. 'Get out of the car,' he said softly.

'What?'

'I'm going to punch you on the nose,' said Doc, 'if you aren't out of this car before I count ten. One – two – three . . .'

The man fumbled at the door catch and backed hurriedly out of the car. But once outside he howled: 'I'm going to find an officer. I'm going to have you arrested.'

Doc opened the box on the dashboard and took out a monkey wrench. His guest saw the gesture and walked hurriedly away.

Doc walked angrily to the counter of the stand.

The waitress, a blonde beauty with just the hint of a goitre, smiled at him. 'What'll it be?'

'Beer milk-shake,' said Doc.

'What?'

Well here it was and what the hell. Might just as well get it over with now as some time later.

The blonde asked: 'Are you kidding?'

Doc knew wearily that he couldn't explain, couldn't tell the truth. 'I've got a bladder complaint,' he said. 'Bipaly-chaetsonectomy, the doctors call it. I'm supposed to drink a *beer milk-shake*. Doctor's orders.'

The blonde smiled reassuringly. 'Oh! I thought you was kidding,' she said archly. 'You tell me how to make it. I didn't know you was sick.'

'Very sick,' said Doc, 'and due to be sicker. Put in some milk, and add half a bottle of beer. Give me the other half in a glass – no sugar in the milk-shake.' When she served it, he tasted it wryly. And it wasn't so bad – it just tasted like stale beer and milk.

'It sounds awful,' said the blonde.

'It's not so bad when you get used to it,' said Doc. 'I've been drinking it for seventeen years.'

CHAPTER XVIII

Doc had driven slowly. It was late afternoon when he stopped in Ventura, so late in fact that when he stopped in Carpentaria he only had a cheese sandwich and went to the toilet. Besides, he intended to get a good dinner in Los Angeles, and it was dark when he got there. He drove on through and stopped at a big Chicken-in-the-Rough place he knew about. And there he had fried chicken, julienne potatoes, hot biscuits and honey, and a piece of pineapple-pie and blue cheese. And here he filled his thermos-bottle with hot coffee, had them make up six ham sandwiches, and bought two quarts of beer for breakfast.

It was not so interesting driving at night. No dogs to see, only the highway lighted with his headlights. Doc speeded up to finish the trip. It was about two o'clock when he got to La Jolla. He drove through the town and down to the cliff below which his tidal flat lay. There he stopped the car, ate a sandwich, drank some beer, turned out the lights, and curled up in the seat to sleep.

He didn't need a clock. He had been working in a tidal pattern so long that he could feel a tide change in his sleep. In the dawn he awakened, looked out through the windshield, and saw that the water was already retreating down the bouldery flat. He drank some hot coffee, ate three sandwiches, and had a quart of beer.

The tide goes out imperceptibly. The boulders show and seem to rise up and the ocean recedes, leaving little pools, leaving wet weed and moss and sponge, iridescence and brown and blue and China red. On the bottoms lie the incredible refuse of the sea, shells broken and chipped and bits of skeleton, claws, the whole sea bottom a fantastic cemetery on which the living scamper and scramble.

Doc pulled on his rubber-boots and set his rain hat fussily. He took his buckets and jars and his crowbar, and put his sandwiches in one pocket and his thermos-bottle in another pocket, and he went down the cliff to the tidal flat. Then

he worked down the flat after the retreating sea. He turned
over the boulders with his crowbar and now and then his
hand darted quickly into the standing-water and brought
out a little angry squirming octopus, which blushed with
rage and spat ink on his hand. Then he dropped it into a jar
of sea water with the others, and usually the newcomer was
so angry that it attacked its fellows.

It was good hunting that day. He got twenty-two little
octopi. And he picked off several hundred sea cradles and
put them in his wooden bucket. As the tide moved out he
followed it, while the morning came and the sun arose. The
flat extended out two hundred yards and then there was a
line of heavy weed-crusted rocks before it dropped off to
deep water. Doc worked out to the barrier edge. He had
about what he wanted now and the rest of the time he looked
under stones, leaned down, and peered into the tide pools
with their brilliant mosaics and their scuttling, bubbling
life. And he came at last to the outer barrier, where the long
leather brown algae hung down into the water. Red star
fish clustered on the rocks, and the sea pulsed up and down
against the barrier, waiting to get in again. Between two
weeded rocks on the barrier Doc saw a flash of white under
water and then the floating weed covered it. He climbed
to the place over the slippery rocks, held himself firmly, and
gently reached down and parted the brown algae. Then he
grew rigid. A girl's face looked up at him, a pretty, pale girl
with dark hair. The eyes were open and clear and the face
was firm and the hair washed gently about her head. The
body was out of sight, caught in the crevice. The lips were
slightly parted and the teeth showed, and on the face was
only comfort and rest. Just under water it was and the clear
water made it very beautiful. It seemed to Doc that he
looked at it for many minutes, and the face burned into his
picture memory.

Very slowly he raised his hand and let the brown weed
float back and cover the face. Doc's heart pounded deeply
and his throat felt tight. He picked up his bucket and his
jars and his crowbar and went slowly over the slippery rocks
back toward the beach.

And the girl's face went ahead of him. He sat down on the beach in the coarse dry sand and pulled off his boots. In the jar the little octopi were huddled up, each keeping as far as possible from the others. Music sounded in Doc's ears, a high thin piercingly sweet flute carrying a melody he could never remember, and against this, a pounding surf-like wood-wind section. The flute went up into regions beyond the hearing range and even there it carried its unbelievable melody. Goose pimples came out on Doc's arms. He shivered and his eyes were wet the way they get in the focus of great beauty. The girl's eyes had been grey and clear and the dark hair floated, drifted lightly over the face. The picture was set for all time. He sat there while the first little spout of water came over the reef, bringing the returning tide. He sat there hearing the music, while the sea crept in again over the bouldery flat. His hand tapped out the rhythm, and the terrifying flute played in his brain. The eyes were grey and the mouth smiled a little or seemed to catch its breath in ecstasy.

A voice seemed to awaken him. A man stood over him. 'Been fishing?'

'No, collecting.'

'Well – what are them things?'

'Baby octopi.'

'You mean devil-fish? I didn't know there was any there. I've lived here all my life.'

'You've got to look for them,' said Doc listlessly.

'Say,' said the man, 'aren't you feeling well? You look sick.'

The flute climbed again and plucked cellos sounded below and the sea crept in and in toward the beach. Doc shook off the music, shook off the face, shook the chill out of his body. 'Is there a police station near?'

'Up in town. Why, what's wrong?'

'There's a body out on the reef.'

'Where?'

'Right out there – wedged between two rocks. A girl.'

'Say . . .' said the man. 'You get a bounty for finding a body. I forget how much.'

Doc stood up and gathered his equipment. 'Will you report it? I'm not feeling well.'

'Give you a shock, did it? Is it – bad? Rotten or eat up?'

Doc turned away. 'You take the bounty,' he said. 'I don't want it.' He started toward the car. Only the tiniest piping of the flute sounded in his head.

CHAPTER XIX

PROBABLY nothing in the way of promotion Holman's Department Store ever did attracted so much favourable comment as the engagement of the flag-pole skater. Day after day, there he was up on his little round platform skating round and round, and at night he could be seen up there too, dark against the sky, so that everybody knew he didn't come down. It was generally agreed, however, that a steel rod came up through the centre of the platform at night and he strapped himself to it. But he didn't sit down and no one minded the steel rod. People came from Jamesburg to see him and from down the coast as far as Grimes Point. Salinas people came over in droves and the Farmers Mercantile of that town put in a bid for the next appearance when the skater could attempt to break his own record and thus give the new world's record to Salinas. Since there weren't many flag-pole skaters and since this one was by far the best, he had for the last year gone about breaking his own world's record.

Holman's was delighted about the venture. They had a white sale, a remnant sale, an aluminium sale, and a crockery sale all going at the same time. Crowds of people stood in the street watching the lone man on his platform.

His second day up, he sent down word that someone was shooting at him with an air-gun. The display department used its head. It figured the angles and located the offender. It was old Doctor Merrivale, hiding behind the curtains of his office, plugging away with a Daisy air-rifle. They didn't denounce him and he promised to stop. He was very prominent in the Masonic Lodge.

Henri the painter kept his chair at Red Williams' service station. He worked out every possible philosophic approach to the situation and came to the conclusion that he would have to build a platform at home and try it himself. Everyone in the town was more or less affected by the skater. Trade fell off out of sight of him and got better the nearer you came to Holman's. Mack and the boys went up and looked for a moment and then went back to the Palace. They couldn't see that it made much sense.

Holman's set up a double bed in their windows. When the skater broke the world's record he was going to come down and sleep right in the window without taking off his skates. The trade name of the mattress was on a little card at the foot of the bed.

Now in the whole town there was interest and discussion about this sporting event, but the most interesting question of all and the one that bothered the whole town was never spoken of. No one mentioned it, and yet it was there haunting everyone. Mrs Trolat wondered about it as she came out of the Scotch bakery with a bag of sweet buns. Mr Hall in men's furnishings wondered about it. The three Willoughby girls giggled whenever they thought of it. But no one had the courage to bring it into the open.

Richard Frost, a highly-strung and brilliant young man, worried about it more than anyone else. It haunted him. Wednesday night he worried and Thursday night he fidgeted. Friday night he got drunk and had a fight with his wife. She cried for a while and then pretended to be asleep. She heard him slip from bed and go into the kitchen. He was getting another drink. And then she heard him dress quietly and go out. She cried some more then. It was very late. Mrs Frost was sure he was going down to Dora's Bear Flag.

Richard walked sturdily down the hill through the pines until he came to Lighthouse Avenue. He turned left and went up toward Holman's. He had the bottle in his pocket and just before he came to the store he took one more slug of it. The street lights were turned down low. The town was deserted. Not a soul moved. Richard stood in the middle of the street and looked up.

Dimly on top of the high mast he could see the lonely figure of the skater. He took another drink. He cupped his hands and called huskily: 'Hey!' There was no answer. 'Hey!' he called louder, and looked around to see if the cops had come out of their place beside the bank.

Down from the sky came a surly reply: 'What do you want?'

Richard cupped his hands again. 'How – how do you – go to the toilet?'

'I've got a can up here,' said the voice.

Richard turned and walked back the way he had come. He walked along Lighthouse and up through the pines and he came to his house and let himself in. As he undressed he knew his wife was awake. She bubbled a little when she was asleep. He got into bed and she made room for him.

'He's got a can up there,' Richard said.

CHAPTER XX

In mid-morning the Model T truck rolled triumphantly home to Cannery Row and hopped the gutter and creaked up through the weeds to its place behind Lee Chong's. The boys blocked up the front wheels, drained what petrol was left into a five-gallon can, took their frogs, and went wearily home to the Palace Flophouse. Then Mack made a cere-monious visit to Lee Chong while the boys got a fire going in the big stove. Mack thanked Lee with dignity for lending the truck. He spoke of the great success of the trip, of the hundreds of frogs taken. Lee smiled shyly and waited for the inevitable.

'We're in the chips,' Mack said enthusiastically. 'Doc pays us a nickel a frog and we got about a thousand.'

Lee nodded. The price was standard. Everybody knew that.

'Doc's away,' said Mack. 'Jesus, is he gonna be happy when he sees all them frogs.'

Lee nodded again. He knew Doc was away and he also knew where the conversation was going.

'Say, by the way,' said Mack as though he had just thought of it. 'We're a little bit short right now ...' He managed to make it sound like a very unusual situation.

'No whisky,' said Lee Chong, and he smiled.

Mack was outraged. 'What would we want whisky for? Why, we got a gallon of the finest whisky you ever laid a lip over – a whole full God-damned-running-over gallon. By the way,' he continued, 'I and the boys would like to have you just step up for a snort with us. They told me to ask you.'

In spite of himself Lee smiled with pleasure. They wouldn't offer it if they didn't have it.

'No,' said Mack, 'I'll lay it on the line. I and the boys are pretty short and we're pretty hungry. You know the price of frogs is twenty for a buck. Now Doc is away and we're hungry. So what we thought is this. We don't want to see you lose nothing, so we'll make over to you twenty-five frogs for a buck. You got a five-frog profit there and nobody loses his shirt.'

'No,' said Lee. 'No money.'

'Well, hell, Lee, all we need is a little groceries. I'll tell you what – we want to give Doc a little party when he gets back. We got plenty of liquor, but we'd like to get maybe some steaks, and stuff like that. He's such a nice guy. Hell, when your wife had that bad tooth, who give her the laudanum?'

Mack had him. Lee was indebted to Doc – deeply indebted. What Lee was having trouble comprehending was how his indebtedness to Doc made it necessary that he give credit to Mack.

'We don't want you to have like a mortgage on frogs,' Mack went on. 'We will actually deliver right into your hands twenty-five frogs for every buck of groceries you let us have and you can come to the party too.'

Lee's mind nosed over the proposition like a mouse in a cheese cupboard. He could find nothing wrong with it. The whole thing was legitimate. Frogs *were* cash as far as Doc was concerned, the price was standard, and Lee had a double profit. He had his five-frog margin and also he had the grocery mark-up. The whole thing hinged on whether they actually had any frogs.

'We go see flog,' Lee said at last.

In front of the Palace he had a drink of the whisky, inspected the damp sacks of frogs, and agreed to the transaction. He stipulated, however, that he would take no dead frogs. Now Mack counted fifty frogs into a can and walked back to the grocery with Lee and got two dollars' worth of bacon and eggs and bread.

Lee, anticipating a brisk business, brought a big packing-case out and put it into the vegetable department. He emptied the fifty frogs into it and covered it with a wet gunny-sack to keep his charges happy.

And business was brisk. Eddie sauntered down and bought two frogs' worth of Bull Durham. Jones was outraged a little later when the price of Coca-Cola went up from one to two frogs. In fact bitterness arose as the day wore on and prices went up. Steak, for instance – the very best steak shouldn't have been more than ten frogs a pound, but Lee set it at twelve and a half. Canned peaches were sky high, eight frogs for a No. 2 can. Lee had a strangelhold on the consumers. He was pretty sure that the Thrift Market or Holman's would not approve of this new monetary system. If the boys wanted steak, they knew they had to pay Lee's prices. Feeling ran high when Hazel, who had coveted a pair of yellow silk arm-bands for a long time, was told that if he didn't want to pay thirty-five frogs for them he could go somewhere else. The poison of greed was already creeping into the innocent and laudable merchandising agreement. Bitterness was piling up. But in Lee's packing-case the frogs were piling up too.

Financial bitterness could not eat too deeply into Mack and the boys, for they were not mercantile men. They did not measure their joy in goods sold, their egos in bank balances, nor their loves in what they cost. While they were mildly irritated that Lee was taking them for an economic ride or perhaps hop, two dollars' worth of bacon and eggs was in their stomachs lying right on top of a fine slug of whisky and right on top of the breakfast was another slug of whisky. And they sat in their own chairs in their own house and watched Darling learning to drink canned milk out of a sardine can. Darling was and was destined to remain a very happy dog, for in the group of five men there were five distinct theories of dog training, theories which clashed so that Darling never got any training at all. From the first she was a precocious bitch. She slept on the bed of the man who had given her the last bribe. They really stole for her sometimes. They wooed her away from one another. Occasionally all five agreed that things had to change and that Darling must be disciplined, but in the discussion of method the intention invariably drifted away. They were in love with her. They found the little puddles she left on the floor charming. They bored all their acquaintances with her cuteness and they would have killed her with food if in the end she hadn't had better sense than they.

Jones made her a bed in the bottom of the grandfather clock, but Darling never used it. She slept with one or another of them as the fancy moved her. She chewed the blankets, tore the mattresses, sprayed the feathers out of the pillows. She coquetted and played her owners against one another. They thought she was wonderful. Mack intended to teach her tricks and go in vaudeville and he didn't even house-break her.

They sat in the afternoon, smoking, digesting, considering, and now and then having a delicate drink from the jug. And each time they warned that they must not take too much, for it was to be for Doc. They must not forget that for a minute.

'What time you figure he'll be back?' Eddie asked.

'Usually gets in about eight or nine o'clock,' said Mack. 'Now we got to figure when we're going to give it. I think we ought to give it tonight.'

'Sure,' the others agreed.

'Maybe he might be tired,' Hazel suggested. 'That's a long drive.'

'Hell,' said Jones, 'nothing rests you like a good party. I've been so dog-tired my pants was draggin' and then I've went to a party and felt fine.'

'We got to do some real thinkin',' said Mack. 'Where we going to give it – here?'

'Well, Doc, he likes his music. He's always got his phonograph going at a party. Maybe he'd be more happy if we give it over at his place.'

'You got something there,' said Mack. 'But I figure it ought to be like a surprise party. And how we going to make like it's a party and not just bringin' over a jug of whisky?'

'How about decorations?' Hughie suggested. 'Like Fourth of July or Halloween.'

Mack's eyes looked off into space and his lips were parted. He could see it all. 'Hughie,' he said, 'I think you got something there. I never would of thought you could do it, but by God you really rang a duck that time.' His voice grew mellow and his eyes looked into the future. 'I can just see it,' he said. 'Doc comes home. He's tired. He drives up. The place is all lit up. He thinks somebody's broke in. He goes up the stairs, and by God the place has got the hell decorated out of it. There's crêpe paper and there's favours and a big cake. Jesus, he'd know it was a party then. And it wouldn't be no little mouse fart party neither. And we're kind of hiding so for a minute he don't know who done it. And then we come out yelling. Can't you see his face? By God, Hughie, 1 don't know how you thought of it.'

Hughie blushed. His conception had been much more conservative, based in fact on the New Year's party at 'La Ida', but if it was going to be like that, why Hughie was willing to take credit. 'I just thought it would be nice,' he said.

'Well, it's a pretty nice thing,' said Mack, 'and I don't mind saying when the surprise kind of wears off, I'm going to tell Doc who thought it up.' They leaned back and considered the thing. And in their minds the decorated laboratory looked like the conservatory at the Hotel del Monte. They had a couple more drinks, just to savour the plan.

Lee Chong kept a very remarkable store. For instance, most stores buy yellow-and-black crêpe paper and black paper cats, masks and papier-mâché pumpkins in October. There is a brisk business for Halloween and then these items disappear. Maybe they are sold or thrown out, but you can't

buy them, say, in June. The same is true of Fourth of July
equipment, flags and bunting and sky-rockets. Where are
they in January? Gone – no one knows where. This was not
Lee Chong's way. You could buy Valentines in November
at Lee Chong's, shamrocks, hatchets, and paper cherry-trees
in August. He had fire-crackers he had laid up in 1920. One
of the mysteries was where he kept his stock since his was
not a very large store. He had bathing-suits he had bought
when long skirts and black stockings and head bandanas
were in style. He had bicycle clips and tatting shuttles and
Mah Jong sets. He had badges that said 'Remember the
Maine' and felt pennants commemorating 'Fighting Bob'.
He had mementos of the Panama Pacific International Ex-
position of 1915 – little towers of jewels. And there was one
other unorthodoxy in Lee's way of doing business. He never
had a sale, never reduced a price, and never remaindered.
An article that cost thirty cents in 1912 still was thirty cents,
although mice and moths might seem to some to have reduced its value. But there was no question about it. If you
wanted to decorate a laboratory in a general way, not being
specific about the season but giving the impression of a
cross between Saturnalia and a pageant of the Flags of all
Nations, Lee Chong's was the place to go for your stuff.

Mack and the boys knew that, but Mack said: 'Where
we going to get a big cake? Lee hasn't got nothing but them
little bakery cakes.'

Hughie had been so successful before he tried again.
'Why'n't Eddie bake a cake?' he suggested. 'Eddie used to
be fry cook at the San Carlos for a while.'

The instant enthusiasm for the idea drove from Eddie's
brain the admission that he had never baked a cake.

Mack put it on a sentimental basis besides. 'It would mean
more to Doc,' he said. 'It wouldn't be like no God damned
old soggy bought cake. It would have some heart in it.'

As the afternoon and the whisky went down the enthusiasm rose. There were endless trips to Lee Chong's. The
frogs were gone from one sack and Lee's packing-case was
getting crowded. By six o'clock they had finished the gallon
of whisky and were buying half-pints of Old Tennis Shoes

at fifteen frogs a crack, but the pile of decorating materials was heaped on the floor of the Palace Flophouse – miles of crêpe paper commemorating every holiday in vogue and some that had been abandoned.

Eddie watched his stove like a mother hen. He was baking a cake in a wash-basin. The recipe was guaranteed not to fail by the company which made the shortening. But from the first the cake had acted strangely. When the batter was completed it writhed and panted as though animals were squirming and crawling inside it. Once in the oven it put up a bubble like a baseball which grew tight and shiny and then collapsed with a hissing sound. This left such a crater that Eddie made a new batch of batter and filled in the hole. And now the cake was behaving very curiously, for while the bottom was burning and sending out a black smoke the top was rising and falling glueyly with a series of little explosions.

When Eddie finally put it out to cool, it looked like one of Bel Geddes's miniatures of a battlefield on a lava bed.

This cake was not forunate, for while the boys were decorating the laboratory Darling ate what she could of it, was sick on it, and finally curled up in its still warm dough and went to sleep.

But Mack and the boys had taken the crêpe paper, the masks, the broomsticks and paper pumpkins, the red, white and blue bunting, and moved over the lot and across the street to the laboratory. They disposed of the last of the frogs for a quart of Old Tennis Shoes and two gallons of 49-cent wine.

'Doc is very fond of wine,' said Mack. 'I think he likes it even better than whisky.'

Doc never locked the laboratory. He went on the theory that anyone who really wanted to break in could easily do it, that people were essentially honest, and that finally there wasn't much the average person would want to steal there, anyway. The valuable things were books and records, surgical instruments and optical glass and such things that a practical working burglar wouldn't look at twice. His theory had been sound as far as burglars, snatch thieves, and kleptomaniacs were concerned, but it had been completely ineffective regarding his friends. Books were often 'borrowed'. No can of beans ever survived his absence, and on several occasions, returning late, he had found guests in his bed.

The boys piled the decorations in the ante-room and then Mack stopped them. 'What's going to make Doc happiest?' he asked.

'The party!' said Hazel.

'No,' said Mack.

'The decorations?' Hughie suggested. He felt responsible for the decorations.

'No,' said Mack, 'the frogs. That's going to make him feel best of all. And maybe by the time he gets here, Lee Chong might be closed and he can't even see his frogs until to-morrow. No, sir,' Mack cried. 'Them frogs ought to be right here, right in the middle of the room with a piece of bunting on it and a sign that says: "Welcome Home, Doc".'

The committee which visited Lee met with stern opposition. All sorts of possibilities suggested themselves to his suspicious brain. It was explained that he was going to be at the party so he could watch his property, that no one questioned that they were his. Mack wrote out a paper transferring the frogs to Lee in case there should be any question.

When his protests weakened a little they carried the packing-case over to the laboratory, tacked red, white, and blue bunting over it, lettered the big sign with iodine on a card, and they started the decorating from there. They had finished the whisky by now and they really felt in a party mood. They criss-crossed the crêpe paper, and put the pumpkins up. Passers-by in the street joined the party and rushed over to Lee's to get more to drink. Lee Chong joined the party for a while, but his stomach was notoriously weak and he got sick and had to go home. At eleven o'clock they fried the steaks and ate them. Someone digging through the records found an album of Count Basie and the great phonograph roared out. The noise could be heard from the boatworks to 'La Ida'. A group of customers from the Bear Flag mistook Western Biological for a rival house and charged up the stairs whooping with joy. They were evicted by the outraged hosts, but only after a long, happy, and bloody battle that took out the front door and broke two windows. The crashing of jars was unpleasant. Hazel going through the kitchen to the toilet tipped the frying-pan of hot grease on himself and the floor and was badly burned.

At one-thirty a drunk wandered in and passed a remark which was considered insulting to Doc. Mack hit him a clip which is still remembered and discussed. The man rose off his feet, described a small arc, and crashed through the packing-case in among the frogs. Someone trying to change a record dropped the tone arm down and broke the crystal.

No one has studied the psychology of a dying party. It may be raging, howling, boiling, and then a fever sets in and a little silence and then quickly quickly it is gone, the guests go home or go to sleep or wander away to some other affair and they leave a dead body.

The lights blazed in the laboratory. The front door hung sideways by one hinge. The floor was littered with broken glass. Phonograph records, some broken, some only nicked, were strewn about. The plates with pieces of steak ends and coagulating grease were on the floor, on top of the bookcases, under the bed. Whisky-glasses lay sadly on their sides. Someone trying to climb the bookcases had pulled out a whole section of books and spilled them in broken-backed confusion on the floor. And it was empty, it was over.

Through the broken end of the packing-case a frog hopped and sat feeling the air for danger, and then another joined him. They could smell the fine, damp, cool air coming in the door and in through the broken windows. One of them sat on the fallen card which said: 'Welcome Home, Doc.' And then the two hopping timidly toward the door.

For quite a while a little river of frogs hopped down the steps, a swirling, moving river. For quite a while Cannery Row crawled with frogs – was overrun with frogs. A taxi which brought a very late customer to the Bear Flag squashed five frogs in the street. But well before dawn they had all gone. Some found the sewer and some worked their way up the hill to the reservoir and some went into culverts and some only hid among the weeds in the vacant lot.

And the lights blazed in the quiet empty laboratory.

CHAPTER XXI

In the back room of the laboratory the white rats in their cages rang and skittered and squeaked. In the corner of a separate cage a mother rat lay over her litter of blind, naked children and let them suckle and the mother stared about nervously and fiercely.

In the rattlesnake cage the snakes lay with their chins resting on their own coils and they stared straight ahead out of their scowling dusty black eyes. In another cage a Gila monster with a skin like a beaded bag reared slowly up and clawed heavily and sluggishly at the wire. The anemones in the aquaria blossomed open, with green and purple tentacles and pale green stomachs. The little sea-water pump whirred softly and the needles of driven water hissed into the tanks, forcing lines of bubbles under the surface.

It was the hour of the pearl. Lee Chong brought his garbage cans out to the kerb. The bouncer stood on the porch of the Bear Flag and scratched his stomach. Sam Malloy crawled out of the boiler and sat on his wood block and looked at the lightening east. Over on the rocks near Hopkins Marine Station the sea-lions barked monotonously. The old Chinaman came up out of the sea with his dripping basket and flip-flapped up the hill.

Then a car turned into Cannery Row and Doc drove up to the front of the laboratory. His eyes were red-rimmed with fatigue. He moved slowly with tiredness. When the car had stopped, he sat still for a moment to let the road jumps get out of his nerves. Then he climbed out of the car. At his step on the stairs, the rattlesnakes ran out their tongues and listened with their waving forked tongues. The rats scampered madly about the cages. Doc climbed the stairs. He looked in wonder at the sagging door and at the broken window. The weariness seemed to go out of him. He stepped quickly inside. Then he went quickly from room to room, stepping round the broken glass. He bent down quickly and picked up a smashed phonograph record and looked at its title.

In the kitchen the spilled grease had turned white on the floor. Doc's eyes flamed red with anger. He sat down on his couch and his head settled between his shoulders and his body weaved a little in his rage. Suddenly he jumped up and turned on the power in his great phonograph. He put on a record and put down the arm. Only a hissing roar came from the loud-speaker. He lifted the arm, stopped the turntable, and sat down on the couch again.

On the stairs there were bumbling uncertain footsteps and through the door came Mack. His face was red. He stood uncertainly in the middle of the room. 'Doc . . .' he said – 'I and the boys . . .'

For the moment Doc hadn't seemed to see him. Now he leaped to his feet. Mack shuffled backward. 'Did you do this?'

'Well, I and the boys . . .' Doc's small hard fist whipped out and splashed against Mack's mouth. Doc's eyes shone with a red animal rage. Mack sat down heavily on the floor. Doc's fist was hard and sharp. Mack's lips were split against his teeth and one front tooth bent sharply inward. 'Get up!' said Doc.

Mack lumbered to his feet. His hands were at his sides. Doc hit him again, a cold, calculated, punishing punch in the mouth. The blood spurted from Mack's lips and ran down his chin. He tried to lick his lips.

'Put up your hands. Fight, you son of a bitch,' Doc cried, and he hit him again and heard the crunch of breaking teeth.

Mack's head jolted, but he was braced now so he wouldn't fall. And his hands stayed at his side. 'Go ahead, Doc,' he said thickly through his broken lips. 'I got it coming.'

Doc's shoulders sagged with defeat. 'You son of a bitch,' he said bitterly. 'Oh, you dirty son of a bitch.' He sat down on the couch and looked at his cut knuckles.

Mack sat down in a chair and looked at him. Mack's eyes were wide and full of pain. He didn't even wipe away the blood that flowed down his chin. In Doc's head the mono-

onal opening of Monteverdi's *Hor ch' el Ciel e la Terra* began
o form, the infinitely sad and resigned mourning of Petrarch
or Laura. Doc saw Mack's broken mouth through the
music, the music that was in his head and in the air. Mack sat
perfectly still, almost as though he could hear the music too.
Doc glanced at the place where the Monteverdi album was
and then he remembered that the phonograph was broken.

He got to his feet. 'Go wash your face,' he said, and he
went out and down the stairs and across the street to Lee
Chong's. Lee wouldn't look at him as he got two quarts of
beer out of the ice-box. He took the money without saying
anything. Doc walked across the street.

Mack was in the toilet cleaning his bloody face with wet
paper towels. Doc opened a bottle and poured gently into a
glass, holding it at an angle so that very little collar rose to
the top. He filled a second tall glass and carried the two into
the front room. Mack came back dabbing at his mouth with
wet towelling. Doc indicated the beer with his head. Now
Mack opened his throat and poured down half the glass
without swallowing. He sighed explosively and stared into
the beer. Doc had already finished his glass. He brought the
bottle in and filled both glasses again. He sat down on his
couch.

'What happened?' he asked.

Mack looked at the floor and a drop of blood fell from his
lips to his beer. He mopped his split lips again. 'I and the
boys wanted to give you a party. We thought you'd be home
last night.'

Doc nodded his head. 'I see.'

'She got out of hand,' said Mack. 'It don't do no good to
say I'm sorry. I been sorry all my life. This ain't no new
thing. It's always like this.' He swallowed deeply from his
glass. 'I had a wife,' Mack said. 'Same thing. Ever'thing
I done turned sour. She couldn't stand it any more. If I
done a good thing it got poisoned up some way. If I give
her a present they was something wrong with it. She only
got hurt from me. She couldn't stand it no more. Same
thing ever' place 'til I just got to clowning. I don't do nothin'
but clown no more. Try to make the boys laugh.'

Doc nodded again. The music was sounding in his head again, complaint and resignation all in one. 'I know,' he said.

'I was glad when you hit me,' Mack went on. 'I thought to myself: "Maybe this will teach me. Maybe I'll remember this." But, hell, I won't remember nothin'. I won't learn nothin'. Doc,' Mack cried, 'the way I seen it, we was all happy and havin' a good time. You was glad because we was givin' you a party. And we was glad. The way I seen it, it was a good party.' He waved his hand at the wreckage on the floor. 'Same thing when I was married. I'd think her out and then – but it never come off that way.'

'I know,' said Doc. He opened the second quart of beer and poured the glasses full.

'Doc,' said Mack. 'I and the boys will clean up here – and we'll pay for the stuff that's broke. If it takes us five years we'll pay for it.'

Doc shook his head slowly and wiped the beer foam from his moustache. 'No,' he said, 'I'll clean it up. I know where everything goes.'

'We'll pay for it, Doc.'

'No you won't, Mack,' said Doc. 'You'll think about it and it'll worry you for quite a long time, but you won't pay for it. There's maybe three hundred dollars in broken museum glass. Don't say you'll pay for it. That will just keep you uneasy. It might be two or three years before you forgot about it and felt entirely easy again. And you wouldn't pay it, anyway.'

'I guess you're right,' said Mack. 'God damn it, I *know* you're right. What can we do?'

'I'm over it,' said Doc. 'Those socks in the mouth got it out of my system. Let's forget it.'

Mack finished his beer and stood up. 'So long, Doc,' he said.

'So long. Say, Mack – what happened to your wife?'

'I don't know,' said Mack. 'She went away.' He walked clumsily down the stairs and crossed over and walked up the lot and up the chicken walk to the Palace Flophouse. Doc watched his progress through the window. And then wearily he got a broom from behind the water-heater. It took him all day to clean up the mess.

CHAPTER XXII

HENRI the painter was not French and his name was not Henri. Also he was not really a painter. Henri had so steeped himself in stories of the Left Bank in Paris that he lived there although he had never been there. Feverishly he followed in periodicals the Dadaist movements and schisms, the strangely feminine jealousies and religiousness, the obscurantisms of the forming and breaking schools. Regularly he revolted against outworn techniques and materials. One season he threw out perspective. Another year he abandoned red, even as the mother of purple. Finally he gave up paint entirely. It is not known whether Henri was a good painter or not, for he threw himself so violently into movements that he had very little time left for painting of any kind.

About his painting there is some question. You couldn't judge very much from his productions in different coloured chicken feathers and nut-shells. But as a boat-builder he was superb. Henri was a wonderful craftsman. He had lived in a tent years ago when he started his boat and until galley and cabin were complete enough to move into. But once he was housed and dry he had taken his time on the boat. The boat was sculptured rather than built. It was thirty-five feet long and its lines were in a constant state of flux. For a while it had a clipper bow and a fan-tail like a destroyer. Another time it had looked vaguely like a caravel. Since Henri had no money, it sometimes took him months to find a plank or a piece of iron or a dozen brass screws. That was the way he wanted it, for Henri never wanted to finish his boat.

It sat among the pine-trees on a lot Henri rented for five dollars a year. This paid the taxes and satisfied the owner. The boat rested in a cradle on concrete foundations. A rope ladder hung over the side except when Henri was at home. Then he pulled up the rope ladder and only put it down

when guests arrived. His little cabin had a wide padded seat
that ran round three sides of the room. On this he slept and
on this his guests sat. A table folded down when it was
needed and a brass lamp hung from the ceiling. His galley
was a marvel of compactness, but every item in it had been
the result of months of thought and work.

Henri was swarthy and morose. He wore a beret long
after other people abandoned them, he smoked a calabash
pipe and his dark hair fell about his face. Henri had many
friends whom he loosely classified as those who could feed
him and those whom he had to feed. His boat had no name.
Henri said he would name it when it was finished.

Henri had been living in and building his boat for ten
years. During that time he had been married twice and had
promoted a number of semi-permanent liaisons. And all of
these young women had left him for the same reason. The
seven-foot cabin was too small for two people. They resented
bumping their heads when they stood up and they definitely
felt the need for a toilet. Marine toilets obviously would not
work in a shore-bound boat, and Henri refused to com-
promise with a spurious landsman's toilet. He and his friend
of the moment had to stroll away among the pines. And one
after another his loves left him.

Just after the girl he had called Alice left him, a very
curious thing happened to Henri. Each time he was left
alone, he mourned formally for a while, but actually he felt
a sense of relief. He could stretch out in his little cabin. He
could eat what he wanted. He was glad to be free of the endless female biologic functions for a while.

It had become his custom, each time he was deserted, to
buy a gallon of wine, to stretch out on the comfortably hard
bunk and get drunk. Sometimes he cried a little all by himself, but it was luxurious stuff and he usually had a wonderful feeling of well-being from it. He would read Rimbaud
aloud with a very bad accent, marvelling the while at his
fluid speech.

It was during one of his ritualistic mournings for the lost
Alice that the strange thing began to happen. It was night
and his lamp was burning and he had just barely begun to

get drunk when suddenly he knew he was no longer alone. He let his eye wander cautiously up and across the cabin, and there on the other side sat a devilish young man, a dark, handsome young man. His eyes gleamed with cleverness and spirit and energy and his teeth flashed. There was something very dear and yet very terrible in his face. And beside him sat a golden-haired little boy, hardly more than a baby. The man looked down at the baby and the baby looked back and laughed delightedly as though something wonderful were about to happen. Then the man looked over at Henri and smiled and he glanced back at the baby. From his upper left vest pocket he took an old-fashioned straight edged razor. He opened it and indicated the child with a gesture of his head. He put a hand among the curls and the baby laughed gleefully, and then the man tilted the chin and cut the baby's throat and the baby went right on laughing. But Henri was howling with terror. It took him a long time to realize that neither the man nor the baby was still there.

Henri, when his shaking had subsided a little, rushed out of his cabin, leaped over the side of the boat and hurried away down the hill through the pines. He walked for several hours and at last he walked down to Cannery Row.

Doc was in the basement working on cats when Henri burst in. Doc went on working while Henri told about it, and when it was over Doc looked closely at him to see how much actual fear and how much theatre was there. And it was mostly fear.

'Is it a ghost, do you think?' Henri demanded. 'Is it some reflection of something that has happened or is it some Freudian horror out of me, or am I completely nuts? I saw it, I tell you. It happened right in front of me as plainly as I see you.'

'I don't know,' said Doc.

'Well, will you come up with me, and see if it comes back?'

'No,' said Doc. 'If I saw it, it might be a ghost and it would scare me badly because I don't believe in ghosts. And if you saw it again and I didn't it would be a hallucination and you would be frightened.'

'But what am I going to do?' Henri asked. 'If I see it again I'll know what's going to happen and I'm sure I'll die. You see, he doesn't look like a murderer. He looks nice and the kid looks nice and neither of them give a damn. But he cut that baby's throat. I saw it.'

'I don't know,' said Doc. 'I'm not a psychiatrist or a witch-hunter and I'm not going to start now.'

A girl's voice called into the basement. 'Hi, Doc, can I come in?'

'Come along,' said Doc.

She was a rather pretty and a very alert girl.

Doc introduced her to Henri.

'He's got a problem,' said Doc. 'He neither has a ghost or a terrible conscience and he doesn't know which. Tell her about it, Henri.'

Henri went over the story again and the girl's eyes sparkled.

'But that's horrible,' she said when he finished. 'I've never in my life even caught the smell of a ghost. Let's go back up and see if he comes again.'

Doc watched them go a little sourly. After all, it had been his date.

The girl never did see the ghost, but she was fond of Henri, and it was five months before the cramped cabin and the lack of a toilet drove her out.

CHAPTER XXIII

A BLACK gloom settled over the Palace Flophouse. All the joy went out of it. Mack came back from the laboratory with his mouth torn and his teeth broken. As a kind of penance, he did not wash his face. He went to his bed and pulled his blanket over his head and he didn't get up all day. His heart was as bruised as his mouth. He went over all the bad things he had done in his life and everything he had ever done seemed bad. He was very sad.

Hughie and Jones sat for a while staring into space and then morosely they went over to the Hediondo Cannery and applied for jobs and got them.

Hazel felt so bad that he walked to Monterey and picked a fight with a soldier and lost it on purpose. That made him feel a little better to be utterly beaten by a man Hazel could have licked without half trying.

Darling was the only happy one of the whole club. She spent the day under Mack's bed happily eating up his shoes. She was a clever dog and her teeth were very sharp. Twice in his black despair, Mack reached under the bed and caught her and put her in bed with him for company, but she squirmed out and went back to eating his shoes.

Eddie mooned on down to 'La Ida' and talked to his friend the bar-tender. He got a few drinks and borrowed some nickels with which he played *Melancholy Baby* five times on the musical-box.

Mack and the boys were under a cloud and they knew it, and they knew they deserved it. They had become social outcasts. All their good intentions were forgotten now. The fact that the party was given for Doc, if it was known, was never mentioned or taken into consideration. The story ran through the Bear Flag. It was told in the canneries. At 'La Ida' drunks discussed it virtuously. Lee Chong refused to comment. He was feeling financially bruised. And the story as it grew went this way: They had stolen liquor and money. They had maliciously broken into the laboratory and systematically destroyed it out of pure malice and evil. People who really knew better took this view. Some of the drunks at 'La Ida' considered going over and beating the hell out of the whole lot of them to show them they couldn't do a thing like that to Doc.

Only a sense of the solidarity and fighting ability of Mack and the boys saved them from some kind of reprisal. There were people who felt virtuous about the affair who hadn't had the material of virtue for a long time. The fiercest of the whole lot was Tom Sheligan, who would have been at the party if he had known about it.

Socially Mack and the boys were beyond the pale. Sam Malloy didn't speak to them as they went by the boiler. They drew into themselves and no one could foresee how they would come out of the cloud. For there are two possible reactions to social ostracism – either a man emerges determined to be better, purer, and kindlier or he goes bad, challenges the world, and does even worst things. This last is by far the commonest reaction to stigma.

Mack and the boys balanced on the scales of good and evil. They were kind and sweet to Darling: they were forbearing and patient with one another. When the first reaction was over they gave the Palace Flophouse a cleaning such as it had never had. They polished the bright work on the stove and they washed all their clothes and blankets. Financially they had become dull and solvent. Hughie and Jones were working and bringing home their pay. They bought groceries up the hill at the Thrift Market because they could not stand the reproving eyes of Lee Chong.

It was during this time that Doc made an observation which may have been true, but since there was one factor missing in his reasoning it is not known whether he was correct. It was the Fourth of July. Doc was sitting in the laboratory with Richard Frost. They drank beer and listened to a new album of Scarlatti and looked out the window. In front of the Palace Flophouse there was a large log of wood where Mack and the boys were sitting in the mid-morning sun. They faced down the hill toward the laboratory.

Doc said: 'Look at them. There are your true philosophers. I think,' he went on, 'that Mack and the boys know everything that has ever happened in the world and possibly everything that will happen. I think they survive in this particular world better than other people. In a time when people tear themselves to pieces with ambition and nervousness and covetousness, they are relaxed. All of our so-called successful men are sick men, with bad stomachs, and bad souls, but Mack and the boys are healthy and curiously clean. They can do what they want. They can satisfy their appetites without calling them something else.' This speech so dried out Doc's throat that he drained his beer glass. He waved two fingers in the air and smiled. 'There's nothing like that first taste of beer,' he said.

Richard Frost said: 'I think they're just like anyone else. They just haven't any money.'

'They could get it,' Doc said. 'They could ruin their lives and get money. Mack has qualities of genius. They're all very clever if they want something. They just know the nature of things too well to be caught in that wanting.'

If Doc had known of the sadness of Mack and the boys he would not have made the next statement, but no one had told him about the social pressure that was exerted against the inmates of the Palace.

He poured beer slowly into his glass. 'I think I can show you proof,' he said. 'You see how they are sitting facing this way? Well – in about half an hour the Fourth of July Parade is going to pass on Lighthouse Avenue. By just turning their heads they can see it, by standing up they can watch it, and by walking two short blocks they can be right beside it. Now I'll bet you a quart of beer they won't even turn their heads.'

'Suppose they don't?' said Richard Frost. 'What will that prove?'

'What will it prove?' cried Doc. 'Why, just that they know what will be in the parade. They will know that the Mayor will ride first in an automobile with bunting streaming back from the hood. Next will come Long Bob on his white horse with the flag. Then the city council, then two companies of soldiers from the Presidio, next the Elks with purple umbrellas, then the Knights Templars in white ostrich feathers and carrying swords. Next the Knights of Columbus with red ostrich feathers and carrying swords. Mack and the boys know that. The band will play. They've seen it all. They don't have to look again.'

'The man doesn't live who doesn't have to look at a parade,' said Richard Frost.

'Is it a bet then?'

'It's a bet.'

'It has always seemed strange to me,' said Doc. 'The things we admire in men, kindness and generosity, openness, honesty, understanding, and feeling are the concomitants of failure in our system. And those traits we detest, sharpness, greed, acquisitiveness, meanness, egotism, and self-interest are the traits of success. And while men admire the quality of the first they love the produce of the second.'

'Who wants to be good if he has to be hungry too?' said Richard Frost.

'Oh, it isn't a matter of hunger. It's something quite different. The sale of souls to gain the whole world is completely voluntary and almost unanimous – but not quite. Everywhere in the world there are Mack and the boys. I've seen them in an ice-cream seller in Mexico and in an Aleut in Alaska. You know how they tried to give me a party and something went wrong. But they wanted to give me a party. That was their impulse. Listen,' said Doc. 'Isn't that the band I hear?' Quickly he filled two glasses with beer and the two of them stepped close to the window.

Mack and the boys sat dejectedly on their log and faced the laboratory. The sound of the band came from Lighthouse Avenue, the drums echoing back from the buildings. And suddenly the Mayor's car crossed and it sprayed bunting from the radiator – then Long Bob on his white horse carrying the flag, then the band, then the soldiers, the Elks, the Knights Templar, the Knights of Columbus. Richard and the Doc leaned forward tensely, but they were watching and the line of men sitting on the log.

And not a head turned, not a neck straightened up. The parade filed past and they did not move. And the parade was gone. Doc drained his glass and waved two fingers gently in the air and he said: 'Hah! There's nothing in the world like that first taste of beer.'

Richard started for the door. 'What kind of beer do you want?'

'The same kind,' said Doc gently. He was smiling up the hill at Mack and the boys.

It's all fine to say: 'Time will heal everything, this too shall pass away. People will forget' – and things like that when you are not involved, but when you are there is no passage of time, people do not forget, and you are in the middle of something that does not change. Doc didn't know

the pain and self-destructive criticism in the Palace Flophouse or he might have tried to do something about it. And
Mack and the boys did not know how he felt or they would
have held up their heads again.

It was a bad time. Evil stalked darkly in the vacant lot.
Sam Malloy had a number of fights with his wife and she
cried all the time. The echoes inside the boiler made it
sound as though she were crying under water. Mack and
the boys seemed to be the node of trouble. The nice bouncer
at the Bear Flag threw out a drunk, but threw him too hard
and too far and broke his back. Alfred had to go over to
Salinas three times before it was cleared up, and that didn't
make Alfred feel very well. Ordinarily he was too good a
bouncer to hurt anyone. His A and C was a miracle of
rhythm and grace.

On top of that a group of high-minded ladies in the town
demanded that the dens of vice must close to protect young
American manhood. This happened about once a year in
the dead period between the Fourth of July and the County
Fair. Dora usually closed the Bear Flag for a week when it
happened. It wasn't so bad. Everyone got a vacation and
little repairs to the plumbing and the walls could be made.
But this year the ladies went on a real crusade. They wanted
somebody's scalp. It had been a dull summer and they were
restless. It got so bad that they had to be told who actually
owned the property where vice was practised, what the rents
were, and what little hardships might be the result of their
closing. That was how close they were to being a serious
menace.

Dora was closed a full two weeks and there were three
conventions in Monterey while the Bear Flag was closed.
Word got around and Monterey lost five conventions for the
following year. Things were bad all over. Doc had to get a
loan at the bank to pay for the glass that was broken at the
party. Elmer Rechati went to sleep on the Southern Pacific
track and lost both legs. A sudden and completely unex-
pected storm tore a purse-seiner and three lampara boats
loose from their moorings and tossed them broken and sad
on Del Monte beach.

There is no explaining a series of misfortunes like that. Every man blames himself. People in their black minds remember sins committed secretly and wonder whether they have caused the evil sequence. One man may put it down to sun-spots while another invoking the law of probabilities doesn't believe it. Not even the doctors had a good time of it, for while many people were sick none of it was good-paying sickness. It was nothing a good physic or a patent medicine wouldn't take care of.

And to cap it all, Darling got sick. She was a very fat and lively puppy when she was struck down, but five days of fever reduced her to a little skin-covered skeleton. Her liver-coloured nose was pink and her gums were white. Her eyes glazed with illness and her whole body was hot, although she trembled sometimes with cold. She wouldn't eat and she wouldn't drink and her fat little belly shrivelled up against her spine, and even her tail showed the articulations through the skin. It was obviously distemper.

Now a genuine panic came over the Palace Flophouse. Darling had come to be vastly important to them. Hughie and Jones instantly quit their jobs so they could be near to help. They sat up in shifts. They kept a cool, damp cloth on her forehead and she got weaker and weaker. Finally, although they didn't want to, Hazel and Jones were chosen to call on Doc. They found him working over a tide-chart while he ate a chicken stew of which the principal ingredient was not chicken but sea cucumber. They thought he looked at them a little coldly.

'It's Darling,' they said. 'She's sick.'

'What's the matter with her?'

'Mack says it's distemper.'

'I'm no veterinarian,' said Doc. 'I don't know how to treat these things.'

Hazel said: 'Well, couldn't you just take a look at her? She's sick as hell.'

They stood in a circle while Doc examined Darling. He looked at her eyeballs and her gums and felt in her ear for fever. He ran his finger over the ribs that stuck out like spokes and at the poor spine. 'She won't eat?' he asked.

'Not a thing,' said Mack.

'You'll have to force feed her – strong soups and eggs and cod liver oil.'

They thought he was cold and professional. He went back to his tide-charts and his stew.

But Mack and the boys had something to do now. They boiled meat until it was as strong as whisky. They put cod liver oil far back on her tongue so that some of it got down her. They held up her head and made a little funnel of her chops and poured the cool soup in. She had to swallow or drown. Every two hours they fed her and gave her water. Before they had slept in shifts – now no one slept. They sat silently and waited for Darling's crisis.

It came early in the morning. The boys sat in their chairs half asleep, but Mack was awake and his eyes were on the puppy. He saw her ears flip twice, and her chest heave. With infinite weakness she climbed slowly to her spindly legs, dragged herself to the door, took four laps of water, and collapsed on the floor.

Mack shouted the others awake. He danced heavily. All the boys shouted at one another. Lee Chong heard them and snorted to himself as he carried out the garbage cans. Alfred the bouncer heard them and thought they were having a party.

By nine o'clock Darling had eaten a raw egg and half a pint of whipped cream by herself. By noon she was visibly putting on weight. In a day she romped a little and by the end of the week she was a well dog.

At last a crack had developed in the wall of evil. There were evidences of it everywhere. The purse-seiner was hauled back into the water and floated. Word came down to Dora that it was all right to open up the Bear Flag. Earl Wakefield caught a sculpin with two heads and sold it to the museum for eight dollars. The wall of evil and of waiting was broken. It broke away in chinks. The curtains were drawn at the laboratory that night and the Gregorian music played until two o'clock and then the music stopped and no one came out. Some force wrought with Lee Chong's heart and all in an Oriental moment he forgave Mack and the

boys and wrote off the frog debt, which had been a monetary headache from the beginning. And to prove to the boys
that he had forgiven them he took a pint of Old Tennis
Shoes up and presented it to them. Their trading at the
Thrift Market had hurt his feelings, but it was all over now.
Lee's visit coincided with the first destructive healthy impulse Darling had since her illness. She was completely
spoiled now and no one thought of housebreaking her. When
Lee Chong came in with his gift, Darling was deliberately
and happily destroying Hazel's only pair of rubber-boots,
while her happy masters applauded her.

Mack never visited the Bear Flag professionally. It would
have seemed a little like incest to him. There was a house
out by the baseball park he patronized. Thus, when he went
into the front bar, everyone thought he wanted a beer. He
stepped up to Alfred. 'Dora around?' he asked.

'What do you want with her?' Alfred asked.

'I got something I want to ask her.'

'What about?'

'That's none of your God damn business,' said Mack.

'Okay. Have it your way. I'll see if she wants to talk to
you.'

A moment later he led Mack into the sanctum. Dora sat
at a roll-top desk. Her orange hair was piled in ringlets on
her head and she wore a green eyeshade. With a stub pen
she was bringing her books up-to-date, a fine old double-
entry ledger. She was dressed in a magnificent pink silk
wrapper with lace at the wrists and throat. When Mack
came in she whirled her pivot-chair about and faced him.
Alfred stood in the door and waited. Mack stood until
Alfred closed the door and left.

Dora scrutinized him suspiciously. 'Well – what can I do
for you?' she demanded at last.

'You see, ma'am,' said Mack. 'Well I guess you heard
what we done over at Doc's some time back.'

Dora pushed the eyeshade back up on her head and she
put the pen in an old-fashioned coil-spring holder. 'Yeah!'
she said. 'I heard.'

'Well, ma'am, we did it for Doc. You may not believe it,

but we wanted to give him a party. Only he didn't get home in time and – well, she got out of hand.'

'So I heard,' said Dora. 'Well, what you want me to do?'

'Well,' said Mack, 'I and the boys thought we'd ask you. You know what we think of Doc. We wanted to ask you what you thought we could do for him that would kind of show him.'

Dora said: 'Hum,' and she flopped back in her pivot-chair and crossed her legs and smoothed her wrapper over her knees. She shook out a cigarette, lighted it, and studied. 'You gave him a party he didn't get to. Why don't you give him a party he does get to?' she said.

'Jesus,' said Mack afterwards talking to the boys. 'It was just as simple as that. Now there is one hell of a woman. No wonder she got to be madam. There is one hell of a woman.'

CHAPTER XXIV

MARY TALBOT, Mrs Tom Talbot, that is, was lovely. She had red hair with green lights in it. Her skin was golden, with a green under-cast, and her eyes were green, with little golden spots. Her face was triangular, with wide cheek-bones, wide-set eyes, and her chin was pointed. She had long dancer's legs and dancer's feet, and she seemed never to touch the ground when she walked. When she was excited, and she was excited a good deal of the time, her face flushed with gold. Her great-great-great-great-great grandmother had been burned as a witch.

More than anything in the world Mary Talbot loved parties. She loved to give parties and she loved to go to parties. Since Tom Talbot didn't make much money Mary couldn't give parties all the time, so she tricked people into giving them. Sometimes she telephoned a friend and said bluntly: 'Isn't it about time you gave a party?'

Regularly, Mary had six birthdays a year, and she organized costume parties, surprise parties, holiday parties. Christmas Eve at her house was a very exciting thing. For

Mary glowed with parties. She carried her husband along on the wave of her excitement.

In the afternoons when Tom was at work Mary sometimes gave tea-parties for the neighbourhood cats. She set a foot-stool with doll cups and saucers. She gathered the cats, and there were plenty of them, and then she held long and de-tailed conversations with them. It was a kind of play she en-joyed very much – a kind of satiric game, and it covered and concealed from Mary the fact that she didn't have very nice clothes and the Talbots didn't have any money. They were pretty near absolute bottom most of the time, and when they really scraped, Mary managed to give some kind of a party.

She could do that. She could infect a whole house with gaiety and she used her gift as a weapon against the despon-dency that lurked always around outside the house waiting to get in at Tom. That was Mary's job as she saw it – to keep the despondency away from Tom because everyone knew he was going to be a great success some time. Mostly she was successful in keeping the dark things out of the house, but sometimes they got in at Tom and laid him out. Then he would sit and brood for hours, while Mary frantically built up a back-fire of gaiety.

One time when it was the first of the month and there were curt notes from the water company and the rent wasn't paid and a manuscript had come back from *Collier's* and the cartoons had come back from *The New Yorker* and pleurisy was hurting Tom pretty badly, he went into the bedroom and lay down on the bed.

Mary came softly in, for the blue-grey colour of his gloom had seeped out under the door and through the keyhole. She had a little bouquet of candytuft in a collar of paper lace. 'Smell,' she said and held the bouquet to his nose. He smelled the flowers and said nothing. 'Do you know what day this is?' she asked and thought wildly for something to make it a bright day.

Tom said: 'Why don't we face it for once? We're down. We're going under. What's the good kidding ourselves?'

'No we're not,' said Mary. 'We're magic people. We al-ways have been. Remember that ten dollars you found in a book – remember when your cousin sent you five dollars? Nothing can happen to us.'

'Well, it has happened,' said Tom. 'I'm sorry,' he said. 'I just can't talk myself out of it this time. I'm sick of pretending everything. For once I'd like to have it real – just for once.'

'I thought of giving a little party tonight,' said Mary.

'On what? You're not going to cut out the baked ham picture from a magazine again and serve it on a platter, are you? I'm sick of that kind of kidding. It isn't funny any more. It's sad.'

'I could give a little party,' she insisted. 'Just a small affair. Nobody will dress. It's the anniversary of the founding of the Bloomer League – you didn't even remember that.'

'It's no use,' said Tom. 'I know it's mean, but I just can't rise to it. Why don't you just go out and shut the door and leave me alone? I'll get you down if you don't.'

She looked at him closely and saw that he meant it. Mary walked quietly out and shut the door, and Tom turned over on the bed and put his face down between his arms. He could hear her rustling about in the other room.

She decorated the door with old Christmas things, glass-balls, and tinsel, and she made a placard that said: 'Welcome Tom, our Hero'. She listened at the door and she couldn't hear anything. A little disconsolately she got out the foot-stool and spread a napkin over it. She put her bouquet in a glass in the middle of the footstool and set out four little cups and saucers. She went into the kitchen, put the tea in the teapot and set the kettle to boil. Then she went out into the yard.

Kitty Randolph was sunning herself by the front fence. Mary said: 'Miss Randolph – I'm having a few friends in to tea if you would care to come.' Kitty Randolph rolled over languorously on her back and stretched in the warm sun. 'Don't be later than four o'clock,' said Mary. 'My husband and I are going to the Bloomer League Centennial Reception at the Hotel.'

She strolled round the house to the backyard, where the blackberry vines clambered over the fence. Kitty Casini was squatting on the ground growling to herself and flicking her tail fiercely. 'Mrs Casini,' Mary began, and then she stopped for she saw what the cat was doing. Kitty Casini had a mouse. She patted it gently with her unarmed paw and the mouse squirmed horribly away, dragging its paralysed hind legs behind it. The cat let it get nearly to the covert of the blackberry vines and then she reached delicately out and white thorns had sprouted on her paw. Daintily she stabbed the mouse through the back and drew it wriggling to her and her tail flicked with tense delight.

Tom must have been at least half asleep when he heard his name called over and over. He jumped up shouting: 'What is it? Where are you?' He could hear Mary crying. He ran out into the yard and saw what was happening. 'Turn your head,' he shouted and he killed the mouse. Kitty Casini had leaped to the top of the fence, where she watched him angrily. Tom picked up a rock and hit her in the stomach and knocked her off the fence.

In the house Mary was still crying a little. She poured the water into the teapot and brought it to the table. 'Sit there,' she told Tom and he squatted down on the floor in front of the footstool.

'Can't I have a big cup?' he asked.

'I can't blame Kitty Casini,' said Mary. 'I know how cats are. It isn't her fault. But – Oh, Tom! I'm going to have trouble inviting her again. I'm just not going to like her for a while no matter how much I want to.' She looked closely at Tom and saw that the lines were gone from his forehead and that he was not blinking badly. 'But then I'm so busy with the Bloomer League these days,' she said. 'I just don't know how I'm going to get everything done.'

Mary Talbot gave a pregnancy party that year. And everyone said: 'God! A kid of hers is going to have fun.'

CHAPTER XXV

CERTAINLY all of Cannery Row and probably all of Monterey felt that a change had come. It's all right not to believe in luck and omens. Nobody believes in them. But it doesn't do any good to take chances with them and no one takes chances. Cannery Row, like every other place else, is not superstitious, but will not walk under a ladder or open an umbrella in the house. Doc was a pure scientist and incapable of superstition and yet when he came in late one night and found a line of white flowers across the door-sill he had a bad time of it. But most people in Cannery Row simply do not believe in such things and then live by them.

There was no doubt in Mack's mind that a dark cloud had hung on the Palace Flophouse. He had analysed the abortive party and found that a misfortune had crept into every crevice, that bad luck had come up like hives on the evening. And once you got into a routine like that the best thing to do was just go to bed until it was over. You couldn't buck it. Not that Mack was superstitious.

Now a kind of gladness began to penetrate into the Row and to spread out from there. Doc was almost supernaturally successful with a series of lady visitors. He didn't half try. The puppy at the Palace was growing like a pole bean, and, having a thousand generations of training behind her, she began to train herself. She got disgusted with wetting on the floor and took to going outside. It was obvious that Darling was going to grow up a good and charming dog. And she had developed no chorea from her distemper.

The benignant influence crept like gas through the Row. It got as far as Herman's hamburger stand, it spread to the San Carlos Hotel. Jimmy Brucia felt it and Johnny his singing bar-tender. Sparky Evea felt it and joyously joined battle with three new out-of-town cops. It even got as far as the County Jail in Salinas, where Gay, who had lived a good life by letting the sheriff beat him at draughts, suddenly grew cocky and never lost another game. He lost his privileges that way, but he felt a whole man again.

The sea-lions felt it and their barking took on a tone and a cadence that would have gladdened the heart of St Francis. Little girls studying their catechism suddenly looked up and giggled for no reason at all. Perhaps some electrical finder could have been developed so delicate that it could have located the source of all this spreading joy and fortune. And triangulation might possibly have located it in the Palace Flophouse and Grill. Certainly the Palace was lousy with it. Mack and the boys were charged. Jones was seen to leap from his chair only to do a quick tap dance and sit down again. Hazel smiled vaguely at nothing at all. The joy was so general and so suffused that Mack had a hard time keeping it centred and aimed at its objective. Eddie, who had worked at 'La Ida' pretty regularly was accumulating a cellar of some promise. He no longer added beer to the wining jug. It gave a flat taste to the mixture, he said.

Sam Malloy had planted morning glories to grow over the boiler. He had put out a little awning and under it he and his wife often sat in the evening. She was crocheting a bedspread.

The joy even got into the Bear Flag. Business was good. Phyllis Mae's leg was knitting nicely and she was nearly ready to go to work again. Eva Flanegan got back from East St Louis very glad to be back. It had been hot in East St Louis and it hadn't been as fine as she remembered it. But then she had been younger when she had had so much fun there.

The knowledge or conviction about the party for Doc was no sudden thing. It did not burst out full blown. People knew about it, but let it grow gradually, like a pupa in the cocoons of their imaginations.

Mack was realistic about it. 'Last time we forced her,' he told the boys. 'You can't never give a good party that way. You got to let her creep up on you.'

'Well, when's it going to be?' Jones asked impatiently.

'I don't know,' said Mack.

'Is it gonna be a surprise party?' Hazel asked.

'It ought to, that's the best kind,' said Mack.

Darling brought him a tennis ball she had found and he threw it out the door into the weeds. She bounced away after it.

Hazel said: 'If we knew when was Doc's birthday, we could give him a birthday-party.'

Mack's mouth was open. Hazel constantly surprised him.

'By God, Hazel, you got something,' he cried. 'Yes, sir, if it was his birthday there'd be presents. That's just the thing. All we got to find out is when it is.'

'That ought to be easy,' said Hughie. 'Why don't we ask him?'

'Hell,' said Mack. 'Then he'd catch on. You ask a guy when is his birthday and especially if you've already give him a party like we done, and he'll know what you want to know for. Maybe I'll just go over and smell around a little and not let on.'

'I'll go with you,' said Hazel.

'No – if two of us went, he might figure we were up to something.'

'Well, hell, it was my idear,' said Hazel.

'I know,' said Mack. 'And when it comes off why I'll tell Doc it was your idear. But I think I better go over alone.'

'How is he – friendly?' Eddie asked.

'Sure, he's all right.'

Mack found Doc way back in the downstairs part of the laboratory. He was dressed in a long rubber apron and he wore rubber gloves to protect his hands from the formaldehyde. He was injecting the veins and arteries of small dog-fish with colour mass. His little ball mill rolled over and over, mixing the blue mass. The red fluid was already in the pressure-gun. Doc's fine hands worked precisely, slipping the needle into place and pressing the compressed-air trigger that forced the colour into the veins. He laid the finished fish in a neat pile. He would have to go over these again to put the blue mass in the arteries. The dog-fish made good dissection specimens.

'Hi, Doc,' said Mack. 'Keepin' pretty busy?'

'Busy as I want,' said Doc. 'How's the pup?'

'Doin' just fine. She would of died if it hadn't been for you.'

For a moment a wave of caution went over Doc and then slipped off. Ordinarily a compliment made him wary. He had been dealing with Mack for a long time. But the tone had nothing but gratefulness in it. He knew how Mack felt about the pup. 'How are things going up at the Palace?'

'Fine, Doc, just fine. We got two new chairs. I wish you'd come up and see us. It's pretty nice up there now.'

'I will,' said Doc. 'Eddie still bring back the jug?'

'Sure,' said Mack. 'He ain't puttin' beer in it no more and I think the stuff is better. It's got more zip.'

'It had plenty of zip before,' said Doc.

Mack waited patiently. Sooner or later Doc was going to wade into it and he was waiting. If Doc seemed to open the subject himself it would be less suspicious. This was always Mack's method.

'Haven't seen Hazel for some time. He isn't sick, is he?'

'No,' said Mack and he opened the campaign. 'Hazel is all right. Him and Hughie are havin' one hell of a battle. Been goin' on for a week,' he chuckled. 'An' the funny thing is it's about somethin' they don't neither of them know nothin' about. I stayed out of it because I don't know nothin' about it neither, but not them. They've even got a little mad at each other.'

'What's it about?' Doc asked.

'Well, sir,' said Mack, 'Hazel's all the time buyin' these here charts and lookin' up lucky days and stars and stuff like that. And Hughie says it's all a bunch of malarky. Hughie, he says if you know when a guy is born you can tell about him and Hughie says they're just sellin' Hazel them charts for two bits apiece. Me, I don't know nothin' about it. What do you think, Doc?'

'I'd kind of side with Hughie,' said Doc. He stopped the ball mill, washed out the colour-gun and filled it with blue mass.

'They got goin' hot the other night,' said Mack. 'They ask me when I'm born so I tell 'em April 12 and Hazel he goes and buys one of them charts and read all about me. Well it did seem to hit in some places. But it was nearly all good stuff and a guy will believe good stuff about himself. It said I'm brave and smart and kind to my friends. But Hazel says it's all true. When's your birthday, Doc?' At the end of the long discussion it sounded perfectly casual. You couldn't put your finger on it. But it must be remembered that Doc had known Mack a very long time. If he had not he would have said December 18, which was his birthday, instead of October 27, which was not. 'October 27,' said Doc. 'Ask Hazel what that makes me.'

'It's probably so much malarky,' said Mack, 'but Hazel he takes it serious. I'll ask him to look you up, Doc.'

When Mack left, Doc wondered casually what the build-up was. For he had recognized it as a lead. He knew Mack's technique, his method. He recognized his style. And he wondered to what purpose Mack could put the information. It was only later, when rumours began to creep in, that Doc added the whole thing up. Now he felt slightly relieved, for he had expected Mack to put the bite on him.

CHAPTER XXVI

THE two little boys played in the boat works yard until a cat climbed the fence. Instantly they gave chase, drove it across the tracks, and there filled their pockets with granite stones from the roadbed. The cat got away from them in the tall weeds, but they kept the stones because they were perfect in weight, shape, and size for throwing. You can't ever tell when you're going to need a stone like that. They turned down Cannery Row and whanged a stone at the corrugated-iron front of Morden's Cannery. A startled man looked out the office window and then rushed for the door, but the boys were too quick for him. They were lying behind a wooden stringer in the lot before he even got near the door. He couldn't have found them in a hundred years.

'I bet he could look all his life and he couldn't find us,' said Joey.

They got tired of hiding after a while with no one looking for them. They got up and strolled on down Cannery Row. They looked a long time in Lee's window, coveting the pliers, the hacksaws, the engineers' caps, and the bananas. Then they crossed the street and sat down on the lower step of the stairs that went to the second storey of the laboratory.

Joey said: 'You know, this guy in here got babies in bottles.'

'What kind of babies?' Willard asked.

'Regular babies, only before they're borned.'

'I don't believe it,' said Willard.

'Well, it's true. The Sprague kid seen them and he says they ain't no bigger than this and they got little hands and feet and eyes.'

'And hair?' Willard demanded.

'Well, the Sprague kid didn't say about hair.'

'You should of asked him. I think he's a liar.'

'You better not let him hear you say that,' said Joey.

'Well, you can tell him I said it. I ain't afraid of him and I ain't afraid of you. I ain't afraid of anybody. You want to make something of it?' Joey didn't answer. 'Well, do you?'

'No,' said Joey. 'I was thinkin', why don't we just go up and ask the guy if he's got babies in bottles? Maybe he'd show them to us, that is if he's got any.'

'He ain't there,' said Willard. 'When he's here, his car's here. He's away some place. I think it's a lie. I think the Sprague kid is a liar. I think you're a liar. You want to make something of that?'

It was a lazy day. Willard was going to have to work hard to get up any excitement. 'I think you're a coward too. You want to make something of that?' Joey didn't answer. Willard changed his tactics. 'Where's your old man now?' he asked in a conversational tone.

'He's dead,' said Joey.

'Oh yeah? I didn't hear. What'd he die of?'

For a moment Joey was silent. He knew Willard knew, but he couldn't let on he knew, not without fighting Willard, and Joey was afraid of Willard.

'He committed – he killed himself.'

'Yeah?' Willard put on a long face. 'How'd he do it?'

'He took rat poison.'

Willard's voice shrieked with laughter. 'What'd he think he was – a rat?'

Joey chuckled a little at the joke, just enough, that is.

'He must of thought he was a rat,' Willard cried. 'Did he go crawling around like this – look Joey – like this? Did he wrinkle up his nose like this? Did he have a big old long tail?' Willard was helpless with laughter. 'Why'n't he just get a rat-trap and put his head in it?' They laughed themselves out on that one. Willard really wore it out. Then he probed for another joke. 'What'd he look like when he took it – like this?' He crossed his eyes and opened his mouth and stuck out his tongue.

'He was sick all day,' said Joey. 'He didn't die 'til the middle of the night. It hurt him.'

Willard said: 'What'd he do it for?'

'He couldn't get a job,' said Joey. 'Nearly a year he couldn't get a job. And you know a funny thing? The next morning a guy come around to give him a job.'

Willard tried to recapture his joke. 'I guess he just figured he was a rat,' he said, but it fell through even for Willard.

Joey stood up and put his hands in his pockets. He saw a little coppery shine in the gutter and walked toward it, but just as he reached it Willard shoved him aside and picked up the penny.

'I saw it first,' Joey cried. 'It's mine.'

'You want to try and make something of it?' said Willard. 'Why'n't you go and take rat poison?'

CHAPTER XXVII

MACK and the boys – the Virtues, the Beatitudes, the Beauties. They sat in the Palace Flophouse and they were the stone dropped in the pool, the impulse which sent out ripples to all of Cannery Row and beyond, to Pacific Grove, to Monterey, even over the hill to Carmel.

'This time,' said Mack, 'we got to be sure he gets to the party. If he don't get there, we don't give it.'

'Where we going to give it this time?' Jones asked.

Mack tipped his chair back against the wall and hooked his feet around the front legs. 'I've give that a lot of thought,' he said. 'Of course we could give it here, but it would be pretty hard to surprise him here. And Doc likes his own place. He's got his music there.' Mack scowled around the room. 'I don't know who broke his phonograph last time,' he said. 'But if anybody so much as lays a finger on it next time I personally will kick the hell out of him.'

'I guess we'll just have to give it at his place,' said Hughie.

People didn't get the news of the party – the knowledge of it just slowly grew up in them. And no one was invited. Everyone was going. October 27 had a mental red circle around it. And since it was to be a birthday party there were presents to be considered.

Take the girls at Dora's. All of them had at one time or another gone over to the laboratory for advice or medicine or simply for unprofessional company. And they had seen Doc's bed. It was covered with an old faded red blanket full of fox tails and burrs and sand, for he took it on all his collecting trips. If money came in he bought laboratory equipment. It never occurred to him to buy a new blanket for himself. Dora's girls were making a patchwork quilt, a beautiful thing of silk. And since most of the silks available came from underclothing and evening dresses, the quilt was glorious in strips of flesh pink and orchid and pale-yellow and cerise. They worked on it in the late mornings and in the afternoons before the boys from the sardine fleet came in. Under the community of effort, those fights and ill feelings that always are present in a whore-house completely disappeared.

Lee Chong got out and inspected a twenty-five-foot string of fire-crackers and a big bag of China lily bulbs. These to his way of thinking were the finest things you could have for a party.

Sam Malloy had long had a theory of antiques. He knew that old furniture and glass and crockery, which had not been very valuable in its day, had when time went by taken on desirability and cash value out of all proportion to its beauty or utility. He knew of one chair that had brought five hundred dollars. Sam collected pieces of historic automobiles and he was convinced that some day his collection, after making him very rich, would repose on black velvet in the best museums. Sam gave the party a good deal of thought and then he went over his treasures, which he kept in a big locked box behind the boiler. He decided to give

Doc one of his finest pieces – the connecting-rod and piston from a 1916 Chalmers. He rubbed and polished this beauty until it gleamed like a piece of ancient armour. He made a little box for it and lined it with black cloth.

Mack and the boys gave the problem considerable thought and came to the conclusion that Doc always wanted cats and had some trouble getting them. Mack brought out his double cage. They borrowed a female in an interesting condition and set their trap under the cypress-tree at the top of the vacant lot. In the corner of the Palace they built a wire cage and in it their collection of angry tom-cats grew every night. Jones had to make two trips a day to the canneries for fish heads to feed their charges. Mack considered correctly that twenty-five tom-cats would be as nice a present as they could give Doc.

'No decorations this time,' said Mack. 'Just a good solid party with lots of liquor.'

Gay heard about the party clear over in the Salinas jail, and he made a deal with the sheriff to get off that night, and borrowed two dollars from him for a round-trip bus ticket. Gay had been very nice to the sheriff, who wasn't a man to forget it, particularly because election was coming up and Gay could, or said he could, swing quite a few votes. Besides, Gay could give the Salinas jail a bad name if he wanted to.

Henri had suddenly decided that the old-fashioned pin-cushion was an art form which had flowered and reached its peak in the 'Nineties and had since been neglected. He revived the form and was delighted to see what could be done with coloured pins. The picture was never completed – you could change it by re-arranging the pins. He was preparing a group of these pieces for a one-man show when he heard about the party, and he finally abandoned his own work and began a giant pin-cushion for Doc. It was to be an intricate and provocative design in green, yellow, and blue pins, all cool colours, and its title was Pre-Cambrian Memory.

Henri's friend Eric, a learned barber who collected the first editions of writers who never had a second edition or a second book, decided to give Doc a rowing-machine he had got at the bankruptcy proceedings of a client with a three-year barber bill. The rowing-machine was in fine condition. No one had rowed it much. No one ever uses a rowing-machine.

The conspiracy grew and there were endless visits back and forth, discussions of presents, of liquor, of what time will we start and nobody must tell Doc.

Doc didn't know when he first became aware that something was going on that concerned him. In Lee Chong's, conversation stopped when he entered. At first it seemed to him that people were cold to him. When at least half a dozen people asked him what he was doing October 27 he was puzzled, for he had forgotten he had given this date as his birthday. Actually he had been interested in the horoscope for a spurious birthdate, but Mack had never mentioned it again and so Doc forgot it.

One evening he stopped in at the Halfway House because they had a draught beer he liked and kept it at the right temperature. He gulped his first glass and then settled down to enjoy his second when he heard a drunk talking to the bar-tender. 'You goin' to the party?'

'What party?'

'Well,' said the drunk confidentially, 'you know Doc, down in Cannery Row.'

The bar-tender looked up the bar and then back.

'Well,' said the drunk, 'they're givin' him a hell of a party on his birthday.'

'Who is?'

'Everybody.'

Doc mulled this over. He did not know the drunk at all.

His reaction to the idea was not simple. He felt a great warmth that they should want to give him a party and at the same time he quaked inwardly, remembering the last one they had given.

Now everything fell into place – Mack's question and the silences when he was about. He thought of it a lot that night sitting beside his desk. He glanced about, considering what things would have to be locked up. He knew the party was going to cost him plenty.

The next day he began making his own preparations for the party. His best records he carried into the back room, where they could be locked away. He moved every bit of equipment that was breakable back there too. He knew how it would be—his guests would be hungry and they wouldn't bring anything to eat. They would run out of liquor early, they always did. A little wearily he went up to the Thrift Market, where there was a fine and understanding butcher. They discussed meat for some time. Doc ordered fifteen pounds of steak, ten pounds of tomatoes, twelve heads of lettuces, six loaves of bread, a big jar of peanut butter, and one of strawberry jam, five gallons of wine, and four quarts of a good substantial, but not distinguished, whisky. He knew he would have trouble at the bank the first of the month. Three or four such parties, he thought, and he would lose the laboratory.

Meanwhile, on the Row, the planning reached a crescendo. Doc was right, no one thought of food, but there were odd pints and quarts put away all over. The collection of presents was growing and the guest list, if there had been one, was a little like a census. At the Bear Flag a constant discussion went on about what to wear. Since they would not be working, the girls did not want to wear the long beautiful dresses which were their uniforms. They decided to wear street clothes. It wasn't as simple as it sounded. Dora insisted that a skeleton crew remain on duty to take care of the regulars. The girls divided up into shifts, some to stay until they were relieved by others. They had to flip for who would go to the party first. The first ones would see Doc's face when they gave him the beautiful quilt. They had it on a frame in the dining-room and it was nearly finished. Mrs Malloy had put aside her bedspread for a while. She was crocheting six doilies for Doc's beer glasses. The first excitement was gone from the Row now and its place was taken by a deadly cumulative earnestness. There were fifteen tomcats in the cage at the Palace Flophouse and their yowling made Darling a little nervous at night.

CHAPTER XXVIII

SOONER or later Frankie was bound to hear about the party. For Frankie drifted about like a small cloud. He was always on the edge of groups. No one noticed him or paid any attention to him. You couldn't tell whether he was listening or not. But Frankie did hear about the party and he heard about the presents and a feeling of fullness swelled in him and a feeling of sick longing.

In the window of Jacob's Jewellery Store was the most beautiful thing in the world. It had been there a long time. It was a black onyx clock with a gold face, but on top of it was the real beauty. On top was a bronze group – St George killing the dragon. The dragon was on his back with his claws in the air and in his breast was St George's spear. The Saint was in full armour, with the visor raised, and he rode a fat, big-buttocked horse. With his spear he pinned the dragon to the ground. But the wonderful thing was that he wore a pointed beard and he looked a little like Doc.

Frankie walked to Alvarado Street several times a week to stand in front of the window and look at this beauty. He dreamed about it too, dreamed of running his fingers over the rich, smooth bronze. He had known about it for months when he heard of the party and the presents.

Frankie stood on the pavement for an hour before he went inside. 'Well?' said Mr Jacobs. He had given Frankie a visual searching as he came in and he knew there wasn't seventy-five cents on him.

'How much is that?' Frankie asked huskily.

'What?'

'That.'

'You mean the clock? Fifty dollars – with the group seventy-five dollars.'

Frankie walked out without replying. He went down to the beach and crawled under an overturned rowboat and peeked out at the little waves. The bronze beauty was so strong in his head that it seemed to stand out in front of him. And a frantic trapped feeling came over him. He had to get the beauty. His eyes were fierce when he thought of it.

He stayed under the boat all day and at night he emerged and went back to Alvarado Street. While people went to the movies and came out and went to the Golden Poppy, he walked up and down the block. And he didn't get tired or sleepy, for the beauty burned in him like fire.

At last the people thinned out and gradually disappeared from the streets and the parked cars drove away and the town settled to sleep.

A policeman looked closely at Frankie. 'What you doing out?' he asked.

Frankie took to his heels and fled around the corner and hid behind a barrel in the alley. At two-thirty he crept to the door of Jacob's and tried the knob. It was locked. Frankie went back to the alley and sat behind the barrel and thought. He saw a broken piece of concrete lying beside the barrel and he picked it up.

The policeman reported that he heard the crash and ran to it. Jacob's window was broken. He saw the prisoner walking rapidly away and chased him. He didn't know how the boy could run that far and that fast carrying fifty pounds of clock and bronze, but the prisoner nearly got away. If he had not blundered into a blind street he would have got away.

The chief called Doc the next day. 'Come on down, will you? I want to talk to you.'

They brought Frankie in very dirty and frowzy. His eyes were red, but he held his mouth firm and he even smiled a little welcome when he saw Doc.

'What's the matter, Frankie?' Doc asked.

'He broke into Jacob's last night,' the chief said. 'Stole some stuff. We got in touch with his mother. She says it's not her fault, because he hangs around your place all the time.'

'Frankie — you shouldn't have done it,' said Doc. The heavy stone of inevitability was on his heart. 'Can't you parole him to me?' Doc asked.

'I don't think the judge will do it,' said the chief. 'We've got a mental report. You know what's wrong with him?'

'Yes,' said Doc. 'I know.'

'And you know what's likely to happen when he comes into puberty?'

'Yes,' said Doc, 'I know,' and the stone weighed terribly on his heart.

'The doctor thinks we better put him away. We couldn't before, but now he's got a felony on him, I think we better.'

As Frankie listened the welcome died in his eyes.

'What did he take?' Doc asked.

'A great big clock and a bronze statue.'

'I'll pay for it.'

'Oh, we got it back. I don't think the judge will hear of it. It'll just happen again. You know that.'

'Yes,' said Doc softly, 'I know. But maybe he had a reason. Frankie,' he said, 'why did you take it?'

Frankie looked a long time at him. 'I love you,' he said.

Doc ran out and got in his car and went collecting in the caves below Pt Lobos.

CHAPTER XXIX

At four o'clock on October 27 Doc finished bottling the last of a lot of jelly-fish. He washed out the formaline jug, cleaned his forceps, powdered and took off his rubber-gloves. He went upstairs, fed the rats, and put some of his best records and his microscopes in the back room. Then he locked it. Sometimes an illuminated guest wanted to play with the rattlesnakes. By making careful preparations, by foreseeing possibilities, Doc hoped to make this party as non-lethal as possible without making it dull.

He put on a pot of coffee, started the *Great Fugue* on the phonograph, and took a shower. He was very quick about it, for he was dressed in clean clothes and was having his cup of coffee before the music was completed.

He looked out through the window at the lot and up at the Palace, but no one was moving. Doc didn't know who or how many were coming to his party. But he knew he was watched. He had been conscious of it all day. Not that he had seen anyone, but someone or several people had kept him in sight. So it was to be a surprise party. He might as well be surprised. He would follow his usual routine, as though nothing were happening. He crossed to Lee Chong's and bought two quarts of beer. There seemed to be a suppressed Oriental excitement at Lee's. So they were coming too. Doc went back to the laboratory and poured out a glass of beer. He drank the first off for thirst and poured a second one to taste. The lot and the street were still deserted.

Mack and the boys were in the Palace and the door was closed. All afternoon the stove had roared, heating water for baths. Even Darling had been bathed and she wore a red bow round her neck.

'What time you think we should go over?' Hazel asked.

'I don't think before eight o'clock,' said Mack. 'But I don't see nothin' against us havin' a short one to kind of get warmed up.'

'How about Doc getting warmed up?' Hughie said. 'Maybe I ought to just take him a bottle like it was just nothing.'

'No,' said Mack. 'Doc just went over to Lee's for some beer.'

'You think he suspects anything?' Jones asked.

'How could he?' asked Mack.

In the corner cage two tom-cats started an argument and the whole cageful commented with growls and arched backs. There were only twenty-one cats. They had fallen short of their mark.

'I wonder how they'll get them cats over there?' Hazel began. 'We can't carry that big cage through the door.'

'We won't,' said Mack. 'Remember how it was with the frogs. No, we'll just tell Doc about them. He can come over and get them.' Mack got up and opened one of Eddie's wining jugs. 'We might as well get warmed up,' he said.

At five-thirty the old Chinaman flap-flapped down the hill, past the Palace. He crossed the lot, crossed the street, and disappeared between Western Biological and the Hediondo.

At the Bear Flag the girls were getting ready. A kind of

anchor watch had been chosen by straws. The ones who stayed were to be relieved every hour.

Dora was splendid. Her hair freshly dyed orange was curled and piled on her head. She wore her wedding ring and a big diamond brooch on her breast. Her dress was white silk, with a black bamboo pattern. In the bedrooms the reverse of ordinary procedure was in practice.

Those who were staying wore long evening dresses, while those who were going had on short print dresses and looked very pretty. The quilt, finished and backed, was in a big cardboard box in the bar. The bouncer grumbled a little, for it had been decided that he couldn't go to the party. Someone had to look after the house. Contrary to orders, each girl had a pint hidden and each girl watched for the signal to fortify herself a little for the party.

Dora strode magnificently into her office and closed the door. She unlocked the top drawer of the roll-top desk, took out a bottle and a glass, and poured herself a snort. And the bottle clinked softly on the glass. A girl listening outside the door heard the clink and spread the word. Dora would not be able to smell breaths now. And the girls rushed for their rooms and got out their pints. Dusk had come to Cannery Row, the grey time between daylight and street light. Phyllis Mae peeked round the curtain in the front parlour.

'Can you see him?' Doris asked.

'Yeah. He's got the lights on. He's sitting there like he's reading. Jesus, how that guy does read. You'd think he'd ruin his eyes. He's got a glass of beer in his hand.'

'Well,' said Doris, 'we might as well have a little one, I guess.'

Phyllis Mae was still limping a little, but she was as good as new. She could, she said, lick her weight in City Councilmen. 'Seems kind of funny,' she said. 'There he is, sitting over there and he don't know what's going to happen.'

'He never comes in here for a trick,' Doris said a little sadly.

'Lots of guys don't want to pay,' said Phyllis Mae. 'Costs them more, but they figure it different.'

'Well, hell, maybe he likes them.'

'Likes who?'

'Them girls that go over there.'

'Oh, yeah – maybe he does. I been over there. He never made a pass at me.'

'He wouldn't,' said Doris. 'But that don't mean if you didn't work here you wouldn't have to fight your way out.'

'You mean he don't like our profession.'

'No, I don't mean that at all. He probably figures a girl that's workin' has got a different attitude.'

They had another small snort.

In her office Dora poured herself one more, swallowed it, and locked the drawer again. She fixed her perfect hair in the wall mirror, inspected her shining red nails, and went out to the bar. Alfred the bouncer was sulking. It wasn't anything he said nor was his expression unpleasant, but he was sulking just the same. Dora looked him over coldly. 'I guess you figure you're getting the blocks, don't you?'

'No,' said Alfred. 'No, it's quite all right.'

That quite threw Dora. 'Quite all right, is it? You got a job, Mister. Do you want to keep it or not?'

'It's quite all right,' Alfred said frostily. 'I ain't putting out no beef.' He put his elbows on the bar and studied himself in the mirror. 'You just go and enjoy yourself,' he said. 'I'll take care of everything here. You don't need to worry.'

Dora melted under his pain. 'Look,' she said. 'I don't like to have the place without a man. Some lush might get smart and the kids couldn't handle him. But a little later you can come over and you could kind of keep your eye on the place out of the window. How would that be? You could see if anything happened.'

'Well,' said Alfred, 'I would like to come.' He was mollified by her permission. 'Later I might drop over for just a minute or two. They was a mean drunk in last night. An' I don't know, Dora – I kind of lost my nerve since I bust that guy's back. I just ain't sure of myself no more. I'm gonna pull a punch some night and get took.'

'You need a rest,' said Dora. 'Maybe I'll get Mack to fill in and you can take a couple of weeks off.' She was a wonderful madam, Dora was.

Over at the laboratory, Doc had a little whisky after his

beer. He was feeling a little mellow. It seemed a nice thing to him that they would give him a party. He played the *Pavane to a Dead Princess* and felt sentimental and a little sad. And because of his feeling he went on with *Daphnis and Chloe*. There was a passage in it that reminded him of something else. The observers in Athens before Marathon reported seeing a great line of dust crossing the Plain, and they heard the clash of arms and they heard the Eleusinian Chant. There was part of the music that reminded him of that picture.

When it was done he got another whisky and he debated in his mind about the *Brandenburg*. That would snap him out of the sweet and sickly mood he was getting into. But what was wrong with the sweet and sickly mood? It was rather pleasant. 'I can play anything I want,' he said aloud. 'I can play *Clair de Lune* or *The Maiden with Flaxen Hair*. I'm a free man.'

He poured a whisky and drank it. And he compromised with the *Moonlight Sonata*. He could see the neon light of 'La Ida' blinking on and off. And then the street light in front of the Bear Flag came on.

A squadron of huge brown beetles hurled themselves against the light and then fell to the ground and moved their legs and felt around with their antennae. A lady cat strolled lonesomely along the gutter looking for adventure. She wondered what had happened to all the tom-cats who had made life interesting and the nights hideous.

Mr Malloy on his hands and knees peered out of the boiler door to see if anyone had gone to the party yet. In the Palace the boys sat restlessly watching the black hands of the alarm clock.

CHAPTER XXX

The nature of parties has been imperfectly studied. It is, however, generally understood that a party has a pathology, that it is a kind of an individual, and that it is likely to be a very perverse individual. And it is also generally understood that a party hardly ever goes the way it is planned or intended. This last, of course, excludes those dismal slave parties, whipped and controlled and dominated, given by ogreish professional hostesses. These are not parties at all, but acts and demonstrations, about as spontaneous as peristalsis and as interesting as its end product.

Probably everyone in Cannery Row had projected his imagination to how the party would be – the shouts of greeting, the congratulations, the noise and good feeling. And it didn't start that way at all. Promptly at eight o'clock Mack and the boys, combed and clean, picked up their jugs and marched down the chicken-walk, over the railroad track, through the lot across the street and up the steps of Western Biological. Everyone was embarrassed. Doc held the door open and Mack made a little speech. 'Being as how it's your birthday, I and the boys thought we would wish you happy birthday and we got twenty-one cats for you for a present.'

He stopped and they stood forlornly on the stairs.

'Come on in,' said Doc. 'Why – I'm – surprised. I didn't even know you knew it was my birthday.'

'All tom-cats,' said Hazel. 'We didn't bring 'em down.'

They sat down formally in the room at the left. There was a long silence. 'Well,' said Doc, 'now you're here, how about a little drink?'

Mack said: 'We brought a little snort,' and he indicated the three jugs Eddie had been accumulating. 'They ain't no beer in it,' said Eddie.

Doc covered his early evening reluctance. 'No,' he said. 'You've got to have a drink with me. It just happens I laid in some whisky.'

They were just seated formally, sipping delicately at the whisky, when Dora and the girls came in. They presented the quilt. Doc laid it over his bed and it was beautiful. And they accepted a little drink. Mr and Mrs Malloy followed with their presents.

'Lots of folks don't know what this stuff's going to be worth,' said Sam Malloy as he brought out the Chalmers 1916 piston and connecting-rod. 'There probably isn't three of these here left in the world.'

And now people began to arrive in droves. Henri came in with a pin-cushion three by four feet. He wanted to give a lecture on his new art form, but by this time the formality was broken. Mr and Mrs Gay came in. Lee Chong presented the great string of fire-crackers and the China lily bulbs. Someone ate the lily bulbs by eleven o'clock, but the fire-crackers lasted longer. A group of comparative strangers came in from 'La Ida'. The stiffness was going out of the party quickly. Dora sat in a kind of throne, her orange hair flaming. She held her whisky-glass daintily, with her little finger extended. And she kept an eye on the girls to see that they conducted themselves properly. Doc put dance music on the phonograph and he went to the kitchen and began to fry the steaks.

The first fight was not a bad one. One of the group from 'La Ida' made an immoral proposal to one of Dora's girls. She protested and Mack and the boys, outraged at this breach of propriety, threw him out quickly and without breaking anything. They felt good then, for they knew they were contributing.

Out in the kitchen Doc was frying steaks in three skillets, and he cut up tomatoes and piled up sliced bread. He felt very good. Mack was personally taking care of the phonograph. He had found an album of Benny Goodman's trios. Dancing had started, indeed the party was beginning to take on depth and vigour. Eddie went into the office and did a tap-dance. Doc had taken a pint with him to the kitchen and he helped himself from the bottle. He was feeling better and better. Everyone was surprised when he served the meat. Nobody was really hungry and they cleaned it up instantly. Now the food set the party into a kind of rich digestive sadness. The whisky was gone and Doc brought out the gallons of wine.

Dora, sitting enthroned, said: 'Doc, play some of that nice music. I get Christ awful sick of that musical-box over home.'

Then Doc played *Ardo* and the *Amor* from an album of Monteverdi. And the guests sat quietly and their eyes were inward. Dora breathed beauty. Two newcomers crept up the stairs and entered quietly. Doc was feeling a golden pleasant sadness. The guests were silent when the music stopped. Doc brought out a book and he read in a clear, deep voice:

Even now
If I see in my soul the citron-breasted fair one
Still gold-tinted, her face like our night stars,
Drawing unto her; her body beaten about with flame,
Wounded by the flaring spear of love,
My first of all by reason of her fresh years,
Then is my heart buried alive in snow.

Even now
If my girl with lotus eyes came to me again
Weary with the dear weight of young love,
Again I would give her to these starved twins of arms
And from her mouth drink down the heavy wine,
As a reeling pirate bee in fluttered ease
Steals up the honey from the nenuphar.

Even now
If I saw her lying all wide eyes
And with collyrium the indent of her cheek
Lengthened to the bright ear and her pale side
So suffering the fever of my distance,
Then would my love for her be ropes of flowers, and night
A black-haired lover on the breasts of day.

Even now
My eyes that hurry to see no more are painting, painting
Faces of my lost girl. O golden rings
That tap against cheeks of small magnolia-leaves,
O whitest so soft parchment where
My poor divorcèd lips have written excellent
Stanzas of kisses, and will write no more.

Even now
Death sends me the flickering of powdery lids
Over wild eyes and the pity of her slim body
All broken up with the weariness of joy;
The little red flowers of her breasts to be my comfort
Moving above scarves, and for my sorrow
Wet crimson lips that once I marked as mine.

Even now
They chatter her weakness through the two bazaars
Who was so strong to love me. And small men
That buy and sell for silver being slaves
Crinkles the fat about their eyes; and yet
No Prince of the Cities of the Sea has taken her,
Leading to his grim bed. Little lonely one,
You cling to me as a garment clings; my girl.

Even now
I love long black eyes that caress like silk,
Ever and ever sad and laughing eyes,
Whose lids make such sweet shadow when they close
It seems another beautiful look of hers.
I love a fresh mouth, ah, a scented mouth,
And curving hair, subtle as a smoke,
And light fingers, and laughter of green gems.

Even now
I remember that you made answer very softly,
We being one soul, your hand on my hair,
The burning memory rounding your near lips;
I have seen the priestesses of Rati make love at moon fall
And then in a carpeted hall with a bright gold lamp
Lie down carelessly anywhere to sleep.*

Phyllis Mae was openly weeping when he stopped and Dora herself dabbed at her eyes. Hazel was so taken by the sound of the words that he had not listened to their meaning. But a little world sadness had slipped over all of them. Everyone was remembering a lost love, everyone a call.

Mack said: 'Jesus, that's pretty. Reminds me of a dame . . .' and he let it pass. They filled the wineglasses and became quiet. The party was slipping away in sweet sadness. Eddie went out in the office and did a little tap-dance and came back and sat down again. The party was about to recline and go to sleep when there was a tramp of feet on the stairs. A great voice shouted: 'Where's the girls?'

Mack got up almost happily and crossed quickly to the door. And a smile of joy illuminated the faces of Hughie and Jones. 'What girls you got in mind?' Mack asked softly.

* *Black Marigolds*, translated from the Sanskrit by E. Powys Mathers.

'Ain't this a whore-house? Cab-driver said they was one down here.'

'You made a mistake, Mister.' Mack's voice was gay.

'Well, what's them dames in there?'

They joined battle then. They were the crew of a San Pedro tuna-boat, good, hard, happy, fight-wise men. With the first rush they burst through to the party. Dora's girls had each one slipped off a shoe and held it by the toe. As the fight raged by they would clip a man on the head with the spike heel. Dora leaped for the kitchen and came roaring out with a meat grinder. Even Doc was happy. He flailed about with the Chalmers 1916 piston and connecting-rod.

It was a good fight. Hazel tripped and got kicked in the face twice before he could get to his feet again. The Franklin stove went over with a crash. Driven to a corner the newcomers defended themselves with heavy books from the bookcases. But gradually they were driven back. The two front windows were broken out. Suddenly Alfred, who had heard the trouble from across the street, attacked from the rear with his favourite weapon, an indoor ball bat. The fight raged down the steps and into the street and across into the lot. The front door was hanging limply from one hinge again. Doc's shirt was torn off and his slight strong shoulder dripped blood from a scratch. The enemy was driven halfway up the lot when the sirens sounded. Doc's birthday party had barely time to get inside the laboratory and wedge the broken door closed and turn out the lights before the police car cruised up. The cops didn't find anything. But the party was sitting in the dark giggling happily and drinking wine. The shift changed at the Bear Flag. The fresh contingent raged in full of hell. And then the party really got going. The cops came back, looked in, clicked their tongues and joined it. Mack and the boys used the squad car to go to Jimmy Brucia's for more wine and Jimmy came back with them. You could hear the roar of the party from end to end of Cannery Row. The party had all the best qualities of a riot and a night on the barricades. The crew from the San Pedro tuna-boat crept humbly back and joined the party. They were embraced and admired. A woman five

blocks away called the police to complain about the noise
and couldn't get anyone. The cops reported their own car
stolen and found it later on the beach. Doc sitting cross-
legged on the table smiled and tapped his fingers gently on
his knee. Mack and Phyllis Mae were doing Indian wrest-
ling on the floor. And the cool bay wind blew in through the
broken windows. It was then that someone lighted the
twenty-five-foot string of fire-crackers.

CHAPTER XXXI

A WELL-GROWN gopher took up residence in a thicket of
mallow weeds in the vacant lot on Cannery Row. It was a
perfect place. The deep green luscious mallows towered up
crisp and rich, and as they matured their little cheeses hung
down provocatively. The earth was perfect for a gopher-
hole too, black and soft and yet with a little clay in it so that
it didn't crumble and the tunnels didn't cave in. The gopher
was fat and sleek and he had always plenty of food in his
cheek pouches. His little ears were clean and well set and
his eyes were as black as old-fashioned pin-heads and just
about the same size. His digging hands were strong and the
fur on his back was glossy brown and the fawn-coloured fur
on his chest was incredibly soft and rich. He had long curving yellow teeth and a little short tail. Altogether he was a
beautiful gopher and in the prime of his life.

He came to the place over-land and found it good and he
began his burrow on a little eminence where he could look
out among the mallow weeds and see the trucks go by on
Cannery Row. He could watch the feet of Mack and the
boys as they crossed the lot to the Palace Flophouse. As he
dug down into the coal-black earth he found it even more
perfect, for there were great rocks under the soil. When he
made his great chamber for the storing of food it was under
a rock so that it could never cave in, no matter how hard it
rained. It was a place where he could settle down and raise
any number of families and the burrow could increase in all
directions.

It was beautiful in the early morning when he first poked his head out of the burrow. The mallows filtered green light down on him and the first rays of the rising sun shone into his hole and warmed it so that he lay there content and very comfortable.

When he had dug his great chamber and his four emergency exits and his waterproof deluge room, the gopher began to store food. He cut down only the perfect mallow stems and trimmed them to the exact length he needed and he took them down the hole and stacked them neatly in his great chamber, and arranged them so they wouldn't ferment or get sour. He had found the perfect place to live. There were no gardens about, so no one would think of setting a trap for him. Cats there were, many of them, but they were so bloated with fish-heads and guts from the canneries that they had long ago given up hunting. The soil was sandy enough, so that water never stood about or filled a hole for long. The gopher worked and worked until he had his great chamber crammed with food. Then he made little side chambers for the babies who would inhabit them. In a few years there might be thousands of his progeny spreading out from this original hearthstone.

But as time went on the gopher began to be a little impatient, for no female appeared. He sat in the entrance of his hole in the morning and made penetrating squeaks that are inaudible to the human ear but can be heard deep in the earth by other gophers. And still no female appeared. Finally in a sweat of impatience he went up across the track until he found another gopher-hole. He squeaked provocatively in the entrance. He heard a rustling and smelled female, and then out of the hole came an old battle-torn bull gopher who mauled and bit him so badly that he crept home and lay in his great chamber for three days recovering and he lost two toes from one front paw from that fight.

Again he waited and squeaked beside his beautiful burrow in the beautiful place, but no female ever came, and after a while he had to move away. He had to move two blocks up the hill to a dahlia garden where they put out traps every night.

CHAPTER XXXII

Doc awakened very slowly and clumsily like a fat man getting out of a swimming-pool. His mind broke the surface and fell back several times. There was red lipstick on his beard. He opened one eye, saw the brilliant colours of the quilt, and closed his eye quickly. But after a while he looked again. His eye went past the quilt to the floor, to the broken plate in the corner, to the glasses standing on the table turned over on the floor, to the spilled wine and the books like heavy fallen butterflies. There were little bits of curled red paper all over the place and the sharp smell of fire-crackers. He could see through the kitchen door to the steak plates stacked high and the skillets deep in grease. Hundreds of cigarette-butts were stamped out on the floor. And under the fire-cracker smell was a fine combination of wine and whisky and perfume. His eye stopped for a moment on a little pile of hairpins in the middle of the floor.

He rolled over slowly and supporting himself on one elbow he looked out the broken window. Cannery Row was quiet and sunny. The boiler door was open. The door of the Palace Flophouse was closed. A man slept peacefully among the weeds in the vacant lot. The Bear Flag was shut up tight.

Doc got up and went into the kitchen and lighted the gas water-heater on his way to the toilet. Then he came back and sat on the edge of his bed and worked his toes together while he surveyed the wreckage. From up the hill he could hear the church bells ringing. When the gas heater began rumbling he went back to the bathroom and took a shower and he put on blue jeans and a flannel shirt. Lee Chong was closed, but he saw who was at the door and opened it. He went to the refrigerator and brought out a quart of beer without being asked. Doc paid him.

'Good time?' Lee asked. His brown eyes were a little inflamed in their pouches.

'Good time!' said Doc, and he went back to the laboratory with his cold beer. He made a peanut-butter sandwich

to eat with his beer. It was very quiet in the street. No one
went by at all. Doc heard music in his head – violas and 'cellos, he thought. And they played cool, soft, soothing music
with nothing much to distinguish it. He ate his sandwich
and sipped his beer and listened to the music. When he had
finished his beer, Doc went into the kitchen, and cleared the
dirty dishes out of the sink. He ran hot water in it and
poured soap chips under the running water so that the foam
stood high and white. Then he moved about collecting all
the glasses that weren't broken. He put them in the soapy
hot water. The steak-plates were piled high on the stove
with their brown juice and their white grease sticking them
together. Doc cleared a place on the table for the clean
glasses as he washed them. Then he unlocked the door of the
back room and brought out one of his albums of Gregorian
music and he put a Paternoster and Agnus Dei on the turntable and started it going. The angelic, disembodied voices
filled the laboratory. They were incredibly pure and sweet.
Doc worked carefully washing the glasses so that they would
not clash together and spoil the music. The boys' voices carried the melody up and down, simply but with the richness
that is in no other singing. When the record had finished,
Doc wiped his hands and turned it off. He saw a book lying
half under his bed and picked it up and he sat down on the
bed. For a moment he read to himself, but then his lips
began to move and in a moment he read aloud – slowly,
pausing at the end of each line.

> Even now
> I mind the coming and talking of wise men from towers
> Where they had thought away their youth. And I, listening,
> Found not the salt of the whispers of my girl,
> Murmur of confused colours, as we lay near sleep;
> Little wise words and little witty words,
> Wanton as water, honied with eagerness.

In the sink the high white foam cooled and ticked as the
bubbles burst. Under the piers it was very high tide and the
waves splashed on rocks they had not reached in a long
time.

Even now
I mind that I loved cypress and roses, clear,
The great blue mountains and the small grey hills,
The sounding of the sea. Upon a day
I saw strange eyes and hands like butterflies;
For me at morning larks flew from the thyme
And children came to bathe in little streams.

Doc closed the book. He could hear the waves beat under
the piles and he could hear the scampering of white rats
against the wire. He went into the kitchen and felt the cool-
ing water in the sink. He ran hot water into it. He spoke
aloud to the sink and the white rats, and to himself:

Even now
I know that I have savoured the hot taste of life
Lifting green cups and gold at the great feast.
Just for a small and a forgotten time
I have had full in my eyes from off my girl
The whitest pouring of eternal light . . .

He wiped his eyes with the back of his hand. And the
white rats scampered and scrambled in their cages. And
behind the glass the rattlesnakes lay still and stared into
space with their dusty, frowning eyes.